VICE IN A
VICIOUS SOCIETY

VICE IN A
VICIOUS SOCIETY

Crime and Convicts in
Mid-Nineteenth Century
New South Wales

MICHAEL STURMA

University of Queensland Press
St Lucia • London • New York

© University of Queensland Press, St Lucia, Queensland 1983

Typeset by University of Queensland Press
Printed and bound by Silex Enterprise & Printing Co., Hong Kong

Distributed in the United Kingdom, Europe, the Middle East, Africa, and the Caribbean by Prentice-Hall International, International Book Distributors Ltd, 66 Wood Lane End, Hemel Hempstead, Herts., England.

National Library of Australia Cataloguing-in-Publication data

Sturma, Michael, 1950– .
 Vice in a vicious society.

 Bibliography.
 Includes index.
 ISBN 0 7022 1911 8.

 1. Crime and criminals – New South Wales – History.
 I. Title.
364'.9944

Library of Congress Cataloging in Publication Data

Sturma, Michael, 1950–
 Vice in a vicious society.

 Bibliography: p.
 Includes index.
 1. Crime and criminals–Australia–New South Wales–History–19th century. 2. Law enforcement–Australia–New South Wales–History–19th century. I. Title.
HV7174.N4S85 1983   364'.9944   82-8636
ISBN 0-7022-1911-8   AACR2

For Joan, Rudy, Susan, Barbara and Lee

Contents

Figures

Tables

Preface

The main title of this work is intended to be ironic, because although both contemporaries and historians have generally viewed colonial New South Wales as a "vicious society", I attempt to show that the degree of criminality and vice in the community has been both exaggerated and misunderstood. In the process I deal with two areas of colonial experience which have been relatively neglected by historians — crime and the social consequences of convictism. These two subjects are obviously interrelated, since crime was considered one of the most damaging legacies of penal transportation to New South Wales. It has been commonly assumed, also, that convict vices indelibly stamped the Australian character.

My study concentrates on the years from 1831 to 1861. This is partly due to the nature and availability of official criminal statistics. Moreover, the period is delineated by two developments which give it some historical unity in relation to crime. The first is the governorship of Richard Bourke, who assumed office in 1831, and whose administration was rife with controversy concerning the colony's crime rate. The second is the gold rush, which tended to dominate contemporary concern about crime and public order in the decade after 1851.

For statistical purposes, New South Wales includes the geographical area of Victoria before it became a separate colony in 1851, and Queensland before separation in 1859. Throughout the period the "middle district", as contained by New South Wales' present boundaries, is the main focus of study.

Crime is less easily circumscribed. As a legal category, it may be defined as those acts or kinds of conduct prohibited and punishable under the criminal law. This study deals with both indictable offences, which were considered more serious crimes and were tried before the Supreme Court or courts of quarter sessions, and petty offences, tried summarily before the magistracy. But what is labelled and treated as "crime" is a social process which involves more than simply the violation of a static legal code. With this point in mind, I examine crime within the wider context of community perceptions and relations.

In writing this study I have benefited from the advice of many counsellors. Foremost is John N. Molony, who provided not only academic guidance for my research, but also a generous measure of personal support throughout our association. I have also been fortunate in having three other members of the Australian National University take an especially active interest in my work — A. W. Martin, Susan Magarey and John Merritt. Many other friends and colleagues have given me advice and assistance, and I must at least mention Don Baker, Margaret Browne, Mike Daffy, Maggie Indian, Leanne Kerr, Trish Mercer, Barbara Penny, John Ritchie, David Stephens and especially Lee Sturma. I am indebted to Madeleine Hyson and Elizabeth Wilcox for typing the manuscript. I am grateful to the New South Wales Police Department for permission to examine their records.

Abbreviations

ADB	*Australian Dictionary of Biography*
CO	Colonial Office
Col.Sec.	Colonial Secretary
HRA	*Historical Records of Australia*
JRAHS	*Journal of the Royal Australian Historical Society*
LC	Legislative Council
ML	Mitchell Library
NLA	National Library of Australia
N.S.W.	New South Wales
N.S.W. SA	New South Wales State Archives
PP	*Parliamentary Papers*
SMH	*Sydney Morning Herald*
V&PLA	*Votes and Proceedings of the Legislative Assembly*
V&PLC	*Votes and Proceedings of the Legislative Council*

Introduction

Between 1788 and 1840 about 80,000 male and female prisoners were transported from the United Kingdom to New South Wales. The social consequences of this migration were most forcefully stated by a British select committee in 1838. The committee sounded the death knell of convict transportation to the colony when it concluded that the system not only failed to reform criminals, but also created societies "most thoroughly depraved, as respects both the character and degree of their vicious propensities".[1] According to the committee's chairman, Sir William Molesworth, there existed in Australia "a state of morality worse than that of any other community in the world".[2]

Historians concur that the credibility of the Molesworth Committee was seriously undermined by the prejudices and preconceptions of its chairman and principal witnesses.[3] But they tend to attack the committee's motives rather than to contradict its conclusions. Indeed, Molesworth's portrayal of New South Wales represented less a new departure than the climax of British perceptions of the colony. The committee shared with most accounts of the colony's moral condition two basic assumptions. First, it assumed the existence of a "criminal class". Persons who committed criminal offences were believed to form a class, detached from the working classes, which lived entirely off the proceeds of crime and which threatened social order. As fear of revolutionary violence subsided in Britain, concern with the "criminal" or "dangerous classes" faded. However, the belief that offenders were mainly drawn from a professional criminal subculture prevailed during the first half of the nineteenth century.[4] The conception of a "criminal class" provided part of the rationale for transportation, since it assumed that offenders were from a distinct group which could be exported.

A second pervasive assumption was that criminality was contagious. Contemporaries summed up the demoralizing influence of criminals in the word "contamination". According to Sydney's superintendent of police, William Augustus Miles, "contamination" resulted because "a convict will talk over his deeds of guilt till crime becomes familiar and romantic".[5] Others believed that the process of contamination was even more insidious. Chief Justice James Dowling, while offering some fatherly advice to his son, warned that, "Vice is so fascinating, that she cannot be looked upon without peril to the beholder".[6] Some held as well that criminal traits were hereditary. Judge Alfred Stephen stated his conviction that "crime *descends*, as surely as physical properties and individual temperament".[7]

These same assumptions, if in a less virulent form, are reflected in the works of major writers on the convict period. Studies by C.M.H. Clark, L.L. Robson and A.G.L. Shaw tend to confirm that most convicts were drawn from a "criminal class". All three writers associate the typical convict with city-dwelling professional criminals. Central to their argument is the high proportion of convicts (estimated at two-thirds of all those transported) with prior convictions in Britain.[8] The hardened and habitual criminals, more or less deserving of their fate, have become the textbook view of convicts exiled to Australia.

The interpretations of Clark, Robson and Shaw serve to correct romanticized characterizations of the convicts. "Obvious victims", in the sense of Tolpuddle Martyrs or Canadian Rebels, comprised only a small percentage of the men and women transported.[9] But the convicts' criminality remains debatable. The statistical data available hardly justify the conclusion that most convicts transported to New South Wales had prior convictions.[10] In any case, changes in the judicial system, criminal law, police force and definitions of offences make prior convictions a very dubious indicator of the convicts' character.[11] It should also be remembered that most people transported were convicted of simple larcenies, rather than robberies, burglaries or other offences usually associated with professional criminals. A study of crime in England's Black Country from 1835 to 1860 indicates that most persons prosecuted for criminal offences were normally employed, and although they occasionally supplemented their incomes by theft, they were not members of a "criminal class".[12] Even assuming the reformatory nature of the transportation system, the high proportion of convicts with good records in the colonies appears as further mute testimony against their alleged recidivism.[13]

The concept of "contamination" is still more problematic, both because of its vague connotations in nineteenth-century usage, and because it is more subtly translated into historical interpretations. Some historians have accepted uncritically the demoralizing influence of convicts on the honesty and moral standards of the general population. More importantly, convict vices and values such as hard drinking, hard swearing and a hatred for the police are viewed as leaving a lasting imprint on Australian culture.[14] Convict "contamination" becomes in effect a component in the development of a distinctively Australian ethos.

Such explanations of convicts' long-term influence are particularly resilient, since they are as difficult to disprove as to prove. It is possible, however, to point to contrary evidence and alternative interpretations. There is reason to doubt, for example, whether convict values differed markedly from those of free immigrants, or whether there is any correlation between a concentration of convicts and the emergence of an unique Australian outlook.[15]

The questionable notion of a criminal class and its contaminating influence is indicative of the wider methodological problems involved in relying on contemporary perceptions of crime in relation to New South Wales. Inseparable from the use of literary evidence is the problem of class bias. Few convicts left records, and those convict narratives which were published, even when genuine, follow a standardized formula.[16] Contemporary accounts dealt mainly with the impressions of upper and middle class observers who were often repelled by colonial morality simply because they scrutinized the working classes more closely in the colony than they had in Britain. To some extent, particularly in travellers' accounts, invective against New South Wales' moral character became a literary convention.

Modern readers may suspect that the less savoury aspects of colonial life so often dealt with were calculated largely to appeal to an English audience, rather than to present a balanced view. Literature about the colony and its penal background sometimes approached a subtle form of pornography. Descriptions of convict floggings were added to the already vast number of publications on flagellation in Victorian England.[17] The suspected prevalence of sodomy and bestiality was hinted at to the limits propriety would permit. Another favourite theme was the corrupting influence of female convict servants, as in the following passage by J.C. Byrne.

> Coming from the very hotbed of vice ... These female convict servants are deeply initiated in all the mysteries of human depravity ... The young mind is pliable, open to impression, and readily imbibes the effects of the language and conduct of those around. The chamber of female youth, as well as that of the other sex, is always open of necessity to servants, and there, in the very inmost recesses of the home, vice is inculcated, and taught, until desire and ability produce practice.[18]

Byrne went on to assure his readers that mothers as well as their children were corrupted, as evidenced by the prevalence of incest between free women settlers and their sons.[19] Not surprisingly, these observations in Byrne's 1848 travelogue failed to merit mention in his *Emigrant's Guide* published the same year.[20]

At a more profound level, works by British writers were influenced by domestic class jealousies, and reflected resentment against the social and economic mobility of ex-convicts and lower class immigrants.

Henry Melville, commenting on New South Wales' moral progress at the mid-century, was most disturbed by the manner in which some members of the lower orders became "elevated above their proper station in life".[21] In part, a belief that poverty was a necessary condition of working class morality was grounded in fears concerning the social and political advancement of the working classes in Britain. The rapid accumulation of wealth by colonists was viewed as both offensive and threatening to social order. Convictism enabled British publicists to parade economic and social resentment, perhaps subconsciously, under the guise of moral concern.[22]

Similar class jealousies affected the works of colonial writers. Labour shortages, high wages and the relative independence of New South Wales' working classes, meant that upper and middle class colonists had more immediate reasons than had British publicists to resent the social and economic mobility of the "lower orders". The affluence of workers and their consequent dissipation was a constant theme. Edward M. Curr, a Port Phillip squatter during the 1840s, was typical in his assertion that a decrease in wages was the first step towards transforming the working classes from "drunkards and idlers" into "tolerable servants and citizens".[23]

Colonists' social, political and religious affiliations further determined the perspective of their publications. The most persistent critics of colonial morality, and often the most prolific writers, were clergymen. Their condemnations are surely suspect. Denunciations of vice were an occupational obligation, and the experience of many ministers was limited to England's rural parishes rather than to large towns.[24] Both denominational competition and more altruistic motives led clergymen to emphasize the necessity for religious instruction in New South Wales. Thus for example, William Ullathorne combined his horrific account of the colony with a solicitation for funds in support of the Catholic mission.[25]

Interpretation of newspapers presents still greater problems. Colonial newspapers not only provided the most available source for gauging community perceptions of crime, but they were also intimately involved in shaping those perceptions. As in the case of colonial publications generally, the press reflected various local prejudices, while evincing predominantly middle class values. Even a "very beery" sporting weekly like *Bell's Life in Sydney* drew a sharp distinction between respectable and non-respectable working men and women. Crime news conformed largely to editorial policy, a desire to attract readers, as well as to pre-existing categories determined by the dominant ideology.

Of course, to point to the prejudices and questionable preconceptions of contemporaries is not to deny the usefulness of their evidence.

It is to suggest rather the need for a critical approach to what they said and wrote, and where possible, methods for checking or taking into account distortions of the evidence. The use of statistics suggests one way of obtaining more objective information about crime. As one eminent social historian notes, statistical measurement is the only means of discerning the "typical specimen", while failure to use such controls can result in fallacious or implausible generalizations based on a few well-documented examples.[26]

Quantitative analysis guarantees no clear-cut answers. For reasons which are elaborated in chapter 4, the interpretation of criminal statistics poses problems which are in some ways more formidable than those associated with evaluating literary evidence. But simply ignoring the available statistics can create problems in itself. Although imperfect, statistics provide a firmer basis for making quantitative judgments than do the often impressionistic and ambiguous testimonies of contemporary observers.[27] At the same time, the views of contemporaries concerning crime were often based on statistical information. In fact, an increasing interest in criminal or "moral statistics" was a feature of the period under study.[28] For these reasons, and because it is often impractical to draw conclusions without some quantitative basis, statistical evidence is an essential element of the following study.

Statistics by themselves tell us little about the social implications of crime. Here some of the concepts associated with sociological studies of deviance suggest a means of dealing with crime as a social process. In particular they underline the need to enlarge the area traditionally considered in relation to crime. The way in which certain behaviour and persons come to be perceived, defined and treated as criminal is as important as the aetiology of crime. Criminals are in fact created in a selective way, so that whether a person who commits a deviant act is labelled a criminal depends on many factors extraneous to his or her behaviour. The law may be used as a powerful political weapon, and notions of criminality may reveal much about the structure of social relations.[29]

This type of perspective seems well suited to an historical study of crime in New South Wales. It serves to direct attention away from the character of individuals, which has so much preoccupied historians in dealing with convicts, to the community in general. By challenging the notion that crime is simply the product of specific factors in individuals or situations, questions are raised about the type of society which generates particular types of crime or criminals. The role of "moral entrepreneurs", or those who define moral categories and have those definitions enforced as public policy, becomes as important as that of those who are treated as immoral. An emphasis on the perceptions and motives of those who initiate rules and define criminals, rather than criminal offenders, has an obvious advantage, considering the one-sided nature of the source material.

Any approach in studying crime, whether essentially literary, statistical, or theoretical, is deficient in some respects. An eclectic approach is perhaps the most useful, partly as a means of checking different types of evidence against one another, and partly to avoid reducing crime to a one-dimensional phenomenon. For this reason I have attempted to mesh the literary evidence with statistical analysis, while drawing upon sociological and criminological material when it appears applicable. As the problems outlined above indicate, conclusions drawn must often be equivocal or highly speculative. This is hardly surprising, since many of the issues raised in relation to crime during the first half of the nineteenth century have remained unresolved. But evaluating the evidence in itself can furnish some insight.

The chapters that follow suggest that assumptions concerning a criminal class and contamination are by and large disabling concepts, which obscure more than they reveal about crime in mid-nineteenth-century New South Wales. As such, much of the analysis focuses on the disparity between contemporary perceptions of crime and, as far as can be discerned, the reality of crime. In part, the colony's penal origins acted as a blind in limiting contemporary perceptions of crime. Half a century after transportation ended, some writers still considered that New South Wales laboured under the disadvantage of "a population in whose veins there is an hereditary taint of criminality".[30] The relation between crime and convictism also served an ideological role, in the sense that it was an idea which served the interests of various groups in the community.

While contending that the relation between crime and convicts has been both over-simplified and exaggerated, the following study also suggests other influences at work in shaping perceptions of crime and crimes actually prosecuted in New South Wales. As Leon Radzinowicz points out, crime is made up of such a wide range of behaviour that any attempt to offer a total explanation is doomed to end in broad platitudes.[31] We can, however, shift our attention from the role of a transported criminal class and its contaminating influence by proposing some alternative points of reference.

Crime was not simply grafted on to the colony as contemporaries often implied, but largely reflected environmental determinants, including economic and demographic characteristics as well as physical surroundings. Distance, isolation and pastoral expansion provided opportunities for certain types of offences such as stock theft, bush-ranging and forgery, and affected the degree to which such offences were prosecuted. Relations with Aborigines encouraged a tradition of inter-personal violence. Although there was a high degree of urbanization from early settlement, what might be loosely termed frontier conditions such as a preponderance of males profoundly affected New South Wales' official crime rate. The colony's relative affluence was a further environmental characteristic, which for contemporaries often seemed to make crime all the more inexplicable except in terms of convict depravity. Prosperity could also, however, create a sense of relative deprivation among the less fortunate, provide additional opportunities for offences, and foster materialist values which were conducive to the commission and prosecution of offences against property. Economic conditions played a still more tangible role in relation to the incidence of drunkenness. It could equally be argued that favourable economic conditions inhibited collective violence.

These influences will be considered relative to the incidence and range of offences prosecuted in the colony, as distinct from the social processes which largely determined perceptions of crime and criminals. In this latter sense, the concept of respectability serves as a focal point. The word permeates contemporary literature, although its precise meaning varies.[32] In part, respectability may be associated with the diffusion of middle class values. As the following discussion suggests, it was largely a code of middle class propriety which displaced the convict code in regulating the boundaries of socially acceptable behaviour once transportation ended. More importantly, respectability may be viewed as a product of social relationships. One can be considered moral and respectable only if there are others regarded as immoral and disreputable. To the extent that individuals or groups wish to create a moral image, they are in a "competitive struggle" to morally upgrade themselves, and morally downgrade others not identified with themselves. The more successful they are in stigmatizing others as immoral, the greater their chances of being themselves regarded as law-abiding and respectable.[33]

Within the context of a "competitive struggle" for respectability, the identification of convicts as a "criminal class" assumes social, economic and political significance. Socially, convicts provided a counter-image for free immigrants anxious to enhance their status and consolidate their position in the community. Economically, stigmatizing convicts as hardened criminals was one technique for combating the threat posed by cheap convict labour. The same technique could be used for neutralizing political opponents, and was particularly effective in New South Wales, given the affinity between respectability and authority. On a community level, relegating convicts to the role of "criminals" and "outsiders" represented an attempt to repudiate the colony's penal origins and to project a moral image.

These points of reference facilitate consideration of crime in the broader context of the community. They may also serve as signposts in a society undergoing rapid change. With colonial births and large-scale immigration, the proportion of convicts and ex-convicts in the population diminished from about two-thirds in 1828, to slightly over a third in 1841. By 1851 persons originally transported made up fifteen per cent of the population, before the mass immigration which accompanied the gold rush reduced them to an even smaller minority in the community. It is this dilution of a "sick" and "vicious" society with "virtuous and industrious" immigrants which both contemporaries and historians often view as the central factor in New South Wales' transformation from a convict dumping ground to a free society. At the same time, a legacy of vice is viewed as one of the most conspicuous after-effects of convictism.[34] The following study suggests that New South Wales' transition from a penal colony, at least in relation to colonial crime, was a good deal more complicated.

Three "crime waves", characterized by "a rash of publicity, a movement of excitement and alarm, a feeling that something needs to be done", which were not necessarily connected with an actual increase in crime, form the subject matter of the first three chapters.[35] Although each crime wave was ostensibly precipitated by the menace of convicts, they were in fact largely symptomatic of the colony's changing economic, political and social circumstances. The historical "slices" dealt with in these chapters have by no means been neglected by historians. Nor has the relationship between the alleged criminality of convicts and other issues escaped their notice, especially in regard to the anti-transportation movement. My approach is revisionist to the extent that I try to throw into relief the crucial role perceptions of crime assumed in the community, and the factors shaping those perceptions. While some emphasis on statistical evidence is included in these opening chapters, chapters 4 and 5 deal with New South Wales' official crime rate in greater detail. Both these later chapters underline the fallacy of interpreting the colony's criminal statistics simply in terms of the changing proportion of convicts in the population. Further evidence of "immorality" is examined in chapters 6 and 7, focusing on two vices often associated with convictism — swearing and drinking. The final chapter queries another alleged convict characteristic, antipathy to the police, and deals with the changing nature of public order. Throughout the book I have endeavoured to put in perspective the influence crime and convicts exercised on the colony's consciousness. Ultimately the community's reaction to its convict origins proved of more lasting and profound significance than convictism itself.

Notes

1. Report of the Select Committee on Transportation, *PP* 1837–38, vol. 22 (669), pp. 22, 41.
2. Quoted in M. Clark (ed.), *Sources of Australian History* (London, 1957), p. 154.
3. The influences and prejudices shaping the Molesworth Committee are dealt with by Alison M. Priestly, "The Molesworth Committee and New South Wales" (M.A. thesis, Australian National University, 1967), especially pp. 189–94; James George Menham, "The Molesworth Committee: British Ideas and Colonial Reality" (B.A. honours thesis, Australian National University, 1973), especially pp. 45–52; John Ritchie, "Towards Ending an Unclean Thing: The Molesworth Committee and the Abolition of Transportation to N.S.W., 1837–40", *Historical Studies* vol. 17, no. 67 (October 1976), pp. 149–53; Norma Townsend, "The Molesworth Enquiry: Does the Report Fit the Evidence", *Journal of Australian Studies* no. 1 (June 1977), especially pp. 50–1.
4. See Leon Radzinowicz, *Ideology and Crime: A Study of Crime in its Social and Historical Context* (London, 1966), pp. 38–40; Allan Silver, "The Demand for Order in Civil Society: A Review of Some Themes in the History of Urban Crime, Police and Riot", in David J. Bordua (ed.), *The Police: Six Sociological Essays* (New York, 1967), pp. 3–5; Margaret May and Peter Linebaugh, "Conference Report", *Society for the Study of Labour History Bulletin* no. 25 (Autumn 1972), pp. 8, 11; J.F.C. Harrison, *The Early Victorians 1832–1851* (London, 1971), p. 51; Lenora Ann Ritter, "Concepts and Treatment of Juvenile Delinquency in Nineteenth-Century England, New South Wales and South Australia" (M.A. thesis, University of New England, 1974), pp. 15–16.
5. Evidence of William Augustus Miles to the Select Committee on the Insecurity of Life and Property, N.S.W., *V & PLC*, 1844, vol. 2, p. 384.
6. James Dowling to son, 16 February 1839, Dowling Correspondence, ML, A 486–1.
7. Alfred Stephen to James Macarthur, *c.* 1857–58, Macarthur Papers, ML, A 2924, vol. 28, p. 132. Stephen's emphasis.
8. M. Clark, "The Origins of the Convicts Transported to Eastern Australia, 1787–1852", *Historical Studies* vol. 7, no. 26–7 (May and November 1956), pp. 132–33, 327; L.L. Robson, *The Convict Settlers of Australia. An Enquiry into the Origin and Character of the Convicts Transported to New South Wales and Van Diemen's Land 1787–1852* (Melbourne, 1965), especially pp. 147, 157; A.G.L. Shaw, *Convicts and the Colonies. A Study of Penal Transportation from Great Britain and Ireland to Australia and Other Parts of the British Empire* (London, 1966), especially pp. 164–65; A.G.L. Shaw, "The British Criminal and Transportation", *Tasmanian Historical Research Association, Papers and Proceedings* vol. 2, no. 2 (March 1953), pp. 31–32.
9. The phrase is used by Lloyd Evans and Paul Nicholls (eds.), *Convicts and Colonial Society 1788–1853* (Sydney, 1976), p. 113. Of approximately 162,000 prisoners transported to Australia between 1788 and 1868, George Rudé identifies only 3,600 convicts as "political and social protesters", or about one in forty-five of all those transported. George Rudé, *Protest and Punishment. The Story of the Social and Political Protesters Transported to Australia 1788–1868* (Oxford, 1978), pp. 8, 10.
10. L.L. Robson's sample of the convict ship indents indicates that only eighteen per cent of the convicts transported to New South Wales had previous con-

victions, compared to fifty-eight per cent of those sent to Van Diemen's
Land. Part of this disparity may be explained by the fact that there is no
information concerning the former offences of a large proportion of those
transported to New South Wales. Even so, thirty-five per cent of the convicts
transported to the colony were recorded as having no prior convictions.
Robson, *Convict Settlers,* pp. 209, 212.

11. Susan Magarey, "The Invention of Juvenile Delinquency in Early Nineteenth-
    Century England", *Labour History* no. 34 (May 1978), p. 24.
12. David Philips, *Crime and Authority in Victorian England. The Black Country
    1835–1860* (London, 1977), p. 287.
13. See James F.H. Moore, *The Convicts of Van Diemen's Land 1840–1853*
    (Hobart, 1976), especially pp. 92–3; Robson, *Convict Settlers,* p. 157.
14. This interpretation is best articulated by Russel Ward, *The Australian Legend*
    (London, 1958; reprint ed., Melbourne 1970), especially chapter 2. See also
    Russel Ward, "The Australian Legend Re-Visited", *Historical Studies* vol. 18,
    no. 71 (October 1978), pp. 171–90.
15. See Humphrey McQueen, *A New Britannia. An Argument Concerning the
    Social Origins of Australian Radicalism and Nationalism* (Ringwood, 1970;
    revised ed., 1975), pp. 126–36; H. McQueen, "Convicts and Rebels", *Labour
    History* no. 15 (November 1968), pp. 28, 30; Alan Atkinson, "Four Patterns
    of Convict Protest", *Labour History* no. 37 (November 1979), pp. 48–9;
    H. Reynolds, " 'That Hated Stain': The Aftermath of Transportation in
    Tasmania", *Historical Studies* vol. 14, no. 53 (October 1969), p. 31.
16. Anne Conlon, " 'Mine is a Sad yet True Story': Convict Narratives 1818–
    1850", *JRAHS* vol. 55, pt 1 (March 1969), pp. 44–45.
17. See Steven Marcus, *The Other Victorians. A Study of Sexuality and Porno-
    graphy in Mid-Nineteenth-Century England,* 4th ed. (New Yori, 1974), p.
    252.
18. J.C. Byrne, *Twelve Years' Wanderings in the British Colonies; From 1835–
    1847* (London, 1848), vol. 1, pp. 231–32.
19. Ibid., vol. 1, p. 233.
20. J.C. Byrne, *Emigrant's Guide to New South Wales Proper, Australia Felix,
    and South Australia,* 7th ed. (London, 1848).
21. Henry Melville, *The Present State of Australia, including New South Wales,
    Western Australia, South Australia, Victoria and New Zealand, with Practical
    Hints on Emigration; to which are added the Land Regulations, and Descrip-
    tion of the Aborigines and their Habits* (London, 1851), p. 47.
22. F.G. Clarke, *The Land of Contrarieties: British Attitudes to the Australian
    Colonies 1828–1855* (Melbourne, 1977), pp. 29–37.
23. Edward M. Curr, *Recollections of Squatting in Victoria; Then called the Port
    Phillip District (From 1841 to 1851)* (Melbourne, 1883; facsimile ed.,
    Adelaide, 1968), p. 438.
24. K.S. Inglis, *The Australian Colonists: An Exploration of Social History
    1788–1870* (Melbourne, 1974), pp. 77–78.
25. W. Ullathorne, *The Catholic Mission in Australasia* (Liverpool, 1837; facsimile
    ed., Adelaide, 1963).
26. Lawrence Stone, *The Crisis of the Aristocracy 1558-1641* (London, 1965),
    pp. 3–4.
27. Philips, *Crime in Victorian England,* pp. 16–21.
28. See K.K. Macnab, "Aspects of the History of Crime in England and Wales
    Between 1805–1860" (Ph.D. thesis, University of Sussex, 1965), pp. 33–52.
29. These ideas are principally associated with the "interactionist perspective",
    or more simply "labelling theory", which first came to the fore in socio-

logical studies of deviance during the 1960s. See for example Howard S. Becker, *Outsiders. Studies in the Sociology of Deviance* (London, 1963), pp. 31–34, 161; Kai T. Erikson, *Wayward Puritans. A Study in the Sociology of Deviance* (New York, 1966), pp. 6–7. More recently, labelling theorists have been criticized on a number of counts. This does not, however, negate the usefulness of an interactionist approach, and as a perspective rather than a rigid theory it is flexible enough to be used with other criminological theory. See Ken Plummer, "Misunderstanding Labelling Perspectives", in David Downes and Paul Rock (eds.), *Deviant Interpretations* (Oxford, 1979), especially p. 120; Howard S. Becker, "Labelling Theory Reconsidered", in Paul Rock and Mary McIntosh (eds.), *Deviance and Social Control* (London, 1974), pp. 41–42; John I. Kituse, "The 'New Conceptions of Deviance' and Its Critics", in Walter R. Gove (ed.), *The Labelling of Deviance. Evaluating a Perspective* (New York, 1975), p. 279.

30. Ernest W. Beckett, quoted in Sidney Rosenberg, "Black Sheep and Golden Fleece: A Study of Nineteenth-Century English Attitudes Toward Australian Colonies" (Ph.D. thesis, Columbia University, 1954), pp. 202–3.

31. Radzinowicz, *Ideology and Crime*, p. 82.

32. Michael Roe, *Quest for Authority in Eastern Australia 1835–1851* (Melbourne, 1965), p. 40. See also Barrie Dyster, "The Fate of Colonial Conservatism on the Eve of the Gold-Rush", *JRAHS* vol. 54, pt 4 (December 1968), pp. 347–49.

33. Jack D. Douglas, "Deviance and Respectability: The Social Construction of Moral Meanings", in Jack D. Douglas (ed.), *Deviance and Respectability. The Social Construction of Moral Meanings* (New York, 1970), p. 6. See also Peter L. Berger, *Invitation to Sociology: A Humanistic Perspective* (New York, 1973), p. 159.

34. The impact of a large convict population is most thoroughly explored by Henry Reynolds, who emphasizes the convict toll on Tasmania's crime rate, drunkenness and fear of disorder, which only gradually dissipated once transportation ceased. Reynolds, " 'That Hated Stain' ", especially pp. 20–22, 24.

35. Erikson, *Wayward Puritans*, p. 69. Erikson, in discussing the Massachussetts Bay Colony during the seventeenth century, examines the Antinomian controversy, Quaker invasion and witches of Salem in terms of crime waves which served to unite the community in preserving its identity. Although the analysis presented here is essentially different, Erikson's study suggested the structure of the first three chapters.

1

Crime and Convict Discipline

A peculiar feature of the transition was the manner in which attention focused on certain more or less spectacular evils in this very year 1835 . . . An outburst of outrages in every direction threw a flash of interpretation on the real nature of the convict system, just at the moment when the Governor's laxity was the subject of so much complaint.[1]

The "spectacular evils" of 1835 included foremost an alleged increase in crime. Fears were expressed in the press concerning lawlessness and convict insubordination, while some residents called for urgent action by the government. Others, however, denied that crime was on the increase. Widespread fear of personal violence or the loss of property which is usually associated with a crime wave, tended to be over-shadowed by a statistical debate. A struggle for power, rather than an impending breakdown of law and order, underpinned much of the apparent concern about crime. Crime served as a catchword in attacks on the administration of Governor Bourke and on the aspirations of ex-convicts. Perceptions of crime also served to shore up the shaky authority of the colony's élites.

Judge William Westbrooke Burton's charge to the jury at the close of the Supreme Court sessions in November 1835 occupied a central place in discussions of crime during the mid-1830s. Observations from the bench on the state of the criminal calendar were common in England, but Burton's oration was unprecedented in New South Wales. Referring to both the number of capital convictions before the Supreme Court and the heinous nature of individual offences, Judge Burton drew a harrowing picture. To one looking down on the community, he told the jury, it would appear that its main business was "the commission of crime and the punishment of it; as if the whole Colony were continually in motion towards, the several Courts of Justice". The "grand cause" of this state of affairs, Burton asserted, was a lack of religious principle. To this he added as causes of crime the state of convict road parties, the occupation of waste lands by unauthorized persons, the congregation of convicts in Sydney, the licensing of improper persons as publicans, and the poor superintendence of assigned servants by masters.[2]

Burton assumed office as a puisne judge of the New South Wales Supreme Court in January 1833, after occupying the same position at the Cape of Good Hope from 1827.[3] His appointment was welcomed by Governor Bourke, who had befriended him while serving as acting governor of the Cape Colony. Once in New South Wales, however, Burton quickly showed signs of disenchantment. He was repulsed by the Supreme Court's "filth and looseness of proceedings and want of all order and convenience".[4] He was even more unhappy to contemplate that any prospect of promotion would depend on the "un-Christian like foundation" of his colleagues' death. Burton confided to his brother that if he were not promoted to chief justice of the colony, he would resign his post as soon as he was out of debt.[5] Shortly before delivering his charge to the jury in 1835, Burton had even more reason to feel his ambitions thwarted. Despite his claim for the office of acting chief justice, Governor Bourke recommended James Dowling for the position on the basis of his seniority in New South Wales.

Burton's remarks were perhaps delivered in a fit of pique at having been passed over for the office of acting chief justice, as Bourke's biographer implies.[6] On the other hand, the emphasis on the need for religious instruction was characteristic of his strong sense of Anglican duty. Whatever his motives, Burton's charge to the jury assumed an importance which it seems unlikely he could have predicted. In a tone of both triumph and alarm, the *Sydney Herald* proclaimed that the criminal statistics and offences referred to by Burton demonstrated "a combination of crime, which for its aggregate amount, and the malignity of its nature, is unexampled in the criminal records of any country".[7] At the same time, the *Australian* expressed satisfaction with Burton's jury charge on the grounds that it showed crime had not increased in proportion to the colony's population, and that it provided hope that "some silent causes" were resulting in its decrease.[8]

These opposing interpretations are indicative of both socio-political divisions in New South Wales during the mid-1830s, and the socio-political significance of crime. The *Sydney Herald* reflected conservative opinion and was identified with the "exclusive" faction of wealthy free immigrants. The *Australian*, on the other hand, articulated a liberal viewpoint, and supported the "emancipist" group which was primarily associated with ex-convicts. The emancipists tended to support Governor Bourke's administration and favour political reform, while exclusives opposed Bourke and the aspirations of ex-convicts.

In practice these groups are more difficult to define.[9] The typical view of each faction is largely a caricature popularized by their opponents. The exclusive-emancipist conflict was primarily a struggle for social, economic and political power waged by different segments of the upper and middle classes. To some extent there was also a town and country division, with exclusives drawing support from rural districts and Sydney residents taking the side of emancipists.[10] Debate in the mid-1830s obscured the community of interest between the two groups which became more apparent once transportation ended. That debate centred largely on the issue of ex-convicts' eligibility for civil liberties and the role of convicts in the community. At the core of opposition to Governor Bourke were accusations that his administration tended "to elevate the criminal, and to depress in various ways, the man of untainted character".[11]

The relation between crime and the status of convicts was made explicit by the *Sydney Herald* in its critique of Burton's jury charge. Judge Burton's contention that crime resulted mainly from a lack of religious instruction was dismissed as being for the most part unfounded. Instead, the *Herald* attributed the "alarming increase of crime" allegedly proven by Burton to two innovations which went unmentioned in his charge. The first was an alteration in the summary jurisdiction of magistrates, and the second a recent change in the mode of criminal trials which permitted ex-convicts to serve as jurors.[12]

For Governor Bourke's opponents, the Summary Jurisdiction Act of 1832 was the most conspicuous evidence that he was prepared to sacrifice the security of respectable free immigrants to a lenient convict policy. Before 1832 male prisoners summarily convicted of drunkenness, disobedience, neglect of work, or other disorderly conduct could be punished by a month in solitary confinement, a month on the treadmill, or up to one hundred and fifty lashes with a cat-of-nine-tails. Women convicts guilty of the same offences were liable to one month solitary confinement, or up to two years imprisonment with hard labour.[13] Under the 1832 Act the maximum punishments were reduced to fourteen days solitary confinement and two months imprisonment at hard labour, though the time males could be punished on the treadmill was increased to two months. Greater restraints were placed on flogging. A single magistrate could award no more than fifty lashes, although this number could be doubled by two or more JPs sitting in petty sessions for a second offence.[14]

The limitation imposed on flogging was the most controversial aspect of the Act. Corporal punishment was increasingly criticized, not only on the grounds of its inhumanity, but also for its failure as a deterrent. Far from being stimulated into any kind of reform, it was widely believed that victims of the cat were often angered or frightened into committing further crimes. On the other hand, the lash provided landholders with a cheap instrument of coercion. Not only were scourgers less expensive than prisons, but assigned servants could be returned to work with a minimum of time lost. Even where magistrates were disinclined to inflict floggings, the absence of prison accommodation in many districts meant that their discretionary powers were inoperative.[15]

Although Bourke asserted that most magistrates quietly accepted the new constraints on their authority,[16] the Act stimulated virulent opposition in some quarters. According to the *Sydney Herald,* it overturned the whole system of convict discipline.[17] Residents of the Hunter River area in particular alleged that the reduction in magistrates' powers caused a corresponding increase of insubordination and crime.[18] A dramatic example of this contention was provided in November 1833 when six assigned servants on the Hunter Valley estate of James Mudie absconded after robbing his house and attempting to kill his partner. Exclusives pointed to the "revolt" as a side-effect of the Summary Jurisdiction Act, while Bourke's supporters attributed the convicts' actions to ill-treatment.[19]

As historians have noted, the composition of the Hunter Valley's population goes far toward explaining why agitation against the Act was concentrated there. Because of the convict establishment at Newcastle, settlement in the Valley was officially discouraged until the 1820s. When the area was opened to large-scale settlement it was quickly populated by recently arrived free immigrants. By 1828 the district included about half of the colony's population outside Cumberland County. Not only did free immigrants make up a disproportionate number of the population (excluding convicts under sentence, forty-three per cent of the district's adult males were free immigrants compared to twenty-four per cent in the colony as a whole), but they owned most of the Valley's large land grants. At the same time, a disproportionate number of the colony's assigned servants were located in the district, since they were required to work large estates which combined grazing and farming.[20] The large proportion of free immigrants in the Hunter Valley, the fact that they settled in New South Wales under the repressive regime of Governor Darling, and the heavy dependence on convict labour, provides at least a partial explanation of the region's intense concern about convict discipline and crime.

The most recent study of the revolt on Mudie's estate suggests that convict insubordination was in fact a growing problem in the Hunter Valley, and was probably aggravated by Bourke's lenient policies. While allowing some latitude for Mudie's character, it is contended that master-servant relations on his property, Castle Forbes, were typical of the area.[21] At least one Hunter Valley resident, however, provides a different view. Edward John Eyre, who moved to the district in 1833, considered the assigned servants were extraordinarily well behaved, while most masters, either through disposition or self-interest, abstained from cruelty or tyranny. While misconduct was dealt with severely, he was surprised that convicts, considering their numbers and the meagre machinery for their control, submitted so quietly.[22]

The bench records for Patrick's Plains, where James Mudie served as a magistrate until his name was struck from the commission of the peace in 1836, also suggest that Castle Forbes was something less than typical. Of convict cases brought before the bench during 1834 and 1835, over ten per cent involved servants assigned to Mudie or his partner John Larnach (see table 1). The offences with which his servants were charged were common enough; mostly neglect of work, insolence, absconding or being absent without leave, losing sheep, and suspected pilfering. But the large number of cases indicates that Mudie, his servants, or both, were unrepresentative of the district. Overall there was a marked increase in cases brought before the court between 1834 and 1835, which tends to substantiate charges of increasing crime. But this increase was made up almost entirely of minor breaches of discipline rather than more serious offences. The offences themselves were often extremely trivial or vaguely defined, such as "lurking in a suspicious manner", "allowing a man to come to kitchen at improper hour", "improper conduct", "bad language", "working on overtime against orders", and "troublesome to mistress". One assigned servant, Peter Kench, was sentenced to seven days solitary confinement on bread and water for failing to take some medicine procured for him by his master.[23] It is possible either that convicts were indeed becoming more insubordinate, or simply that masters were adopting a more rigid attitude towards the conduct of assigned servants.

The Patrick's Plains records also indicate the extent to which the lash was relied upon for coercion. Over seventy per cent of the punishments awarded by the bench during 1834 and 1835 were floggings. Most of the remaining convicts punished were sentenced to short terms of imprisonment, or to an iron gang for six to twelve months.[24] Floggings exceeding fifty lashes required the supervision of a doctor, and initially convicts were forwarded to Newcastle to receive such punishments. To reduce further the time assigned servants were absent from their work, the court engaged the services of a physician in 1835 who could superintend floggings on the spot.[25]

Despite charges that Bourke's regime undermined convict discipline, it is questionable whether prisoners were treated with less severity during his governorship. Magistrates were urged to supervise floggings more closely, on the grounds that "to permit their careless or imperfect infliction is but to invite a repetition of crime".[26] In comparison with the first year of Bourke's administration, there was a decline in the average number of lashes inflicted at each flogging following the Summary Jurisdiction Act. But the number of floggings in the colony, in proportion to the number of male convicts, increased after 1832

Table 1. Convict Cases Brought Before the Patrick's Plains Bench, 1834–35.

Offence	Convicts Assigned to James Mudie and John Larnach				Other Convict Cases				Total			
	1834		1835		1834		1835		1834		1835	
	No.	%	No.	%	No.	%	No.	%	No.	%	No.	%
Absconding and Absent Without Leave	10	14.5	12	16.2	174	34.3	187	29.4	184	31.9	199	28.1
Insolence, Disobedience, or Abusive Language	15	21.7	10	13.5	86	17.0	105	16.5	101	17.5	115	16.2
Losing or Neglect of Livestock	9	13.0	17	23.0	54	10.7	95	15.0	63	10.9	112	15.8
Neglect of Work	14	20.3	8	10.8	33	6.5	63	9.9	47	8.2	71	10.0
Feigning Sickness or Prevarication	1	1.4	4	5.4	32	6.3	24	3.8	33	5.7	28	3.9
Drunkenness and Disorderly Conduct	0	0.0	1	1.4	21	4.1	42	6.6	21	3.6	43	6.1
Offence Against the Person	1	1.4	2	2.7	15	3.0	17	2.7	16	2.7	19	2.7
Offence Against Property	13	18.8	12	16.2	72	14.2	77	12.1	85	14.8	89	12.5
Other Miscellaneous Offences	6	8.7	8	10.8	20	3.9	25	3.9	26	4.5	33	4.7
Total	69		74		507		635		576		709	

Source: **Register** of Convict Cases Tried Before the Singleton (Patrick's Plains) Bench, January 1834 – December 1835, N.S.W. SA 7/3714.

(see table 2).[27] Again this may reflect an increase in convict insubordination, or simply a reaction against Bourke's reforms and the widespread
belief that convicts were becoming more intractable.

Table 2.   Floggings Administered to Convicts in New South Wales,
1830–37.

Year	No. of Floggings	Average No. of Lashes Inflicted at Each Flogging	No. of Floggings per 100 Male Convicts
1830	2,985	41	16
1831	3,163	58	14
1832	3,816	43	16
1833	5,824	41	25
1834	6,328	38	25
1835	7,103	46	26
1836	6,904	44	23
1837	5,916	45	18

Source: Return of Floggings, enclosed in Gipps to Glenelg, 8 November
1838, *HRA*, ser. 1, vol. 19, p. 644.

In either case, magistrates might contrive to circumvent the new
regulations. In order to award more than fifty lashes for an infraction
of convict discipline, it was allegedly common practice at some benches
to "split offences".[28] A convict charged with disobedience while
drunk, for example, might be penalized fifty lashes for drunkenness,
and another fifty for disobedience. Thus Edward Hickie, tried before
the Patrick's Plains bench in 1835, received seventy-five lashes, partly
for being absent all night, and partly for "impertinence". His master,
Archibald Bell, explained that Hickie said impertinent things such as
that "he worked quite hard enough for the rations I gave him".[29] If
convicts felt smug about the restraints imposed on JPs, it was also easy,
as John Blanch discovered, for masters to think up additional charges.
Richard Carter told the bench that he discovered Blanch drunk one
night, and that when he ordered him to take a flock of sheep out he
insolently refused. When Carter threatened to bring him to court,
Blanch allegedly replied he didn't care, and that "they could give him
no more than fifty". Perhaps to counter such bravado, Carter complained at the same time Blanch had gone several times into his kitchen
"to make attempts upon the chastity of a married woman". Although
Carter noted the woman, a servant, had complained repeatedly of this,
it had apparently not been worth a trip to the bench before. The court
sentenced Blanch to fifty lashes for drunkenness, and another fifty for
"attempting the chastity of a woman".[30] The same day, Terence Riley

was sentenced to one hundred lashes for losing sheep on two occasions.[31]

At the same time, convicts with grievances against their masters remained largely at the mercy of self-interested magistrates. Despite the *Sydney Herald's* claim that masters were brought almost daily before the bench at the instigation of their convict servants under Bourke's administration,[32] complaints by servants were relatively few. Many would-be complainants were probably deterred by the necessity of requesting a pass from their master in order to appear before the court. Indeed, William Wellbec was sentenced to twenty-five lashes by the Patrick's Plains bench for the impertinent manner in which he demanded a pass, so that he might inquire whether or not he was compelled to work for another man as ordered by his master.[33] Not uncommonly, convicts initiating complaints against their masters ended up being flogged for making "trifling and frivolous charges". Even if the charge were proved, an assigned servant might find himself penalized. In another case before the Patrick's Plains bench, Thomas Graves complained about the quality of the rations issued to him. The bench agreed that part of the meat, which was brought to the court for inspection, was "very bad indeed", and considered he had just reason to complain. Nevertheless, he was sentenced to twenty-five lashes for insolence to his overseer when insisting that his ration be exchanged.[34]

Aside from the possibility of suffering at the hands of the local JPs, there were two further reasons why assigned servants were probably discouraged from seeking redress through the courts. First, the penalties which masters received were relatively innocuous. In 1835 John Larnach, the partner and son-in-law of James Mudie who was the intended victim of the Castle Forbes revolt, was brought before the Patrick's Plains bench for assaulting an assigned servant with a cane. In his defence, Larnach told the court that the servant's manner was so annoying and indifferent that he was unable to restrain himself. The fact that Larnach was fined one pound was presumably small consolation to a man who for a similar act would have faced a flogging at the least, and more probably twelve months in an iron gang.[35]

A second deterrent to complaints by convicts was the knowledge that their masters could subsequently make their lives miserable. William Phillips, assigned to William Brooks, told the Patrick's Plains bench that since he brought his master before the magistrates some time ago he had been continually abused. Brooks called him names such as "vagabond" and "villain". Although he was formerly a house servant, he had been turned out, and was no longer allowed into the yard even to receive his rations. He was forbidden to talk to the other men, and they were told not to have any intercourse with him. He was refused a knife to cut his meat with, and had no thread to mend his pants.

Brooks denied the charges, stating that while he may have called him a name once, he refused Phillips entry to the yard because his wife was afraid of him. He had forgotten about the thread, and had ordered the prisoner to be given a knife, which he assumed he received. As a result, Phillips was sentenced to twenty-five lashes for making a frivolous complaint against Brooks.[36]

This is not to imply that convicts were treated with unmitigated brutality. Practices varied from bench to bench. Not infrequently, masters intervened to have punishments prescribed by the court reduced, either through compassion for their assigned servants, or so that they would not be deprived of their labour. But the Patrick's Plains records suggest that Bourke's policies did not overturn the authority of JPs and masters in the Hunter Valley.

Governor Bourke's liberality seems more apparent in relation to ex-convicts than prisoners under sentence. In this respect, a new jury law became the focal point of attacks on his administration. As provided under the New South Wales Act of 1823, criminal cases before the Supreme Court were tried by a jury of seven military officers.[37] The likelihood that the issue of jurors' qualifications would inflame relations between free immigrants and ex-convicts was a principal reason why trial by civilian juries was not introduced.[38] Before leaving England, however, Bourke had been given permission to introduce civil juries in criminal cases. An Act was narrowly passed by the Legislative Council in 1833, which while retaining military juries, provided that defendants in criminal cases might choose to be tried by a jury of twelve civilians.[39] The option of military juries was retained until after Bourke's departure, when they were abolished by the Jury Trials Act of 1839.[40]

Under the Act of 1833, ex-convicts who fulfilled the prescribed property qualifications, and who were not of "bad repute" or convicted of an offence in the colony, were eligible to serve as jurors. The exclusive faction attacked the so-called "convict jury law" as intolerable. It was unfair, they contended, to expect "untainted" persons to sit in the jury box with or be tried by convicted felons. More importantly, it was argued that the sympathies of ex-convict jurors lay with the accused, and resulted in improper verdicts, and stimulated an increase of crime.[41]

The 1833 Jury Act seemed a direct threat to exclusives, since if ex-convicts were eligible as jurors they would in all probability be considered eligible as future electors. The exclusives were further alarmed by the activities of the emancipist or "liberal" faction, who in May 1835 organized the Australian Patriotic Association to press for reforms including trial by jury in all criminal cases and a representative legislature elected on a wide franchise. Exclusives stated their views in two

petitions sent to England in 1836. Central to their arguments was a
"fearful increase of crime" which they alleged Burton's jury charge confirmed. They cited the prevalence of crime in the colony as evidence of
its lack of fitness for free institutions. Furthermore, they contended
that if ex-convicts were admitted to all the rights and privileges of
citizenship, transportation would no longer act as a punishment, but an
incitement to crime in Britain.[42]

The petitioners' views were amplified in two books published in
1837. James Mudie returned to England in 1836, incensed at Bourke's
initiation of an inquiry into the treatment of convicts on his estate, and
the subsequent omission of his name from the commission of the peace
despite the fact that no charges of misconduct were proven against him.
The professed object of his book, *The Felonry of New South Wales,*
was to expose Bourke's government and its "criminal collusion with
convicts".[43] The second and more important work, at least in terms of
credibility, was by James Macarthur, who left the colony in 1836 to
support the petitioners' demands in London. His book, *New South
Wales; Its Present State and Future Prospects,* was basically an extended
essay in support of the exclusive petitions, which included special
emphasis on the colony's criminal statistics.

In order to reinforce their demands for civil juries and a representative legislature, the emancipist faction adopted a counter-petition. The
petition denied that the condition of convicts in New South Wales
served as a temptation to the commission of crime. Moreover, it was
argued that the exclusion of ex-convicts from civil liberties would
destroy the most powerful stimulus to reform and divide colonists into
castes. As for the colony's crime rate, the petitioners pointed out that
the statistics alluded to by Burton in his jury charge, which were for
capital convictions between 1833 and 1835, demonstrated a decrease
rather than an increase in crime. Although the number of capital convictions increased from 135 to 148 between 1833 and 1834, the
number fell to 116 in 1835. This was in spite of the colony's increasing
population.[44] Governor Bourke as well contradicted the alleged prevalence of crime in the colony, pointing out that Burton himself denied
ever expressing an opinion in public or private as to whether crime was
increasing or decreasing.[45]

Whether the colony's crime rate appeared to be increasing or
decreasing depended in fact on the criminal statistics referred to (see
figure 1). There was an erratic decline in capital convictions relative to
the colony's population during Bourke's administration. The rate of
conviction for all offences tried before the Supreme Court showed a
similar trend. But as James Macarthur pointed out in his book, correspondence with the Colonial Office and his evidence to the Molesworth
Committee, there were strong grounds for arguing that crime had

increased. By including convictions before courts of quarter sessions, Macarthur indicated that the total number of criminal convictions by the superior courts in New South Wales more than doubled between 1831 and 1835.[46]

Was crime increasing or decreasing? The complexity of variables affecting criminal statistics makes any interpretation difficult. In relation to the early 1830s, the problem is magnified by important changes in the criminal law and judicial system. Both exclusives and

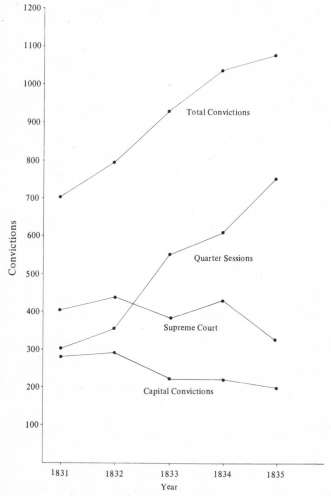

Figure 1. Convictions before the Superior Courts per 100,000 Inhabitants in New South Wales, 1831–35.

emancipists overlooked or chose to ignore factors which would have an obvious impact on the statistics, but which undermined their respective arguments.

Reference by emancipists to the declining number of capital convictions in New South Wales ignored a recent reduction in the number of capital offences. Under an Act of 1833, the colony adopted British legislation abolishing the death penalty for cattle, horse and sheep stealing, stealing in a dwelling house property worth five pounds or more and forgery.[47] A decrease in the number of capital convictions from 1833 may have reflected nothing more than the fact that these crimes were no longer capital offences.

James Macarthur was quick to point this out, but for two reasons the same change in the criminal law almost certainly artificially inflated the colony's total conviction rate which he referred to in asserting crime had increased. First, the knowledge that offenders would no longer be executed probably increased the likelihood of juries convicting persons charged with stock theft, stealing in a dwelling house and forgery. At least in England and Wales the ratio of convictions to acquittals greatly increased following the abrogation of the death penalty.[48] Second, the change in the criminal law probably increased the number of prosecutions initiated for these offences. Prosecutors were no longer compelled to travel to Sydney, where all capital offences were tried before the Supreme Court, but might attend courts of quarter sessions located nearer the place of the offence. Since there were continual complaints that people were deterred from prosecuting offences because of the time and money involved in travelling great distances to the superior courts, this would presumably increase the number of offences brought to trial.

A more publicized factor affecting the criminal statistics was the change in the colony's jury system. Exclusives contended that the introduction of civil juries, with ex-convict jurors, encouraged crime because of the facilities offered for acquittal. To the extent that returns are available, they suggest that convictions were less likely to result in cases tried by civil than military juries.[49] It is unclear, however, whether this reflects on the composition of the juries, or the types of defendants who chose different modes of trial. The colony's judicial officers, at Bourke's solicitation, expressed their satisfaction with the verdicts of civil juries.[50] There was also some contradiction in exclusives arguing that the improper acquittals of civil juries encouraged crime, while pointing to the colony's conviction rate as proof that crime was increasing.

There was one further change of profound significance. This was the restriction of magistrates' authority under the Summary Jurisdiction Act of 1832. Although the Act's limitation of flogging received greatest attention, it also limited the penalties which could be awarded for more serious offences. Before 1832, magistrates were empowered to sentence convicts to transportation for up to three years.[51] Two or more JPs sitting together were also vested with the same powers of summary jurisdiction over convicts exercised by courts of quarter sessions.[52] Under the 1832 Act, the maximum penalty which JPs could award to male convicts was twelve months on the public roads, and six months hard labour in prison for women. More importantly, the jurisdiction of magistrates sitting in petty sessions was restricted to simple larcenies involving property worth less than five pounds.[53] This meant that many cases previously disposed of by magistrates were from 1832 tried by courts of quarter sessions. The upsurge in convictions before courts of quarter sessions during the early 1830s was almost certainly due in large part to the transfer of business from the lower courts.[54]

Changes in the criminal law, jury system and magistrates' jurisdiction make the assertions of the emancipist and exclusive factions concerning New South Wales' crime rate extremely dubious. Emancipists could justifiably claim that capital convictions and convictions before the Supreme Court declined. But this overlooked a reduction in the number of capital offences, and a consequent reduction in cases handled by the Supreme Court. Exclusives could demonstrate that total convictions before the superior courts increased during the same period. But this reflected in part the greater ease with which prosecutions could be undertaken for a number of offences, as well as the transfer of cases previously tried by JPs to the quarter sessions. The absence of comparable statistics for the periods immediately preceding and following the years between 1831 and 1835 makes any apparent trend still more difficult to assess. It was perhaps through a recognition of these problems that both sides hedged their interpretations. The *Australian* asserted that even if crime had increased, this was usually the case in advancing societies, where "men are stimulated to increasing activity in every way".[55] The *Sydney Herald* explained that if the number of serious offences committed in the colony had recently decreased, this was due largely to tighter convict discipline implemented under the pressure of free immigrants.[56]

Whether crime was actually increasing or decreasing was in fact of secondary importance to the social and political significance invested in crime. By emphasizing the prevalence of crime in the colony, exclusives could hope to discredit Bourke's liberal policies, while indicating the unfitness of ex-convicts to assume a responsible role in government. The concept of a "criminal class" provided a convenient rationale for exclusive pretensions. Ex-convicts, it was asserted, managed to become wealthy only through dishonest or questionable practices. They acquired money through keeping grog shops and gambling houses, receiving stolen goods, or plundering the government. In rural areas crime was attributed almost entirely to ex-convicts and ticket of leave holders occupying crown lands.[57] Stigmatizing one's opponents as criminals was an obvious expedient in countering the emancipist faction's claim for a share of political power. Their petition for jury trial and a legislature was attacked as a display of names, which included the signatures of "the very lowest grades of persons in this vicious society".[58]

The criminality imputed to emancipists and their supporters was counterbalanced by the importance exclusives attached to their own respectability. As Michael Roe points out, the concept of respectability gave the colonial gentry much of their cohesion.[59] The same concept served as a linchpin of authority. Since ex-convicts were included among the wealthiest sections of the community, property alone could not form the basis of exclusive claims for political dominance. There was, one anonymous writer noted, a marked "distinction between questionable respectability which, in this Colony, is claimed from the acquisition of wealth *alone*, and that respectability which is naturally inferred from the union of wealth and *unblemished character*."[60] Exclusives based their legitimacy as the colony's natural rulers primarily on their moral superiority. This was clearly understood by the emancipist faction, whose members sarcastically referred to exclusives as the "respectables" and the community's "moral ascendancy".[61] The *Australian* noted that the term "respectability" itself was used as a synonym for what was essentially a political clique.

> By some persons this designation is given to those who are rich — by others to those who are well disposed — who are honest and virtuous — or who are their friends and acquaintances; but there is another and a small class which twice a week receives that designation from the *Herald* — those, namely, who are opposed to the present government.[62]

The same technique was used in an attempt to claim the lion's share of New South Wales' land and labour. In this, however, there was a degree of complicity between wealthy members of the emancipist and exclusive groups, anticipating their co-operation once transportation ended. Large landholders in both factions had reason to resent the issue of new assignment regulations under Bourke's administration in May 1835.[63] The regulations, which placed a ceiling on the number of convicts which could be assigned to any one settler and provided a more generous allocation of convicts to settlers with land under cultivation, were criticized as favouring small farmers at the expense of those with more substantial holdings. The assignment of servants to smallholders or "dungaree" settlers was attacked as contrary to the objects of restraining and reforming the prison population. Significantly, the *Herald* objected to free immigrants as well as ex-convicts on this ground.

> Any man, whether an emancipated Convict or free Emigrant, who drinks, smokes and eats with his Convict servants, will at last also *Rob* with them. Therefore, from all such persons Convict servants should be immediately withdrawn; for it is impossible to preserve discipline, even the distinction between vice and virtue, master and servant, free man and Convict, where such familiarity exists.[64]

Thomas Potter Macqueen, a Hunter Valley settler and magistrate, similarly argued that convicts should not be assigned to anyone possessing insufficient property to maintain themselves "wholly above the *society* of such convicts", including all assisted immigrants who had been in the colony less than seven years.[65]

At the same time, members of the emancipist faction joined exclusives in a law and order campaign against squatting. The term "squatter" initially referred to ex-convicts and ticket of leave holders who took unauthorized possession of crown lands, and allegedly lived by plundering their neighbours.[66] It was largely the squatter menace which stimulated the appointment of a select committee on police and gaols in 1835 chaired by Alexander McLeay, the colony's colonial secretary from 1826 to 1837 and a staunch supporter of the exclusive faction. Witnesses before the committee were virtually unanimous in pointing to the danger squatting posed to the lives and property of settlers, and insisting that they be excluded from crown lands. These included John Jamison, a Penrith JP and the first president of the Australian Patriotic Association. He thought ticket of leave holders should be excluded from occupying crown lands under threat of having their tickets revoked. It was also Jamison who proposed the system of licensing enforced by itinerant JPs and mounted police which was eventually adopted in regulating territory beyond the boundaries of location.[67] The *Sydney Gazette,* which generally supported the emancipist faction before a change of editorship in 1836, also emphasized the necessity of protecting the interests of the "higher orders" against the depredations of squatters.[68]

While expressing concern over the problem, Governor Bourke pointed out that so-called squatters, as far as their unauthorized occupation of crown lands went, were merely following the steps of more influential colonists who held no better title to the land.[69] The rapidity with which "squatting" assumed respectable connotations once the practice was put on a legal basis in 1836 was witness to this fact. It seems likely, as S.H. Roberts suggests, that wealthier settlers raised the bogey of criminal depredators partly to divert attention from their own large-scale egress beyond the boundaries of location.[70] More importantly perhaps, the alleged criminality of small settlers served as a rationale for their exclusion from crown lands. Large landholders raised the same charges of rampant crime against selectors following new land legislation in the 1860s.[71] The exclusion of "small men" from crown lands would not only ensure the settlement of the land by wealthier colonists, but also augment the supply of labour. As one Bathurst settler complained, the facilities afforded to ticket of leave holders for acquiring land and amassing property "by illegal means", meant that they had neither the time nor inclination to work for others.[72]

The similar interests shared by wealthy emancipists and exclusives became still more apparent in their stand on the maintenance of convict labour. In their petitions of 1836, exclusives called for an official investigation into the condition of New South Wales and the transportation system. They perhaps had in mind something along the lines of John Thomas Bigge's commission of inquiry, which was critical of Governor Macquarie's emancipist policies. The upshot was instead the appointment of a select committee on transportation in April 1837, the Molesworth Committee, which laid its final report before the House of Commons in August 1838.

In New South Wales the Molesworth Committee evoked a sharp reaction from both exclusives and emancipists. Even before Molesworth issued his final report, news of the evidence taken by the committee in 1837 adequately foreshadowed his conclusions, and was met by a storm of colonial criticism. In May 1838 a petition was signed by over five hundred citizens of "great respectability" calling upon the Legislative Council to counteract "the evil impression" created in England by the committee.[73] Opposition to the Molesworth Committee resulted largely from its recommendation that transportation and assignment be abolished. Settlers feared losing their cheap convict work force. At the same time, colonists feared the report would discourage immigration to the colony. Molesworth's involvement with the South Australia Company incited charges that he wished to divert immigration away from New South Wales by portraying it as a hotbed of depravity.[74]

Aside from threatening New South Wales' economy, the Molesworth Committee challenged the upper classes' self-image of respectability. The colony's crime rate was seized upon by the committee as evidence of the transportation system's failure. Although the committee confirmed the exclusive stereotype of convicts and ex-convicts, it took their interpretation of the criminal statistics a step further. According to Molesworth's report, not only was crime increasing in a greater proportion than the population, but this indicated "too plainly the progressive demoralization both of the bond and of the free inhabitants of that colony".[75] Not surprisingly, this conclusion offended free immigrants, and especially exclusives, who were prone to emphasize the contaminating influence of convictism, while denying any alteration in their own morals.

The Legislative Council, in defending the efficacy of transportation, resolved that free immigrants "of character and capital", as well as the rising generation of native-born, constituted a body "sufficient to impress a character of respectability upon the Colony at large".[76] The colony's élite was also vigorously defended by Judge William Burton in an article published in 1840. Although his 1835 jury charge was cited almost incessantly by the Molesworth Committee to support its findings, he bitterly resented the committee's conclusion, "rather by process of reasoning than by proof, that the whole society, which is infested by such evils, must be depraved".[77] According to Burton the "superior classes", which included government officers, lawyers, large landholders, merchants and clergy, were "as a class as respectable a body of gentlemen as perhaps were ever associated together in any colony". Their social life did not differ from that of England, while colonial ladies were "precisely what English ladies should be".[78]

The character of New South Wales' upper classes was defended not only by comparison with Britain, but by contrast with the colony's lower orders. Judge Burton's characterization of polite society differed markedly from his perception of the working classes, who were vulnerable to the contaminating influence of convictism.

> Apart from mere dishonesty ... the convict vices manifest themselves continually in the lower order – that of servants of either sex, and labourers especially, in a total absence of good principle – in language profane, disgusting and unclean, and in suspicions of each other and those around them most odious – the offspring only of minds unpure.[79]

In later years the report and evidence of the Molesworth Committee was variously referred to as an accurate description of New South Wales' past demoralization, or as the epitome of Britain's unjust perceptions of the colony. In either case, it left a lasting scar on the community's consciousness. One of its apparent effects was to alter radically portrayals of crime in the press. The *Herald,* formerly so active in fuelling a crime wave, considered the Molesworth Committee's reference to crime and contamination a "monstrous caricature".[80] The *Sydney Gazette,* under Tory management from 1836, made a similar *volte-face.* In spite of the colony's large convict population, it found "that life is safer and property more secure than in any one of the larger towns in England. Sydney may be traversed at any hour of the night with greater safety to purse and person than many parts of

London during the broad light of day."[81] More often, analogies were drawn between the colony and England's port towns. Attorney-General Plunkett, for example, asserted that Sydney's streets were as quiet as those of any English seaport, and that if attacks on drunkards were excepted, robberies were no more numerous.[82] The *Monitor* took the comparison further, noting that the periodic revelry of bush workers sprang largely from the same conditions of isolation which motivated seamen.

> Sir William Molesworth and his compeers think little of English sailors residing on shore in brothels, until they have expended their pay in the lowest haunts of vice. Why then make such a to-do, and open their eyes so wide, and why stands their hair erect on their heads, because the same effects are produced in New South Wales from causes analagous, if not similar?[83]

New South Wales' official crime rate had significantly declined at the time these observations were made. Nevertheless, it is uncertain to what extent the colony experienced a real upsurge in the incidence of criminal activity during the mid-1830s. Aside from the factors already mentioned as artificially inflating the colony's crime rate, it is probable that growing concern stimulated increasing prosecutions. Newspapers in particular were capable of shaping public perceptions of crime in a manner which did not necessarily conform with actual criminal trends. By increasing sensitivity to offences and galvanizing the community and police into action, they might produce a self-fulfilling prophecy.[84]

No doubt some settlers genuinely feared for their lives and property, especially when it was thought that Governor Bourke's administration threatened their control over convict labourers. Residents of the Hunter Valley may have felt particularly vulnerable considering the concentration of assigned servants in the area, and because many landholders were relative newcomers with limited experience in managing convicts. But crime also assumed a significance which was essentially political. This point was clearly stated by Francis Forbes, who served as New South Wales' first chief justice from 1824 to 1836. Although he was a partisan of Bourke, there are strong grounds for accepting his assertion that clamour about a relaxation of convict discipline and increasing crime resulted largely because this was the only cry which colonists supposed would be heard in England.[85]

Perceptions of who were "criminals" also served to enhance the power of the upper classes. Socially, charges of insecurity and a laxity of convict discipline reflected a desire that transported persons be kept in their "proper place" and demonstrate a "proper humility".[86] Not surprisingly, those most insecure about their own moral status were often the most rabid in their denunciation of convict morality. James Mudie apparently tried to defraud the British government and fathered several illegitimate children before emigrating to New South Wales. Ernest Augustus Slade, another principal witness before the Molesworth Committee, was allowed to resign as superintendent of Hyde Park Barracks after he was discovered cohabiting with a convict woman.[87]

Economically, the alleged criminality of ex-convicts served as a rationale for denying them access to labour and land. Politically, their alleged criminality provided a basis for excluding them from participation in democratic institutions. As James Macarthur later conceded, the rhetoric of exclusives was motivated largely by fear of a "convict ascendancy".[88] Already, by the end of the 1830s, portrayals of rampant crime were recanted as fear of political domination by ex-convicts dissipated, and exclusives became convinced of the need for convict labour.

This attempt to relegate convicts to a role of "outsiders" in the community on the basis of their moral inferiority was recurrent, although views of who assigned them this status and why changed over time. The unanimity of wealthy emancipists and exclusives on the squatting issue foreshadowed their closing of ranks against the social aspirations of an increasing number of immigrants. Large landholders became the principal defenders of convict morality. But just as convicts provided a counter-image for exclusive pretensions to respectability, the dangers of a criminal class and contamination were later invoked to buttress the authority of the urban middle classes, and to protect the interests of immigrant wage earners.

Notes

1. Stephen Henry Roberts, *The Squatting Age in Australia 1835–1847* (Melbourne, 1935), p. 24.
2. *Monitor,* 21 November 1835.
3. Concerning Burton's career see Kenneth G. Allars, "Sir William Westbrooke Burton", *JRAHS* vol. 37, pt 5 (1951), pp. 257–94; *ADB*, vol. 2, pp. 184–86.
4. William Burton to Edmund Burton, 29 November 1833 (typescript), Burton Correspondence, ML, MSS. 834, p. 111.
5. Ibid., p. 109.
6. Hazel King, *Richard Bourke* (London, 1971), pp. 174–75.
7. *Sydney Herald,* 30 November 1835.
8. *Australian,* 24 November 1835.
9. Strictly defined, "emancipists" were convicts who received conditional or absolute pardons, as opposed to "expiree" convicts who completed their original sentence. In practice the term "emancipist" was applied to all ex-convicts, and it is in this sense that the word is used. In this chapter, "emancipists" is used also to refer to the faction or party known by that name during the 1830s. The emancipist faction was by no means composed entirely

of ex-convicts. Alan Atkinson indicates that the largest number of subscribers to the Australian Patriotic Association, typically regarded as an emancipist organization, were free immigrants. The Association, however, drew support largely from the ranks of ex-convicts, and was dependent on ex-convict financial support. Alan Thomas Atkinson, "The Political Life of James Macarthur" (Ph.D. thesis, Australian National University, 1976), especially pp. 153, 156.

10. See ibid., pp. 155–56.
11. *Sydney Herald,* 18 May 1835.
12. *Sydney Herald,* 30 November, 3 December 1835.
13. [Colony of N.S.W.] 11 Geo. 4, No. 12, sec. 3.
14. [Colony of N.S.W.] 3 Wm. 4, No. 3, sec. 18, 27.
15. Evidence of John Richard Hardy and John Street to the Committee on Police and Gaols, N.S.W., *V & PLC,* 1839, vol. 2, pp. 271, 287.
16. Bourke to Stanley, 15 January 1834, *HRA,* ser. 1, vol. 17, p. 324.
17. See for example *Sydney Herald,* 30 May 1836.
18. Petition of Landholders and Free Inhabitants of the District of Hunter's River, and Petition of Landholders and Free Inhabitants of the Districts of Newcastle and Port Stephens, N.S.W., *V & PLC,* 1833, pp. 131–32; Petitions of Landholders and Free Inhabitants of the District of Hunter's River, enclosed in Bourke to Secretary of State, 11 December 1834, Despatches from Governor of New South Wales, Enclosures, ML, A1267-B; Appendix to the Select Committee on Transportation, *PP,* 1837, vol. 19 (518), pp. 407–8, 552–54.
19. See Sandra J. Blair, "The Revolt at Castle Forbes: A Catalyst to Emancipist Emigrant Confrontation", *JRAHS* vol. 64, pt 2 (September 1978), pp. 89–107; B. T. Dowd and Averil Fink, "Harlequin of the Hunter. 'Major' James Mudie of Castle Forbes (Part 2)", *JRAHS* vol. 55, pt 1 (March 1969), pp. 86–93.
20. T.M. Perry, *Australia's First Frontier. The Spread of Settlement in New South Wales 1788–1829* (Melbourne, 1963; reprint ed. 1965), especially pp. 72-75, 78. See also King, *Bourke,* pp. 162-63, Blair, "Revolt at Castle Forbes", pp. 93–96.
21. Blair, "Revolt at Castle Forbes", pp. 98–100.
22. Edward John Eyre, "Autobiographical Narrative of the Residence and Exploration in Australia (1832–39) of Edward John Eyre", Unpublished MSS., ML (microfilm), CY reel 118, pp. 60, 62.
23. Singleton (Patrick's Plains) Bench Book, 3 December 1835, N.S.W. SA, 5/7685.
24. Calculated from Register of Convict Cases Tried Before the Singleton (Patrick's Plains) Bench, January 1834–December 1835, N.S.W. SA, 7/3714.
25. Charles Forbes to Col. Sec., 23 April, 10 May 1835, Col. Sec., Letters Received, N.S.W. SA, 4/2292.1; Col. Sec. to Police Magistrate, Patrick's Plains, 4 June 1835, Col. Sec., Letters Sent, N.S.W. SA, 4/3837, p. 276.
26. Circular, 18 May 1833, *New South Wales Government Gazette,* 1833, vol. 2.
27. See also Peter N. Grabosky, *Sydney in Ferment. Crime, Dissent and Official Reaction 1788–1973* (Canberra 1977), pp. 65–66.
28. Report of the Committee on Police and Gaols, N.S.W., *V & PLC,* 1839, vol. 2, p. 209; Evidence of John Street, Henry Fysche Gisborne and Charles Cowper to the Committee, pp. 289, 302, 308.
29. Singleton (Patrick's Plains) Bench Book, 7 September 1835, N.S.W. SA, 5/7685.

30. Singleton (Patrick's Plains) Bench Book, 31 December 1841, N.S.W. SA, 5/7686.
31. Ibid.
32. *Sydney Herald,* 8 August 1835.
33. Singleton (Patrick's Plains) Bench Book, 13 July 1835, N.S.W. SA, 5/7685.
34. Ibid., 3 September 1835.
35. Ibid., 8 October 1835.
36. Ibid., 24 September 1835.
37. 4 Geo. IV, c. 96, sec. 4. Concerning the evolution of trial by jury in New South Wales see J. M. Bennett, "The Establishment of Jury Trial in New South Wales", *Sydney Law Review* vol. 3, no. 2 (March 1961), pp. 463–85; C. H. Currey, "Chapters on the Legal History of New South Wales, 1788–1863", (LL.D. thesis, University of Sydney, 1929), pp. 418–27; A.C.V. Melbourne, *Early Constitutional Development in Australia. New South Wales 1788–1856, Queensland 1859–1922,* edited by R. B. Joyce (London, 1934; 2nd ed., St Lucia, 1963), especially pp. 42–46, 51, 61–63, 78–79, 194.
38. See Report of the Commission of Inquiry on the Judicial Establishments of New South Wales, and Van Diemen's Land, *PP,* 1823, vol. 10 (33), pp. 554–56.
39. [Colony of N.S.W.] 4 Wm. IV, No. 12, sec. 2, 12.
40. [Colony of N.S.W.] 3 Vic., No. 11, sec. 1–2.
41. See for example *Sydney Herald,* 7 May, 2 November 1835; James Macarthur to George Grey, 9 February 1837, Petitions to the King, ML, A 284, especially pp. 102, 107.
42. Petition of Free Inhabitants of New South Wales to the King, and Petition of Free Inhabitants of New South Wales to the House of Commons, enclosed in Bourke to Glenelg, 13 April 1836, *HRA,* ser. 1, vol. 18, pp. 392–99.
43. James Mudie, *The Felonry of New South Wales; Being a Faithful Picture of the Real Romance of Life in Botany Bay with Anecdotes of Botany Bay Society and a Plan of Sydney,* edited by Walter Stone (London, 1837; reprint ed., Melbourne, 1964), p. 52.
44. Counter-Petition of Free Inhabitants of New South Wales to the House of Commons, 12 April 1836, enclosed in Bourke to Glenelg, 13 April 1836, *HRA,* ser. 1, vol. 18, pp. 399–403.
45. Bourke to Glenelg, 18 December 1835, 25 July 1836, *HRA,* ser. 1, vol. 18, pp. 228, 456–57.
46. James Macarthur, *New South Wales; Its Present State and Future Prospects* (London, 1837), especially pp. 34–55, appendix p. 54; Macarthur to Grey, 9, 10 February 1837, CO 201/267, ff. 511–38; Evidence of James Macarthur to the Select Committee on Transportation, *PP,* 1837, vol. 19 (518), pp. 163–64.
47. [Colony of N.S.W.] 4 Wm. IV, No. 4.
48. Macnab, "Crime in England and Wales", pp. 153–56.
49. Returns of Criminal Issues Tried by Juries, N.S.W., *V & PLC,* 1835, p. 371; 1836, p. 484.
50. Opinions of the Judges of the Supreme Court and Law Officers of the Crown upon the Verdicts of Civil Juries, N.S.W., *V & PLC,* 1836, pp. 465–72.
51. [Colony of N.S.W.] 11 Geo. IV, No. 12, sec. 3.
52. [Colony of N.S.W.] 11 Geo. IV, No. 13, sec. 2. See also 10 Geo. IV, No. 1, sec. 2.
53. [Colony of N.S.W.] 3 Wm. IV, No. 3, sec. 16, 18.
54. See William Bland, *New South Wales. Examination of Mr James Macarthur's*

Work, "New South Wales, Its Present State" (Sydney, 1838), pp. 64–66; *Australian,* 30 May 1838.

55. *Australian,* 8 April 1836.

56. *Sydney Herald,* 18 April 1836.

57. See for example Final Report of the Committee on Police and Gaols, N.S.W., *V & PLC,* 1835, p. 437; Evidence of James Mudie and James Macarthur to the Select Committee on Transportation, *PP,* 1837, vol. 19 (518), pp. 38, 107, 195, 223; Macarthur, *New South Wales,* p. 44; John Dunmore Lang, *Transportation and Colonization; or, The Causes of the Comparative Failure of the Transportation System in the Australian Colonies: With Suggestions For Ensuring Its Future Efficiency in Subserviency To Extensive Colonization* (London, 1837), p. 132.

58. *Sydney Herald,* 29 September 1836.

59. Roe, *Quest for Authority,* p. 40. See also R. W. Connell and T. H. Irving, *Class Structure in Australian History. Documents, Narrative and Argument* (Melbourne, 1980), pp. 62–63.

60. "A Colonist" to Editor, *Sydney Herald,* 13 June 1836. *Herald's* emphasis.

61. See Francis Forbes to James Stephen, 13 October 1836, CO 201/257, f. 585; Bland, *New South Wales,* pp. 45–47.

62. *Australian,* 19 February 1836.

63. Regulations for the Assignment of Male Convict Servants, 9 May 1835, *New South Wales Government Gazette,* 1835, pp. 287–94.

64. *Sydney Herald,* 3 December 1835. *Herald's* emphasis.

65. T. Potter Macqueen, *Australia. As She Is and As She May Be* (London, 1840), pp. 12, 23. Macqueen's emphasis.

66. S. H. Roberts takes great pains in distinguishing the term "squatter" as originally applied from its later usage. *Squatting Age,* pp. 67–84.

67. Evidence of John Jamison to Committee on Police and Gaols, N.S.W., *V & PLC,* 1835, pp. 337–38; Roberts, *Squatting Age,* pp. 72, 97.

68. *Sydney Gazette,* 28 April 1835.

69. Bourke to Glenelg, 18 December 1835, *HRA,* ser. 1, vol. 18, p. 230.

70. Roberts, *Squatting Age,* p. 81.

71. See C. M. H. Clark, *A History of Australia,* vol. 4: *The Earth Abideth For Ever 1851–1888* (Melbourne, 1978), p. 169; Atkinson, "James Macarthur", pp. 433–34.

72. "A.B.C." to Editor, *Sydney Herald,* 23 March 1835.

73. Petition from certain Magistrates, Landowners and other Colonists, N.S.W., *V & PLC,* 1838, pp. 229–32.

74. See for example *Sydney Gazette,* 18 January 1838; *Australian,* 8, 22 January 1839; *Sydney Herald,* 8 March 1839.

75. Report of the Select Committee on Tranportation, *PP,* 1837–38, vol. 22 (669), p. 28.

76. Resolutions, N.S.W., *V & PLC,* 1838, p. 262.

77. W. Westbrooke Burton, "State of Society and of Crime in New South Wales, During Six Years' Residence in that Colony", *Colonial Magazine and Commercial-Maritime Journal* vol. 1. (January-April 1840), p. 425.

78. Ibid., pp. 433–36.

79. Burton, "State of Society", *Colonial Magazine* vol. 2 (May-August 1840), p. 51.

80. *Sydney Herald,* 30 April 1841. The *Herald* was at this time under new management, but remained the colony's leading conservative newspaper.

81. *Sydney Gazette,* 26 February 1839.

82. LC, *Sydney Herald,* 6 July 1838.

83. *Monitor,* 30 May 1838.
84. See Stanley Cohen and Jock Young (eds.), *The Manufacture of News. Social Problems, Deviance and the Mass Media* (London, 1973; reprint ed., 1974), especially pp. 343–45; Jock Young, "Mass Media, Drugs, and Deviance", in Rock and McIntosh (eds.), *Deviance,* p. 243; Keith Windshuttle, "Granny Versus the Hooligans", in Paul R. Wilson and John Braithwaite (eds.), *Two Faces of Deviance. Crimes of the Powerless and the Powerful* (St Lucia, 1978), pp. 18–24.
85. Francis Forbes to James Stephen, 13 October 1836, CO 201/257, f. 585.
86. See for example Unsigned Letter to Editor, *Sydney Herald,* 17 September 1835; John Bingle to Secretary of State, 3 January 1837, Bingle Papers, ML, A1825.
87. Dowd and Fink, "James Mudie (Part 1)", *JRAHS* vol. 54, pt 4 (December 1968), pp. 373–75; Townsend, "Molesworth Enquiry", p. 37; *ADB,* vol. 2, p. 450.
88. LC, *SMH,* 28 September 1850.

2

Anatomy of a Crime Wave, 1844

> The year 1844 cannot . . . be rightly understood in its relation to
> the country we inhabit, unless viewed as part of that eventful
> cycle which will never be forgotten by the present generation,
> and which must ever form a dark spot in Australian chronology.[1]

When Judge William Burton departed New South Wales for Madras in
June 1844, the *Sydney Morning Herald* included in its eulogy prominent reference to his "Celebrated Charge" of 1835, which had disclosed
an increasing tide of depravity and crime in "appalling, but factful
colours".[2] During the same month, the *Herald* reported that the colony
was experiencing another crime wave.

> We feel that we are in circumstances of imminent danger to our
> property, and danger to our very lives. Robberies and murders,
> increasing both in numbers and in audacity, infest our streets and
> beset our inhabitations. Anxiety and alarm have seized upon our
> families, and in many instances have almost banished sleep from
> their eyes. . . . In short, a complete sense of insecurity has seized
> upon all classes, and we unanimously feel that something must be
> done — done effectually, and done forthwith.[3]

Crime became a dominant theme in the press, public meetings were
held, and a select committee of the Legislative Council was appointed
to investigate. The city's official crime rate was on the decline, and it
was conceded that crimes had not increased in number but in "inten-
sity".[4] The most apparent reason for citizens' "complete sense of
insecurity" was a rash of robberies and burglaries, and more especially
two homicides. In January 1844 John Thomas Knatchbull was convicted of murdering Ellen Jamieson in order to rob her, and within five
months another attempted robbery resulted in the death of James
Noble.

Homicides occurred with enough frequency in Sydney for one to
question why two deaths should have induced a crime wave. The
sensational Knatchbull murder case has been variously interpreted by
historians as being a diversion from one of the colony's worst economic
depressions, an indication of the community's advancing respectability,
and as the unjust treatment of a criminally insane man.[5] On closer

investigation a more complex explanation begins to unfold. The murder of Ellen Jamieson, like the subsequent murder of James Noble, assumed a largely symbolic importance for the community in relation to a number of long-standing grievances. It was these grievances, related to the continued presence of convicts in the colony after transportation officially ceased, which gave the 1844 crime wave much of its impetus.

On a Saturday evening on 6 January 1844, John Thomas Knatchbull was observed "lurking about" the shop of Ellen Jamieson. A neighbour later saw Knatchbull enter the shop about midnight, and after hearing some suspicious noises, sounded an alarm. The house was quickly surrounded, and on the arrival of the police the back door was broken in with an axe. Knatchbull was discovered behind the front door. Mrs Jamieson was lying in a pool of blood, her brain protruding, and pieces of her skull on the floor. The horror of her condition was magnified by the fact that she lingered on for twelve days before dying.[6]

The most sensational aspect of the crime was not its brutality, but Knatchbull's background. He was the second son of eighth baronet Sir Edward Knatchbull. In 1844 his half-brother, the ninth baronet, was an MP and a member of the Privy Council. Knatchbull was further distinguished for having served as a commander in the Royal Navy for five years, before losing his rank for failing to pay a private debt. Following a conviction for pickpocketing, he arrived in Sydney in 1825 under sentence of fourteen years transportation. A year after his arrival in New South Wales he was employed as a police runner, and in 1829 he received a ticket of leave for good conduct and for his capture of eight runaway convicts. In 1832 he was convicted of forging a cheque, using the inauspicious signature of Judge James Dowling. For this offence he was transported to Norfolk Island for seven years, and was then sent to Port Macquarie to serve the remainder of his original sentence. In 1842 he again received a ticket of leave.[7]

Knatchbull's aristocratic origins and connections raised doubts about whether justice would be impartially administered in his case. Despite his protests of innocence, there was little question of his guilt.[8] In addition to being discovered locked in Jamieson's house, his pants were spattered with blood. When searched by the police money presumably stolen from Mrs Jamieson was found on him, as well as a woman's torn-off pocket. The alleged murder weapon, a tomahawk, was identified as the property of Knatchbull's landlord.

Robert Lowe, a recently-arrived barrister and member of the Legislative Council, acted as counsel for the defence. He argued that if Knatchbull had indeed committed the crime, he suffered from an "insanity of the will" and "an irresistible and overwhelming influence to the commission of crimes".[9] It was a defence inspired partly by desperation, and partly by the newly formulated McNaghten Rules in which British judges defined the legal criterion for insanity.[10] Lowe's argument also owed much to the pseudo-science of phrenology, which among other things claimed that a person's character might be determined by his or her cranial development. Sydney's populace was attuned to such theories, since lectures on phrenology were delivered at the School of Arts from the 1830s.[11] Knatchbull, described as having large features, "particularly in the upper part of the brow", was an obvious candidate for phrenological analysis.

Using the principles of phrenology, Lowe explained that the mind was divided in such a way that the impairment of one portion might render a person "perfectly insane", while in other respects they might appear normal. Knatchbull, he contended, laboured "under some mental infirmity which paralysed his better nature". This line of argument proved unsuccessful. Judge William Burton, who presided at the trial, instructed the jury that the case "might be very easily determined upon without resorting to any such abstract reasoning", and they returned a verdict of guilty without leaving the box.[12] Lowe's wife, Georgiana, alleged in a private letter that Judge Burton's conduct of the trial was prompted largely by vindictiveness, due to her husband's attacks on an Insolvent Act drawn up by Burton.[13] Lowe later attempted to have the penalty of death set aside on the grounds that Burton neglected to give directions for the disposal of Knatchbull's body when he pronounced sentence, but this objection was overruled.[14]

Many citizens considered that Lowe exceeded his duty in his defence of Knatchbull. The prospect that he might escape the gallows on a legal technicality added further indignation to what in some respects approached a public crusade. At one point, following the coroner's inquest into Jamieson's death, police feared that the populace might even take the law into their own hands.[15] Despite rumours of a reprieve, Knatchbull was executed on 13 February before a crowd estimated variously at from four to ten thousand. According to the *Herald*, which wedged its report of the event between the cricket scores and the opening of a Wesleyan chapel, the "solemnity" of the occasion was unbroken.[16]

The cathartic effect of Knatchbull's execution on the community was to prove short-lived. On a Sunday evening, 26 May, James Noble was fatally stabbed during an attempted robbery, just a block from where the murder of Ellen Jamieson occurred. The scenes which followed were reminiscent of the Knatchbull case. The inquest into Noble's death was crowded by respectably dressed people, while an estimated eight hundred to one thousand people assembled outside. The appearance of James Martin, the only one of three suspects so far apprehended, elicited groans and hisses, while the jury men received cheers. George Vigors and Thomas Burdett were captured later after committing a robbery on the Liverpool Road, and indicted for Noble's murder. John Rankin, an aging ticket of leave holder, was also indicted as an accessory, for supplying them with a pistol before Noble was killed. Before a packed courtroom Martin, acting as an "approver" for the prosecution, testified that it was Vigors who stabbed Noble during a struggle. Vigors, Burdett and Rankin were sentenced to death. Vigors and Burdett were executed on 13 August.[17]

Following the death of Noble there was evidence of a public panic. The *Herald* urged respectable householders to attend a public meeting necessitated *"by the first law of nature* – SELF DEFENCE".[18] Residents of at least two city wards had already held meetings asserting that they were in a state of collective terror.[19] In fact the *Australian* claimed that at one ward meeting the participants were beseiged by pickpockets.[20] At a mass assembly in the City Theatre, the citizenry was chillingly informed that "The red hand of murder had been raised", and that "The hour of dark had become the hour of danger; no man was safe".[21] Meanwhile the Legislative Council appointed a select committee to investigate the insecurity of life and property in Sydney. The committee was chaired by Dr Charles Nicholson, who had arrived in Sydney ten years earlier as a physician, but who by 1844 had forsaken private practice to look after his pastoral interests.[22]

The public sense of outrage and alarm created by the two killings can be attributed largely to the respectability of the murder victims. Judge Burton once observed of crime in New South Wales that "Happily the grosser injuries, those affecting life and chastity, are for the most part, confined to the equally worthless associates of those guilty of them".[23] Ellen Jamieson and James Noble were obvious exceptions to this maxim. Jamieson, the widowed mother of two children, supported herself by keeping a shop. Robert Lowe, perhaps to atone for his role as Knatchbull's attorney, became the orphans' legal guardian. James Noble, described as "a man of integrity, of quiet, industrious, plodding habits of business", fitted into a similar mould.[24] Like Ellen Jamieson, he was a member of John Dunmore Lang's Presbyterian congregation, and was reportedly engaged in Bible reading with his wife and sister-in-law only minutes before being stabbed. The fact that the victims had no prior association with their killers, and were seemingly killed at random, contributed to a sense of vulnerability. Underlying this feeling of insecurity, however, were other concerns. Jamieson's and Noble's deaths provided both a new sense of immediacy and a focal point for a number of grievances which were currently being discussed in the press and the Legislative Council.

Agitation about insecurity in Sydney was inspired partly by discontent with the City Council, in particular with its involvement with police administration. In 1843 the City Council had assumed financial responsibility for Sydney's police, although control of the force remained with the central government. Even before the Knatchbull case the *Herald* criticized the Council's handling of police affairs, stressing its intention to further reduce expenses, and hence the number of police.[25] A series of leading articles asserted that the numerical deficiency of the police was resulting in an alarming increase of crime.[26] Other newspapers as well alluded to daily "outrages" which were attributed to police retrenchment.[27] The murders of Jamieson and Noble lent dramatic support to this contention.

Criticism of police inadequacy in Sydney was not without basis. During 1843 the number of ordinary constables in the city was reduced from ninety to seventy in order to bring expenses within the estimate made by the City Council.[28] In January 1844 the Council announced plans for a further reduction in the police by abolishing the offices of chief constable and assistant chief constable, and reducing the number of police magistrates from three to one.[29] Yet not everyone agreed that a reduction in the police was ill-considered. The *Guardian,* an ally of the Council, asserted that public opinion had favoured a reduction rather than an augmentation of the police. It considered that at the time the estimates were framed, outrages against the person were rare, while police activities were directed primarily against unregistered dogs, unruly publicans and suspected drunkards.[30]

In fact, conflict with the City Council and the issue of police inadequacy came to be overshadowed by other concerns. In moving for the appointment of a select committee on insecurity, Dr Nicholson asserted that so long as Hyde Park Barracks and convict gangs in the vicinity of Sydney were improperly superintended, and convicts continued to arrive from Norfolk Island, no corps of police could be expected to maintain order.[31] The committee gave the police relatively little attention in its report, and when the central government resumed control of Sydney's police finances in 1845 the force was augmented by only six men.[32] The "chief objects" of the committee's recommendations were the exclusion of Norfolk Island expirees from the colony, and the removal of convicts from Sydney.[33]

To the community and the committee on insecurity the fact that Vigors and Burdett, as well as Knatchbull, underwent punishment at Norfolk Island before committing crimes in Sydney was extremely significant. Knatchbull returned to New South Wales from Norfolk Island in 1839 following the partial completion of his sentence for forgery. Vigors and Burdett, both sentenced to transportation for life, were returned from Norfolk Island as incurably ill.

The murders of Jamieson and Noble did not initiate concern about convicts returned to New South Wales from Norfolk Island. There had been persistent complaints about the practice from the time that a cessation of transportation appeared imminent. It was argued that the colony continued to suffer the "stain" of convictism without the benefit of assigned convict labour. This objection was intensified by experiments in prison discipline conducted by Alexander Maconochie, who assumed command of the island in March 1840. In contrast to the "separate" system of prison discipline current in Britain, which was essentially a modified form of solitary confinement, Maconochie's ideas were embodied in a "social" system. Prisoners were to be reformed through a gradual reduction of restraints, which would better prepare them for resisting temptation once free.[34]

Many colonists considered Maconochie's administration too lenient. The press ridiculed his regime as "a penal Utopia", which fostered vice rather than reforming criminals.

> To recline upon verdant banks, gazing upon the glories of a southern sky, lulled by the gentle murmuring of a brook ... to saunter in careless indolence through the groves, or along the smooth beach of the magnificent Pacific; ... these are the enviable occupations of the pick-pockets and cut-throats of Norfolk Island.[35]

Governor Gipps reported that the effects of Maconochie's system were universally derided and dreaded in New South Wales, while confidentially predicting that he would be dismissed on the grounds of expense.[36]

In these circumstances, the murders of Janieson and Noble gave an old issue new life. Although Maconochie was replaced in February 1844, his memory was resurrected in that Vigors and Burdett were returned to Sydney on his repeated request less than four months before Noble's death. With reference to "thrice convicted thieves and men of the vilest description" from Norfolk Island, as well as runaways from Van Diemen's Land, the *Australian* noted that:

> Sad indeed is the state of things when, after having wiped off the disgrace of a penal Colony, we are reduced to believe that the Colonists were far safer in that condition than in their present one, when a man cannot venture to stir his tea with a silver spoon, or to walk after dark without fear of assassination.[37]

The select committee on insecurity concluded that the majority of convicts from Norfolk Island were not reformed, but "rendered more hardened in vice, and more prone to the commission of every species of crime". Their continued arrival not only threatened life and property, but was "demoralising and fatal to the habits and character of the rising generation".[38]

The crime wave was also attributed to the prison population in the vicinity of Sydney, and in particular to prisoners confined in Hyde Park Barracks.[39] Like the Norfolk Island expirees, the Barracks prisoners were viewed with a jaundiced eye from the abolition of assignment. The Barracks were completed in 1819 under Governor Macquarie's adminis-tration as a receptacle for convicts, and especially those returned from assigned service. In 1844 the Barracks housed what Governor Gipps bluntly referred to as "the refuse of the convict system in New South Wales".[40] Conspicuously located in the centre of the city, they were a grim reminder of the colony's penal origins. The Barracks were rendered still more offensive in 1844 by a recent increase in inmates, who numbered 828 in May.[41]

Again the murder of Noble assumed importance, since Vigors and Burdett were confined at Hyde Park Barracks. The morning of the crime they slipped away from a gang on their way to church, shed their prison clothing in a privy, and emerged in ordinary dress. According to reports, it appeared that twenty-five prisoners were absent from the Barracks on the night of Noble's stabbing, and over half a dozen convicts were apprehended wearing civilian clothes under their prison uniforms.[42] Vigors, no doubt cognizant of public sentiment, allegedly stated before hanging that "he had never been in a place where so much crime and rascality was carried on", and attributed his downfall to the Barracks.[43]

The conclusions of the select committee were generally supported by the Legislative Council, which resolved that the return of prisoners from Norfolk Island was an "intolerable grievance" and the Hyde Park Barracks a "demoralising influence".[44] Nevertheless, the committee's report appears somewhat dubious in light of the evidence. In contrast to the committee's characterization of Norfolk Island expirees, Sydney's police superintendent testified that of eighty-two expirees not confined in Hyde Park Barracks and known to the police, sixteen were under surveillance, while the others were given a "good character".[45] Maconochie pointed out that the re-conviction rate was twice as high before his administration.[46] The Colonial Secretary also confessed his surprise at learning that of 240 convicts arriving from Norfolk Island between September 1843 and June 1844, those accused of Noble's murder were the only ones committed for trial.[47]

As for the Hyde Park Barracks, Governor Gipps conceded that its presence in Sydney was "a nuisance".[48] He objected to the removal of convicts, on the grounds that their employment on public works in rural areas would only increase their opportunities for crime, and would make the colony responsible for their support. Before the committee on insecurity was appointed, however, Gipps determined to remove as many inmates as possible from Hyde Park Barracks, and one hundred of "the worst characters" were sent to Cockatoo Island.[49] There was also some justice in criticism of the investigating committee by the principal superintendent of convicts. He noted the committee's attempt to connect the cases of Knatchbull and Vigors, although Knatchbull had nothing to do with Hyde Park Barracks. He pointed as well to the committee's "extraordinary credulity" in accepting any impressions which cast the Barracks in an unfavourable light. The committee reiterated in its report, for example, highly questionable testimony concerning gambling at the Barracks for stakes of twenty-five pounds, and the routine lending out of pistols to inmates. Finally, the city's criminal statistics suggested that convicts were not the only perpetrators of crimes.[50] According to the attorney-general, no offences committed during 1844 other than Noble's murder and one robbery were directly traceable to the presence of Hyde Park Barracks.[51]

That the select committee investigating insecurity was less than impartial is not surprising considering the atmosphere in which it worked. Nor do its conclusions concerning Norfolk Island expirees and occupants of Hyde Park Barracks seem surprising since both were objects of long-standing grievance. But underlying the conclusions, and the general disquiet about a crime wave in general, were two further grievances. As Governor Gipps suspected, concern about crime was motivated largely by unemployment, and perennial objections to the expense of maintaining police and gaols.[52]

From July 1835, when the cost of maintaining police and gaols was transferred to the colony, this expense served as a constant irritant. Colonists argued that the high cost of police and prisons was almost entirely the outcome of transportation, and as such at least a portion of the expense should be paid by the mother country. More realistically, as select committees on police periodically noted, the expense of law enforcement was also attributable to a preponderance of males, a widely dispersed population, and the presence of Aborigines.[53] This knowledge did little to quiet objections, and with the abolition of transportation the grievance seemed even more insufferable. While colonists remained subject to "indirect" transportation from Norfolk Island and Van Diemen's Land, they failed to receive the benefits of assigned convict labour. In 1840 the Legislative Council adopted resolutions expressing its opinion that half the cost of police and gaols should be defrayed by Britain, and the following year Governor Gipps reported that their expense was the source of "nearly every difficulty" encountered in administering the government.[54]

For a number of reasons the issue of support for police and gaols became still more pressing in 1844. Under the Constitution Act of 1842, district councils were to raise half the cost of the police in their respective districts.[55] In the light of the colony's economic situation, Governor Gipps agreed to postpone implementation of this portion of the Act.[56] In 1843, however, half the cost of the Sydney police was transferred to the newly incorporated city to be paid by local assessments.[57] Aside from charges against the City Council for mismanagement of the estimates, some citizens protested that the rates they contributed entitled them to better police protection. More importantly, the increased taxation was resented in a period of depression, particularly since the police of other districts continued to be paid out of the general revenue.

The connection between the cost of police and concern about crime became apparent when Sydney residents petitioned the Legislative Council in reference to the "late outrages" committed in the city. According to the petitioners the arrival of convicts from Norfolk Island necessitated more adequate police and prisons. Since these could not be supported by local taxation, it was "only just and reasonable" that at least a portion of the charges be borne by the British treasury. It was further suggested that if the British government refused to bear part of the charges, a means should be devised for granting expiree convicts arriving in Sydney free passages to England.[58]

Bitter feeling concerning support of police and gaols was further aroused in 1844 by plans to remove one of the colony's two military regiments to Van Diemen's Land. The *Sydney Morning Herald* protested against the proposal on the same grounds on which it objected to a reduction in the police. Although New South Wales was no longer subject to direct transportation, it continued to receive "robbers and murderers" from Van Diemen's Land and Norfolk Island.[59] The *Star and Working Man's Guardian,* in the same column which reported Noble's murder, urged colonists to petition for the retention of military regiments, noting that it was better for potential immigrants "to starve at home than to have their throats cut in New South Wales".[60] In a similar vein, the Legislative Council concluded that any reduction in the colony's military force would be "dangerous".[61] The removal of troops was further evidence that the colony would have to rely on its own resources for law enforcement. But concern was probably prompted more through a fear of losing commissariat expenditure than by disorder. The withdrawal of soldiers, the *Australian* pointed out, would mean not only a loss of protectors, but of purchasers.[62] It was asserted that the cost of maintaining police and gaols was all the more burdensome in the face of rapidly decreasing expenditure from the military chest, which was reduced by over one-third between 1839 and 1843.[63]

In a less direct way, the issue of police and gaol expense also gained new vigour from squatting regulations promulgated by Governor Gipps in April 1844. The new regulations, which placed more stringent conditions on the occupation of crown lands, elicited a sharp reaction, particularly since many squatters were in economic difficulties.[64] Like the issue of police expense, the squatting regulations also symbolized imperial restrictions on the colonial legislature. As part of the backlash against them, the Legislative Council enumerated grievances over the administration of crown lands. A select committee on land grievances, chaired by Charles Cowper, was appointed in May, only a few weeks before Noble's murder. The committee members, including Charles Nicholson, were all members of the newly formed Pastoral Association, organized to oppose the new land regulations. Among the grievances outlined by the committee was Governor Gipps' alleged violation of "the compact". It vainly contended that in return for supporting police and gaols, the colony received the right to appropriate revenue from crown lands.[65] Within this context, it is significant that at a public meeting on insecurity in Sydney, William Charles Wentworth protested against not only the injustice of burdening the city with the cost of the police, but also the Legislative Council's lack of control over the territorial revenue.[66]

In moving for a select committee to investigate insecurity in Sydney, Charles Nicholson made his own priorities clear. The landing of convicts from Norfolk Island was not the only grievance, for the colony was compelled "to go to all the expense of maintaining a police for their control, and a gaol establishment for their incarceration".[67] When later moving for resolutions on the committee's report in September, Nicholson pointed out that most crimes in Sydney were committed by persons originally transported, and concluded that "there could not be a stronger argument" against the colony being saddled with the cost of police and prisons.[68] The committee refrained from making any specific recommendations concerning the issue, but this was probably because action was already taken. At the end of August resolutions were adopted by the Legislative Council recommending that two-thirds of police and gaol expenses, including arrears from 1835, be paid by the home government.[69]

Concern about crime in 1844 was also related to unemployment. Underlying some condemnations of the convicts' moral influence was a desire to improve the economic position of free wage earners. During 1843 Sydney labourers held several meetings in protest against the competition of convict labour. In January a proposal by the City Council to employ convicts in repairing the streets resulted in a petition to the governor. Labourers requested that no convict labour be allocated to the city corporation, and that all prisoners be withdrawn from assigned service in the city.[70] Additional petitions were presented in 1843 calling for the removal of all convicts from public works in Sydney on the grounds that large numbers of free persons were unemployed.[71]

These efforts were unsuccessful. A select committee of the Legislative Council appointed to consider the labourers' petition objected to the removal of convicts from Sydney. The committee considered that the petitioners deluded themselves as to the amount of relief such a measure would afford, particularly since convicts were employed on public works which would otherwise not be undertaken at all. Furthermore, convicts in government service were clothed and rationed from the military chest, whereas their removal to the interior would necessitate their support by the colony. The committee recommended instead that as many unemployed as possible be siphoned off to country districts.[72]

The committee's report did not end the issue. The Mutual Protection Association, formed at a meeting of Sydney's unemployed in August 1843, continued to press the government to provide public works. The Association opposed further immigration as well as the arrival of convicts, and considered that convicts should neither be employed on public works nor assigned to service in towns.[73] On 20 May 1844, six days before the murder of James Noble, a public meeting was held at the Sydney School of Arts in order to memorialize the governor again. The meeting resolved that the employment of convict labour in Sydney was injurious to the community and prejudicial to free labour. Convicts should be employed in distant districts where they would not compete with free men.[74] This petition, like its predecessors, was unsuccessful. Incensed, the Mutual Protection Association resolved that the first step toward improving working class conditions must be the removal of Governor Gipps.[75]

In at least some quarters, the death of Noble brought new optimism. Following the public meeting on insecurity at the City Theatre the *Guardian,* mouthpiece of the Mutual Protection Association, reported in jubilant terms that the removal of convicts from Sydney was supported by all parties. It appeared that its object might at last meet with success.[76] It was certainly supported by the select committee on insecurity, which recommended that tickets of leave for the district of Sydney be withheld, and that prisoners in government or assigned service be removed to the interior. In supporting its proposal well-worn allusions were made to the role of convicts in perpetuating crime, and their exposure to temptation in the metropolis. The committee also concluded that, regardless of any other reasons, the large number of labourers unemployed in Sydney was alone sufficient reason to adopt their recommendations.[77]

It seems evident that the crime wave became politicized, and was even in part manufactured, through various interests and grievances. An atmosphere of crisis was created not only by the spectre of crime, but by economic depression. As in the mid-1830s, it was largely other issues which focused public attention on crime. A change in newspaper reportage as much as an actual change in offences committed, possibly contributed to widespread fear.[78] The *Sydney Morning Herald* made crime a daily topic in its columns, while most other newspapers responded to the crime wave with stereotyped allusions to convict depravity. Convicts provided both an explanation for feelings of insecurity, and to some extent scapegoats for economic ills.

At a meeting of residents in Bourke ward to discuss the crime wave, one businessman, R. P. Welsh, was bold enough to suggest that although convicts were responsible for several gross crimes, he believed that on closer inquiry it would be found that a considerable number had been committed by other persons suffering under the privation of the times. For this suggestion he was sternly rebuked. James McEachern, a leading light of the Mutual Protection Association and the *Guardian*'s first editor, retorted that Welsh "had grossly insulted the free portion of the community". While admitting that many immigrants were suffering from poverty, he denied that such suffering led to crime. "On the contrary", McEachern asserted, he was happy "to say that they would rather die than be guilty of such outrages."[79] Under public pressure Welsh retreated. At a subsequent meeting he insisted that he had really been trying to draw attention to the evils the city and colony were subjected to by "criminals from the adjacent islands being poured upon our shores".[80]

The select committee on insecurity reached a conclusion which was consistent with McEachern's. The committee acknowledged the role of unemployment and reduced wages as a cause of crime, but only in a qualified way. While economic distress might result in the commission of offences by persons who had previously evinced a "want of correct principles", the committee concluded that such a causal relation could by no means be applied to the working classes generally.[81] This view fitted in neatly with contemporary conceptions of a "criminal class", which in New South Wales was easily identifiable as that containing persons originally transported.

In opposing convicts the community was drawn together not only by a collective sense of indignation, but also by a mutuality of interests. The Mutual Protection Association and the *Guardian* sided with squatters in opposing Gipps' land regulations, largely because of their animosity to the governor. Given the failure of appeals for public works, radicals also viewed the regulations as obstructing a general revival of the economy. The decision to support squatters split the Mutual Protection Association and the alliance proved only temporary, but their uneasy coalition in 1844 helps to explain in part why Nicholson's committee on insecurity supported the exclusion of all prisoners from Sydney.

By 1844, at least in Sydney, the proportion of convicts in the community had also diminished to the extent that they could be regarded as socially distinct from the working classes, as marginal and outsiders. Between 1841 and 1844 nearly 40,000 free immigrants arrived in New

South Wales. At the census of 1846 the convict-emancipist group made up one-fifth of the colony's population, but less than one-tenth of Sydney's populace.[82] Collective indignation generated by the murders of Jamieson and Noble tended to confirm the moral worth of immigrants, while downgrading the status of convicts.

Although Sydney was relieved of the responsibility for providing partial support for its constabulary after 1844, the expense of supporting police and gaols remained a reason for opposing the reception of convicts in New South Wales. More importantly, fears expressed concerning crime continued to be related largely to fears that convicts would threaten workers' standard of living. The criminality imputed to convicts served not only to combat an economic threat, but also to unite free immigrants with a sense of moral purpose. In these respects, the 1844 crime wave stands out not as an isolated phenomenon, but as a precursor of the anti-transportation movement which gathered momentum at the end of the decade.

Notes

1. *SMH*, 31 December 1844.
2. *SMH*, 18 June 1844.
3. *SMH*, 8 June 1844.
4. Dr Nicholson's Address, LC, *SMH*, 28 September 1844. For Sydney's criminal statistics from 1841 to 1845 see Appendix to the Select Committee on the Insecurity of Life and Property, N.S.W., *V & PLC*, 1844, vol. 2, p. 386; Appendix referred to in Evidence of William Augustus Miles to the Select Committee on Police, N.S.W., *V & PLC*, 1847, vol. 2, p. 60.
5. Ruth Knight, *Illiberal Liberal. Robert Lowe in New South Wales, 1842–1850* (Melbourne, 1966), p. 64; Alan Birch and David S. Macmillan (eds.), *The Sydney Scene 1788–1960* (Melbourne, 1962), p. 91; Colin Roderick, *John Knatchbull. From Quarterdeck to Gallows* (Sydney, 1963), especially pp. 248–52.
6. For details of the case see Notes of Criminal Cases tried before Mr Justice Burton in the Supreme Court of N.S.W. from January 19th 1844, 24 January 1844, Supreme Court, N.S.W. SA, 2/2451, pp. 40–76; Copy of Mr Justice Burton's Report on the case of John Thomas Knatchbull laid before the Executive Council on 27 January 1844, enclosed in Gipps to Stanley, 15 February 1844, *HRA*, ser. 1, vol. 23, pp. 406–7; *SMH*, 8, 19, 25 January 1844; *Weekly Register*, 13, 27 January 1844.
7. Roderick, *Knatchbull*, especially pp. 11–16; John Knatchbull, "The Life of John Knatchbull, written by himself 23 January 1844, in Woolloomooloo Gaol", ML, MSS. 798 (also published in Roderick, *Knatchbull*, pp. 27–131); Roger Therry, *Reminiscences of Thirty Years' Residence in New South Wales and Victoria* (London, 1863, reprint ed., Sydney, 1974), pp. 100–104; Thomas McCombie, "Distinguished Convicts", *Simmonds's Colonial Magazine and Foreign Miscellany* vol. 8 (May-August 1846) pp. 366–67; Anon., *A Memoir of Knatchbull, The Murderer of Mrs Jamieson, Comprising an Account of his English and Colonial History* (Sydney, 1844).

8. Knatchbull later confessed to the crime while awaiting execution. John Thomas Knatchbull's Confession, 10 February 1844, enclosed in J. Long Innes to Col. Sec., 23 February 1844, Col. Sec., Letters Received, N.S.W. SA, 4/2670.

9. *SMH*, 25 January 1844. Concerning Lowe's involvement in the case see Knight, *Illiberal Liberal*, pp. 64–71, 117–18.

10. See Nigel Walker, *Crime and Insanity in England*, Vol. 1: *The Historical Perspective* (Edinburgh, 1968), pp. 84–103.

11. See George Nadel, *Australia's Colonial Culture: Ideas, Men and Institutions in Mid-Nineteenth-Century Eastern Australia* (Melbourne, 1957), pp. 139, 141.

12. *SMH*, 25 January 1844. See also *Atlas*, 8 March 1845.

13. Georgiana Lowe to Mrs Sherbrooke, 28 February 1844 (microfilm), Lowe Papers, NLA, G 2040, Letter 13.

14. Minutes of the Executive Council, 27 January, 10 February 1844, Executive Council, N.S.W. SA, 4/1521; Gipps to Stanley, 10 February, 10 March 1844, *HRA*, ser. 1, vol. 23, pp. 398–99, 448–53.

15. *SMH*, 19 January 1844.

16. *SMH*, 14 February 1844. See also *Australian*, 15 February 1844.

17. *SMH*, 28, 29 May, 12 June, 15, 16, 17 July, 14 August 1844; *Australian*, 29 May, 1, 3, 4, 13 June 1844; *Star*, 1 June, 17 August 1844.

18. *SMH*, 8 June 1844. *Herald*'s emphasis.

19. *SMH*, 31 May, 1 June 1844.

20. *Australian*, 1 June 1844.

21. *SMH*, 10 June 1844.

22. See Victor Windeyer, *Sir Charles Nicholson. A Place in History* (St Lucia, 1978); *ADB*, vol. 2, pp. 283–85.

23. Burton, "State of Society", *Colonial Magazine* vol. 2, p. 50.

24. *SMH*, 28 May 1844.

25. *SMH*, 2, 6 January 1844.

26. *SMH*, 28 March, 16 April, 20, 28 May, 1, 8, 11 June, 12 July 1844.

27. See for example *Australian*, 13, 28 May, 3 June 1844; *Star*, 1 June 1844.

28. Returns of the Colony, "Blue Books", 1842–43 (xerox copy), ML, CY 4/274–276; Col. Sec. to Sydney Bench of Magistrates, 10 November 1843, Col. Sec., Letters Sent, N.S.W. SA, 4/3849, p. 61.

29. *SMH*, 9 January 1844. See also Charles Windeyer and William Augustus Miles to Col. Sec., 7 February 1844, Col. Sec., Letters Received, N.S.W. SA, 2/8022.2.

30. *Guardian*, 22 June 1844.

31. LC, *SMH*, 7 June 1844.

32. Returns of the Colony, "Blue Books", 1845 (xerox copy), ML, CY 4/278.

33. LC, *SMH*, 28 September 1844.

34. See John Vincent Barry, *Alexander Maconochie of Norfolk Island. A Study of a Pioneer in Penal Reform* (London, 1958), especially pp. 69–79.

35. *SMH*, 31 July 1841.

36. Gipps to Stanley, 15 August 1842, *HRA*, ser. 1, vol. 22, p. 209; Gipps to La Trobe, 29 March 1843 (microfilm), Gipps-La Trobe Correspondence, NLA, Letter H 7159.

37. *Australian*, 3 June 1844.

38. Report from the Select Committee on the Insecurity of Life and Property, N.S.W., *V & PLC*, 1844, vol. 2, pp. 372, 375.

39. Ibid., pp. 372–74.

40. Gipps to Stanley, 28 November 1844, *HRA*, ser. 1, vol. 24, p. 84.

41. *Guardian*, 4 May 1844. See also Return of Prisoners in Hyde Park Barracks 1842–1844, Appendix to the Select Committee on the Insecurity of Life and Property, N.S.W., *V & PLC*, 1844, vol. 2, p. 444.
42. *SMH*, 28 May 1844; *Weekly Register*, 1 June 1844.
43. *SMH*, 14 August 1844.
44. LC, *SMH*, 2 October 1844.
45. Evidence of William Augustus Miles to the Select Committee on the Insecurity of Life and Property, N.S.W., *V & PLC*, 1844, vol. 2, p. 383.
46. Captain Maconochie, "Criminal Statistics and Movement of the Bond Population of Norfolk Island, to December, 1843", *Journal of the Statistical Society of London* vol. 8 (1845), pp. 20–21.
47. LC, *SMH*, 7 June 1844.
48. Gipps to Stanley, 28 November 1844, *HRA*, ser. 1, vol. 24, p. 84.
49. LC, *SMH*, 28 November, 2 October 1844.
50. Captain McLean to Col. Sec., 30 September 1844, Col. Sec., Letters Received, N.S.W. SA., 4/2674.3.
51. LC, *SMH*, 2 October 1844.
52. Gipps to Stanley, 28 November 1844, *HRA*, ser. 1, vol. 24, pp. 83–84.
53. Reports from Select Committees on Police, N.S.W., *V & PLC*, 1839, vol. 2, p. 136; 1847, vol. 2, p. 23; 1850, vol. 2, p. 399.
54. Gipps to Russell, 8 October 1840, 24 December 1841, *HRA*, ser. 1, vol. 21, pp. 40, 608.
55. 5 & 6 Vic., c. 76, sec. 47.
56. Gipps to Stanley, 7, 14 October 1843, *HRA*, ser. 1, vol. 23, pp. 182, 190–91.
57. [Colony of N.S.W.] 6 Vic., No. 3, sec. 70; 6 Vic., No. 5.
58. Petition of 682 Inhabitants of Sydney, N.S.W., *V & PLC*, 1844, vol. 2, p. 79.
59. *SMH*, 25 May 1844.
60. *Star*, 1 June 1844.
61. LC, *SMH*, 2 October 1844.
62. *Australian*, 3 June 1844.
63. Address to the Queen and Parliament prepared by the Select Committee on General Grievances, N.S.W., *V & PLC*, 1844, vol. 2, p. 750.
64. Concerning reaction against the regulations see Roberts, *Squatting Age*, pp. 297–303; Sydney Kendall Barker, "The Governorship of Sir George Gipps", *JRAHS* vol. 16, pt 3 (1930), pp. 210–17; K. Buckley, "Gipps and the Graziers of New South Wales, 1841–6", *Historical Studies* vol. 7, no. 26 (May 1956), pp. 179–89; Barrie Dyster, "Support for the Squatters, 1844", *JRAHS* vol. 51, pt 1 (March 1965), pp. 41–59; T. H. Irving, "The Development of Liberal Politics in New South Wales, 1843–1855" (Ph.D. thesis, University of Sydney, 1967), pp. 100–22.
65. Report from the Select Committee on Land Grievances, N.S.W., *V & PLC*, 1844, vol. 2, pp. 132–36.
66. *SMH*, 10 June 1844.
67. LC, *SMH*, 7 June 1844.
68. LC, *SMH*, 28 September 1844.
69. LC, *SMH*, 31 August 1844. The resolutions were referred to the select committee on general grievances, chaired by William Charles Wentworth, for the purpose of preparing an address to the Queen and parliament. The committee laid the address and its report on the Council table in December. LC, *SMH*, 7 December 1844.
70. *SMH*, 9 January 1843.

71. *SMH*, 12 June, 8 August 1843.
72. Report from the Select Committee on the Petition from Distressed Mechanics and Labourers, N.S.W., *V & PLC*, 1843, pp. 3–4.
73. See L. J. Hume, "Working Class Movements in Sydney and Melbourne before the Gold Rushes", *Historical Studies* vol. 9, no. 35 (November 1960), pp. 270–71.
74. *Guardian*, 25 May 1844; *Star*, 25 May 1844.
75. *Guardian*, 1 June 1844.
76. *Guardian*, 15 June 1844.
77. Report from the Select Committee on the Insecurity of Life and Property, N.S.W., *V & PLC*, 1844, vol. 2, p. 375.
78. See Paul Rock, *Deviant Behaviour* (London, 1973), p. 43.
79. *SMH*, 1 June 1844.
80. *SMH*, 10 June 1844.
81. Report from the Select Committee on the Insecurity of Life and Property, N.S.W., *V & PLC*, 1844, vol. 2, p. 372.
82. R. B. Madgwick, *Immigration into Eastern Australia 1788–1851* (London, 1937), p. 223; Census of New South Wales, 1846.

3

Contamination and
Anti-Transportation

> Under the most favourable circumstances we shall always be com-
> pelled to deal with our own crime — a task surely of sufficient
> difficulty to every community. But to draw down upon ourselves
> — to invite the scum of the British Empire merely from pecuniary
> motives, would be to ask from the parent land her curse, instead
> of her blessing — would be to effect the complete destruction of
> the trifling claim to respectability, which we now possess . . .[1]

Although direct transportation to New South Wales ended in 1840,
there were continued efforts to renew transportation, made both by
colonists eager for convict labour and by the British government.[2]
The Colonial Office became particularly anxious to secure an alternative place to send convicts as deteriorating economic conditions in Van
Diemen's Land increased the number supported by the government. It
was determined to forward prisoners, under the sobriquet of "exiles",
to the Australian mainland with pardons after they had served a term in
British penitentiaries. A total of nine ships disembarked 1,727 exiles
at Port Phillip between November 1844 and February 1849.[3] The first
ship carrying exiles to Sydney, the *Hashemy*, was greeted by a mass
protest in June 1849.

Crime and New South Wales' vulnerability to any importation of
British criminals served as a rallying cry for citizens opposing exiles.
In the rhetoric of anti-transportationists, crime and convicts became
synonymous. The convict ship was a "cargo of crime", and a "crime-
freighted vessel", while transportation was referred to variously as an
"importation of crime", "flood of crime", and "influx of crime".
Perceptions of transportation as primarily a moral issue played an
important role which went beyond the alleged criminality of convicts,
or even fears concerning the economic competition of convict labour.
First, the supposed threat convicts posed to the community's morality
added legitimacy, and perhaps more importantly, drama to the anti-
transportation movement. Emphasis on the moral aspects of the transportation issue also served to conceal deep divisions within the anti-
transportation movement itself. Denunciations of convicts' criminality
further served to legitimize the colony's new image as it attempted to
throw off the stigma of its origins.

The anti-transportation movement which developed in response to the exile issue was not, as commonly thought, the spontaneous product of mass indignation. Despite agitation by the press, the movement was inhibited by public apathy. Writing at mid-century, Godfrey Mundy found New South Wales' population usually drowsy and well-fed, noting that their collective comfort made it difficult to inspire discontent and disquiet.[4] The poor voter turnout at elections was another indicator of the community's political indolence.[5]

When an anti-transportation meeting was held at Sydney in early March 1849 to protest against the sending of exiles, the *Herald* confessed it was not as well attended as expected.[6] Preparations for the "Great Protest Meeting" later in the year against the *Hashemy* began almost two months before the ship arrived.[7] Even so, it is questionable how well the protest was attended. The *Herald* estimated the crowd at from four to five thousand, while the *People's Advocate* reported there were seven to eight thousand persons present.[8] On the other hand, the superintendent of police, Joseph Long Innes, asserted that the demonstration was never attended by more than seven hundred people.[9] Part of the discrepancy can be attributed to the difficulty of making an accurate estimate, and to the fact that Innes's low figure referred to the crowd at any one time, while newspaper estimates included all persons who attended during the day. Nevertheless, the difference is so great that one or both of the reports were seemingly fabricated.

Innes is not a particularly reliable source, since he was dismissed from office a short time later for prevaricating before a select committee on Darlinghurst Gaol. One may suspect, however, that the virulence with which his evidence was attacked by the committee owed something to its chairman, leading anti-transportationist Charles Cowper. Was Innes perhaps being punished for his unsympathetic view of the anti-transportation movement? Aside from Innes's report, Governor FitzRoy's assertion that Archibald Michie, a prominent speaker at anti-transportation meetings, was employed writing leading articles for the *Herald,* casts further doubts on the newspaper's credibility.[10]

While it can be assumed that most colonists opposed a renewal of transportation, it is likely that anti-transportationists greatly exaggerated the degree of community participation. At Bathurst, for example, initial attempts to form a branch of the Anti-Transportation Association failed, even though it was believed to express the views of "the people".[11] In part, "crime" served as an emotional lever and catchword in attempting to generate further support and enthusiasm.

As one newspaper noted, fear of crime and "pollution" was effective in stimulating those who were otherwise indifferent to the transportation issue.

these are the persons who cannot understand an opposition to transportation in any other way than as implying a personal dread of the
prisoners. A man of this sort will be up in arms if you tell him that
there is any fear of his pocket being picked; but he will look on with
the most stoical indifference while measures are being adopted for
the political ruin of his country.[12]

The discovery of this reaction perhaps explains the change in tactics
adopted by the *People's Advocate*. The *Advocate* began publication in
December 1848 and endorsed the objectives of the recently-formed
Constitutional Association. Its radical platform included an extension
of the franchise, responsible government and land reform, as well as
opposition to transportation. Initially the *Advocate* scorned talk
"about contamination and pollution" as "the very weakest kind of
argument" against transportation.[13] A short time later, it was referring
to convictism as the "ugly foulness rooted in our blood" which made
the colony a "dunghill".[14] Workers were urged to support the anti-
transportation movement on the grounds that "not only will their
wages be reduced by competition with prisoners, but their wives, and
their children, will be far more exposed to the violence and contamination which must necessarily ensue, than will the wives and children of
their employers."[15]

A similar, if often more subtle, campaign against convicts was waged
by other newspapers. In a leading article entitled "Our Criminal
Statistics", the *Sydney Morning Herald* pointed to New South Wales'
conviction rate as "unequivocal proof" of diminishing crime. Even so,
the comparison with returns for England and Wales was still considered
a source of "shame and humiliation".[16] The following month, the
Herald noted the disproportionate number of convicts and emancipists
tried recently before the Sydney Quarter Sessions.[17] It was asserted
that one beneficial result of the Molesworth inquiry, so long regarded
as a gross slur on the colony, was a complete moral transformation of
the community. Unless the Colonial Office succeeded in "contaminating" the colony again with criminals, "gentlemen of birth and education, accompanied by their accomplished wives and beautiful
daughters", might emigrate to New South Wales with confidence that
it was no less "virtuous, tranquil, and secure" than any place in
Britain.[18]

Crime reportage in the Sydney press reflected not only the
impending threat posed by exiles, but also the continuing problem of
"indirect" transportation. Towards the end of 1849 there were reports
of an "alarming increase" in robberies and burglaries. This increase was
attributed principally to the arrival of ex-convicts from Van Diemen's
Land.[19] In January 1850 the *Sydney Morning Herald* alluded to "immigrating hordes of Van Diemen's Land expirees", noting that "The year

1844 set in with an alarming increase of crime. So has the year 1850. Every day has this journal to report outrages on person or on property, or on both. Not a single night passes without a burglary or an attempt at burglary."[20] The following month Ann Deas Thomson wrote to her father, former governor Richard Bourke, that scarcely a night passed without hearing of some neighbour being robbed. It was rumoured that "a regular gang" was operating in the neighbourhood, "supposed to be expirees from Hobart Town".[21]

Whether the city was in fact being inundated by Van Diemen's Land expirees is questionable. Of about 5,000 convicts freed by servitude or holding conditional pardons recorded leaving Van Diemen's Land between 1847 and 1849, over 3,800 departed for Port Phillip, compared to less than 250 for Sydney.[22] It is possible, of course, that many ex-convicts travelled overland to the east. But it was later reported, in order to "allay unnecessary apprehensions", that very few expiree convicts from Van Diemen's Land arrived in Sydney, and that those who did were kept under close surveillance by the police.[23] As in 1844, it seems likely that the menace of convicts arriving from adjacent colonies was exaggerated. It is also perhaps significant that reports of a "crime wave" precipitated by Van Diemen's Land expirees appeared when the question of direct transportation was temporarily assumed at an end.

Opponents of transportation resurrected the same fears about an influx of crime and contamination at public meetings and in the Legislative Council. At a public meeting held in March 1849 and a subsequent deputation to Governor FitzRoy, anti-transportationists pointed to the probability of convicts forming bands of outlaws which the colony would be powerless to control. Although exiles were to be limited to the interior, it was asserted that it was in these precise areas, beyond the pale of police and church, "where crime may be perpetrated with the boldest chances of impunity".[24] At Maitland a meeting was informed that the relative absence of bushranging and other "outrages" in the district was sufficient reason for opposing any renewal of transportation.[25] Residents of Bathurst heard orations in a similar vein. One speaker asserted that:

> I remember some ten years ago, when you could never take up a paper but accounts of bushranging, robbery, and murder, stared you in the face; and under the assignment system as now proposed, similar scenes will occur again. Runaway prisoners, combining with unemployed operatives, will infest the roads and haunt the bush lands."[26]

Particular emphasis was placed on the vulnerability of women and children to sexual assault. John Dunmore Lang electrified a crowd at

Barrack Square with an example of the transportation system he claimed to be personally acquainted with. In 1834 he had induced a family consisting of a married couple and their three daughters to settle in New South Wales. The husband was frequently absent from their farm, and during one of his absences their house was attacked by some men from a gaol gang who threw his wife in the fire. Although she recovered from the burns she received, the shock of the incident resulted in her death a short time later due to an "organic disease". The father continued to reside at the farm with his daughters. During another of the father's absences, according to Lang, an old convict "perpetrated an outrage upon each of them in succession, fit only for one of the demons from hell to perpetrate, and for which our language has no name".[27]

Such appeals for the protection of wives and daughters were especially effective in the colony, since the small numbers of women and their frequent isolation in the bush was thought to make them more vulnerable to attack. While mitigating other penalties of the criminal law, New South Wales retained the death penalty for rape long after it was abolished in Britain in 1841. The fact that one of the exiles was accused of committing rape assumed special importance in the Legislative Council's debate. Henry Dangar, a pro-transportationist with massive land holdings, asserted that exiles in the colony had been charged only with "minor offences". When enumerating the offences committed by exiles, however, he began by noting that one was accused of rape.[28] Although Dangar later explained that he meant to say exiles "generally" were only accused of minor offences, the damage was done. Speaker after speaker attacked his implication that rape was a minor crime. Dangar's insensitivity was cited as evidence of convicts' contaminating influence, while greater violence to women and children was predicted if transportation were renewed.[29]

At the same time, speakers in the Legislative Council cited the colony's criminal statistics as a measure of convictism's impact. John Nichols pointed to New South Wales' relatively high conviction rate during the mid-1830s, while Edwin Suttor asserted that nine-tenths of the colony's crime was committed by persons originally transported.[30] Although the attorney-general, John Hubert Plunkett, considered the proportion was somewhat less, his observations were hardly less damning. He estimated that while the "transported classes" made up only about twenty per cent of the population, they were responsible for at least sixty per cent of the crime. Plunkett cited return after return of cases tried before various superior courts, noting the small proportion of cases involving the "free classes". Not only did convicts and ex-convicts commit a disproportionate number of offences, but "nearly all the heinous offences".[31] While conceding that thousands were previously transported for petty and political offences, opponents of transportation noted that changes in the English criminal law meant that only the "worst class" would be sent if transportation were renewed.[32] Aside from creating the danger of murder, rape and theft, the presence of convicts would necessarily lead to contamination. "If they were to introduce them, a large number of vicious men, or men who indulged in vicious habits, the inevitable consequence must be that the free population, whether native or transported, must become demoralized".[33]

Throughout the period, the criminal tendencies of exiles received special attention. It was reported that at one session of the criminal court at Port Phillip, exiles made up one-third of the prisoners tried.[34] At Moreton Bay it was alleged that while residents had scarcely considered locking their doors before, the arrival of exiles necessitated their being constantly on the alert for "the numerous sneaks now prowling about after night-fall".[35] In the vicinity of Goulburn, exiles were believed to be responsible for a rash of forgeries.[36] Offences committed by exiles were scrupulously reported by Sydney newspapers, including such minor infractions as disobedience of orders and drunkenness.[37]

While exiles were credited with committing numerous offences, fears concerning their criminal propensities seem greatly exaggerated. Between June 1849, when the *Hashemy* arrived, and June 1850, a total of 1,618 exiles disembarked at New South Wales' middle district and Moreton Bay. During that year forty forfeited their tickets of leave. In three-quarters of the cases this loss was simply for minor breaches of discipline. But ten of the exiles were alleged to have committed what Governor FitzRoy termed "offences of a grave character", including one rape, five cases of larceny, and four cases of assault or felony.[38] A year and a half later, the exiles were credited with an additional 309 offences. Again, most of these were minor breaches of discipline. The most common offences were absence from musters, absconding, breach of the Masters and Servants Act, drunkenness or disorderly conduct. The large numbers absenting themselves, absconding, or breaking agreements must be viewed in the context of the opportunities for alternative employment created by the discovery of gold. Exiles were also punished for an additional fourteen "serious" offences, generally some form of theft.[39] As in the case of convicts and ex-convicts generally, these figures must be considered in the light of community attitudes toward them, and especially discrimination by the police and courts.

The Legislative Council's decision against any renewal of transportation in October 1850 was lauded as a moral victory. According to the *Sydney Morning Herald,* despite temptations "between the expedient and the right, between material gain and moral loss", colonists opted for "the purity of their country".[40] Perceptions of transportation as "a great moral question" served not only to dramatize the anti-transportation movement, but gave the movement much of its cohesion.

Although anti-transportationists contended that all sects, parties, classes, interests and groups were "fused into one compact body",[41] the movement represented an uneasy coalition. While some squatters were active in the movement, squatters in general were the foes of both the workers and the urban middle classes.[42] In turn, workers and the middle classes were divided on such issues as immigration. Middle class proponents of anti-transportation tended to argue that the presence of convicts would discourage suitable immigrants from coming to the colony. Workers, however, often seemed as adamant against immigration as they were against transportation. Even before it was learned that exiles were to be sent to New South Wales, fears were expressed concerning the impact large numbers of immigrants were having on the labour market. Sydney operatives denigrated "such ignorant vendors of misrepresentation" as John Dunmore Lang, and considered proposals to inform British workers of the distress many colonial labourers were suffering, in order to discourage immigration.[43]

There was also tension within the movement between moderates and radicals. The leading role initially taken by members of the Constitutional Association, formed in November 1848 to press the interests of the working classes, created unease. When radicals organized a protest meeting in August 1850 which called for Governor FitzRoy's dismissal, even those who professed support for the anti-transportation cause deprecated the intemperate language used. Possibly because of fears stimulated by the demonstration, moderates like Charles Cowper and John Lamb seized the initiative in directing future anti-transportation activities. When a New South Wales Association for Preventing the Revival of Transportation was formed the following month, its twenty-eight man managing committee included five members of the Legislative Council. The remaining members were mainly drawn from Sydney's business and professional circles, rather than from among the shopkeepers and tradesmen who formed the backbone of the radical movement.[44] The *Freeman's Journal* asserted that the "most peaceable and best disposed" citizens took an active part in the anti-transportation movement with a view to countering the revolutionary projects and dissension fostered by demagogues.[45] The cloak of morality and the perception of convicts as a threat to public safety helped minimize conflict and give the movement at least a superficial consensus.

Even more dramatically than in 1844, the anti-transportation movement relegated convicts to the role of outsiders. Their changed status was reflected officially in a new Vagrancy Act passed by the Legislative Council at the end of 1849, largely on the grounds that expiree convicts from Van Diemen's Land were primarily responsible for robberies in and around Sydney.[46] Throughout the period under study, the Vagrancy Act served as a catch-all law for combating what were perceived as criminal problems. The Act was suggested as a means of excluding disorderly Aborigines from the towns, and later for clearing "disreputable characters" from the goldfields.[47] The *Herald* had urged the necessity of a Vagrancy Act in 1835 for the control of ex-convicts, while during the 1844 crime wave police used the existing Act to deal summarily with suspected thieves.[48] Under the new Act freed convicts from Van Diemen's Land were required to register their residence with the local magistracy, a requirement already imposed on doubly-convicted convicts arriving from Norfolk Island. Ex-convicts who failed to comply with the Act were liable to imprisonment with hard labour for up to two years. All such persons could also be summoned by the magistrates to give an account of themselves, and if unable to demonstrate any lawful means of support they were also liable to two years imprisonment.[49]

The Act was later disallowed by the British government on the grounds that it interfered with the Crown's prerogative of pardon.[50] While some colonists conceded that the penalties prescribed were too severe, they resented British intervention. George Nichols, who initially proposed the Act, claimed that since its disallowance crime in Sydney had increased five-fold.[51] During the Act's operation, however, only one conviction was made under the objectionable clauses.[52] This was compared to 140 convictions in the space of two years in Victoria, where more stringent legislation excluding Van Diemen's Land expirees was subsequently passed.[53] At least in New South Wales, the Act was mainly of symbolic importance. It provided the illusion that something was being done to stem the threat of "immigrating hordes" from Van Diemen's Land, while marking ex-convicts as undersirable settlers.

For the most part, the law-abiding and productive role which most emancipists assumed in the community was ignored by anti-transportationists. The *People's Advocate* on one occasion apologized for any offence it had given ex-convicts, and made a rare appeal for their support. Emancipists, it was argued, were well acquainted with the horrors of transportation, and would suffer as other workers did from an importation of cheap labour. Those with conditional pardons were even more vulnerable than immigrants to economic competition, since they were not free to leave the colony. More generally, there was some attempt to minimize criticism of ex-convicts by emphasizing the brutality of the penal system, and asserting that exiles were worse than those persons transported before 1840.[54]

The anti-transportation movement was primarily, however, a movement of free immigrants, anxious to secure their own place in the community. The movement reflected the social and economic aspirations of immigrants, as well as the emergence of a new community consciousness. In turn, that community consciousness was defined largely by placing convictism beyond its boundaries. To the cheers of anti-transportationists, Archdeacon McEncroe noted that "it is against all reasoning — against all principles of human nature, to imagine that a branded class could come out here to operate harmoniously with those who looked upon them as a branded class."[55] Perceptions of convicts as a "branded" or "criminal" class, as outsiders, enabled free immigrants to deal cohesively with a social, political and economic threat. Those same perceptions served to elevate the status of even the lowliest free immigrant, who became by association with anti-transportationists a member of the respectable classes.

The identification of convicts as outsiders also served to repudiate New South Wales' penal origins. Even allowing for anti-transportationists' bombastic language, there was genuine concern about the "taint" and "stain" of convictism which was apparent when the colony was referred to in English journals and the House of Commons. Charles Cowper argued that anti-transportation "was the only course which they could take to save that which individuals, or at least respectable individuals, prized most dearly — their reputation".[56] According to the *Herald*, if the anti-transportation movement proved anything, "it proved that in this community there exists a general hatred of convict influence and convict association! . . . And is it conceivable that in a society where this feeling is so widely diffused and so deeply seated, the emancipists, *as such*, can exert a dominant influence? The thought is preposterous."[57] Exhibiting contempt for convicts served to legitimate the community's new identity.[58] It was largely with a view to Australia's image that the eastern colonies later opposed transportation to Western Australia.[59]

As in the mid-1830s, the conflicting views of convicts' criminality were indicative of a contest for power. During the 1840s the colony's middle classes grew both in numbers and self-confidence. Their alliance with the working classes in opposing transportation was part of a broader movement against the pastoral interest. The gold rushes which began in 1851 both intensified this movement, and modified the role of convicts.

As far as the Colonial Office was concerned, the presence of gold ended the feasibility of transportation, since exiling convicts to the proximity of goldfields would create an undesirable impression on "the minds of the criminal class".[60] In New South Wales the discovery of gold signalled a new era in colonial crime, inasmuch as it shifted attention from the criminality of convicts to regulating a community in rapid flux. Although there was continued concern about the arrival of convicts from Van Diemen's Land, they no longer seemed such an immediate threat. Indeed crime reportage in the press witnessed a turn-around similar to that in response to the Molesworth Committee a decade earlier.

Initially the gold rush created widespread fears of anarchy. Predictions of rampant crime and social chaos, however, were soon replaced by self-congratulatory descriptions of the goldfields.[61] The colony's good order was contrasted to the lawlessness of both Victoria and California. The discovery of gold in Victoria in August 1851 was viewed as less than an unmixed blessing. "What a contrast! The evils which we feared have fallen heavily upon her. Gold she possesses a plenty, but with it the curse of overriding ruffianism and total insecurity."[62] Starker comparisons were made with California. Colonists bitterly resented insinuations made by American newspapers that New South Welshmen were largely responsible for crimes, especially arson, committed in California. The colonial press retaliated with abundant reports of lynch law and vigilante movements in California, which served both to confirm New South Wales' superior order, and to underline the dangers inherent in Yankee republicanism.[63] Edward Hargraves, the acclaimed discoverer of gold in New South Wales, expressed his opinion that the worst convicts from Van Diemen's Land were better than New Yorkers on the American diggings, who had little scruple about killing and scarcely a semblance of religion.[64] The discovery of gold was heralded as an excellent opportunity for

> demonstrating to California and the world, that much of the odium which has been lavished upon the country is undeserved; and that with all the disadvantage of a penal origin, the inhabitants of New South Wales imported to their new homes that instinctive respect for authority of the law, and regard for social order, which distinguish the brethren of their fatherland.[65]

Underpinning New South Wales' claims to moral superiority, were in fact more fundamental differences. Unlike California, the machinery for government and social control was already firmly established in the colony before gold was discovered. The proximity of settled communities to the diggings provided relatively easy access to police and courts. Established wool and agricultural pursuits in New South Wales also served as a safety valve for frustrated gold seekers by affording alternative employment. In California the presence of hostile Indians stimulated a habit of using armed force, while in New South Wales Aboriginal resistance was already crushed in the gold mining regions.[66] Comparison with Victoria seems similarly unjust, since gold digging was on a much larger and more frenetic scale than in New South Wales. Portrayals of Victorian lawlessness in the Sydney press no doubt owed much to colonial rivalry intensified by recent separation, and a desire to discourage migration.[67]

The idealization of order on New South Wales' goldfields may be viewed partly as a defensive ideology which masked upper and middle class anxieties about the social and economic impact of gold. More importantly, that idealization reflected a concern with establishing New South Wales' new identity. The Victorian and Californian goldfields provided a counter-image for New South Wales' claims to respectability and freedom from the convict stain. When violence later erupted against the Chinese on the diggings, it was rationalized on the basis that if similar circumstances existed in the heart of England, much greater disorders would have occurred than in New South Wales.[68] There were in fact more subtle ways of dealing with groups, such as the Chinese, which seemed to pose a threat. The *Empire,* edited by leading anti-transportationist Henry Parkes, proclaimed in 1851 that it would be more in the colony's moral interest to receive two thousand convicts than five hundred "yellow slaves" accompanied by "all incestuous and murderous crimes".[69] The concepts of a "criminal class" and "contamination" were malleable enough to continue serving various interests in the community.

Notes

1. *Bathurst Free Press,* 11 January 1851.
2. Concerning the transportation question and the anti-transportation movement see Ernest Scott, "The Resistance to Convict Transportation in Victoria, 1844–53", *Victorian Historical Magazine* vol. 1, no. 4 (December 1911), pp. 101–42; John M. Ward, *Earl Grey and the Australian Colonies 1846–1857: A Study of Self-Government and Self-Interest* (Melbourne, 1958), especially pp. 196–226; Shaw; *Convicts and the Colonies,* chapter 14; Irving, "Liberal Politics", pp. 201–22, 325–59; C. M. H. Clark, *A History of Australia,* Vol. 3: *The Beginning of An Australian Civilization 1824–1851* (Melbourne, 1973), especially pp. 348-51, 368-72, 415-27, 329-46; John N. Molony, *An Architect of Freedom: John Hubert Plunkett in New South Wales 1832–1869* (Canberra, 1973), especially pp. 125–33; Alan Powell, *Patrician Democrat: The Political Life of Charles Cowper 1843–1870* (Melbourne, 1977), chapter 3; A. W. Martin, *Henry Parkes. A Biography* (Melbourne, 1980), especially pp. 54–67.
3. Return of Exiles to Port Phillip, N.S.W., *V & PLC,* 1849, vol. 1, p. 902.
4. Godfrey Charles Mundy, *Our Antipodes: or, Residence and Rambles in the Australasian Colonies with A Glimpse of the Gold Fields* (London, 1855), pp. 467, 470.
5. See Martin, *Parkes,* pp. 60, 110; F. A. Larcombe, *A History of Local Government in New South Wales,* vol. 1: *The Origin of Local Government in New South Wales 1831–58* (Sydney, 1973), p. 101; S. G. Foster, *Colonial Improver. Edward Deas Thomson 1800–1879* (Melbourne, 1978), p. 120.
6. *SMH,* 10 March 1849.
7. *People's Advocate,* 21, 28 April, 5, 12 May 1849; Martin, *Parkes,* p. 56; Irving "Liberal Politics", p. 330.
8. *SMH,* 13 June 1849; *People's Advocate,* 16 June 1849.

9. **Confidential** Minute enclosed in FitzRoy to Grey, 30 June 1849, CO 201/414, f. 362.
10. FitzRoy to Grey, 30 June 1849, CO 201/414, ff. 332–3.
11. *Bathurst Free Press*, 11 January 1851.
12. *Moreton Bay Courier*, quoted in *People's Advocate*, 14 July 1849.
13. *People's Advocate*, 10 March 1849.
14. *People's Advocate*, 8 September 1849.
15. *People's Advocate*, 19 October 1850.
16. *SMH*, 10 October 1849.
17. *SMH*, 8 November 1849.
18. *SMH*, 29 October 1849.
19. *Bell's Life*, 29 December 1849; *People's Advocate*, 29 December 1849.
20. *SMH*, 23 January 1850.
21. Ann Deas Thomson to Richard Bourke, 17 February 1850, Bourke Papers, ML, Uncatalogued MSS., Set 403, Item 7.
22. Return of Van Diemen's Land Convicts, N.S.W., *V & PLC*, 1850, vol. 2, p. 583.
23. *People's Advocate*, 21 September 1850. See also *SMH*, 16 October 1850.
24. *SMH*, 10 March, 25, 27 April 1849; *People's Advocate*, 28 April 1849.
25. *SMH*, 16 September 1850.
26. *SMH*, 20 September 1850.
27. *People's Advocate*, 21 September 1850. Lang recounted the same incident in the Legislative Council. LC, *SMH*, 3 October 1850.
28. LC, *SMH*, 4 October 1850.
29. Ibid., LC, *SMH*, 7 October 1850.
30. LC, *SMH*, 1, 4 October 1850.
31. LC, *SMH*, 4 October 1850.
32. Mr Suttor's and Attorney-General's Address, ibid.
33. Mr Bowman's Address, ibid.
34. *People's Advocate*, 24 March 1849.
35. *SMH*, 8 March 1850.
36. *Goulburn Herald*, 15 February, 8 March 1851; *Empire*, 10 May 1851.
37. See for example *People's Advocate*, 8 December 1849; *SMH*, 13 November 1849.
38. FitzRoy to Grey, 5 July 1850, and enclosed return, *PP*, 1851, vol. 45, [1361], pp. 177–78.
39. Return of Offences Committed by Exiles, N.S.W., *V & PLC*, 1851, vol. 2, pp. 431–32. It is unclear whether these "serious" offences referred to arrests, committals or convictions.
40. *SMH*, 4 October 1850.
41. *SMH*, 4 April 1849.
42. See Robin Gollan, *Radical and Working Class Politics: A Study of Eastern Australia 1850–1910* (Melbourne, 1960; reprint ed., 1966), pp. 8–9; Connell and Irving, *Class Structure*, p. 115.
43. *People's Advocate*, 18 August 1849.
44. See Clark, *History of Australia*, vol. 3, p. 445; Powell, *Patrician Democrat*, p. 46; Irving, "Liberal Politics", p. 334.
45. *Freeman's Journal*, 9 October 1851.
46. Mr Nichols's Address, LC, *SMH*, 3 October 1849.
47. R. H. W. Reece, *Aborigines and Colonists. Aborigines and Colonial Society in New South Wales in the 1830s and 1840s* (Sydney, 1974), pp. 9–10; Evidence of Charles Henry Green to the Select Committee on the Gold Fields Management Bill, N.S.W., *V & PLC*, 1853, vol. 2, p. 451.

48. *Sydney Herald,* 15, 18 June 1835; *Australian,* 22 June 1844.
49. [Colony of NSW] 13 Vic., No. 46, sec. 2–3; FitzRoy to Grey, 16 December 1849, *PP*, 1850, vol. 45, [1285], p. 340.
50. Grey to FitzRoy, 4 July 1850, *PP*, 1850, vol. 45, [1285], pp. 359–60.
51. LC, *Empire*, 17 April 1851.
52. Convictions Under Vagrancy Act, N.S.W., *V & PLC*, 1851, vol. 2, p. 463. See also *Press*, 8 January 1851.
53. Geoffrey Serle, *The Golden Age. A History of the Colony of Victoria 1851–1862* (Melbourne, 1963; reprint ed., 1968), p. 127.
54. See for example *People's Advocate*, 10 March, 28 April 1849.
55. *SMH*, 3 May 1851.
56. Address to the Australasian League, *SMH*, 3 May 1851.
57. *SMH*, 18 October 1850. *Herald's* emphasis.
58. See Berger, *Invitation to Sociology*, p. 159.
59. J. E. Thomas and Alex Stewart, *Imprisonment in Western Australia. Evolution, Theory and Practice* (Medlands, 1978), p. 31.
60. Pakington to Denison, 14 December 1852, *PP*, 1852–53, vol. 82 [1601], pp. 117–18.
61. See for example *Empire*, 27 May 1851; *SMH*, 21 June 1851.
62. *Bell's Life*, 6 March 1852.
63. See for example *Freeman's Journal*, 9 October 1851; *Bathurst Free Press*, 15 October 1851. The *Empire*, while denying that California's evils derived from democratic institutions, deprecated American vigilante action as both inhumane and un-British. *Empire*, 22 October 1851.
64. Arthur E. Selwyn to Rose Rusden, 25 February 1852, Selwyn Correspondence, NLA, MS. 3542, pp. 102–3.
65. *Bathurst Free Press*, 7 June 1851.
66. See F. Lancelott, *Australia As It Is: Its Settlements, Farms and Gold Fields* (London, 1853), vol. 1, pp. 208–9; Mundy, *Our Antipodes*, p. 566; *SMH*, 23 August 1851, Andrew Markus, *Fear and Hatred. Purifying Australia and California 1850–1901* (Sydney, 1979), p. 14.
67. Serle, *Golden Age*, p. 36.
68. *Empire*, 20 June 1861.
69. *Empire*, 24 November 1851.

4

Measuring Morality

> Allowing the facts to speak for themselves often masks an ignorance of the meaning of those facts and how they are officially compiled; and speaking for the facts is often a means of selective perception and interpretation to support and further personal or group interests. . . . The source of information that sustains most beliefs about crime and criminals is the official statistics . . . [1]

Contemporaries generally made two quantitative judgements about New South Wales' crime rate. First, it was assumed that as a result of penal transportation the colony's crime rate was extremely high; some believed the highest in the world. Second, it was contended that crime in the colony was almost wholly attributable to persons originally transported. Statistical evidence marshalled to support these contentions, however, was usually scanty or non-existent. A *Colonial Magazine* correspondent, for example, asserted that Australia's criminal statistics demonstrated the country's "low state of morals", "the most fearful debauchery and violence", and "the most corrupt form of civilisation that has yet been recorded", without actually citing any statistics.[2] When criminal statistics were cited by publicists and newspapers, they generally referred to only brief spans of time and were listed without reference to the colony's changing population. In fact, despite intense concern about crime, New South Wales' official statistics provide only a crude index of criminal trends. Returns of committals to trial, available for England and Wales from the beginning of the nineteenth century, were not introduced in New South Wales until 1858. Statistics of police arrests were not systematically compiled until 1874. The only statistics comprehending the years before 1858 are convictions before the Supreme Court, circuit courts and courts of quarter sessions.

Although contemporaries had little doubt that New South Wales' crime rate was almost entirely dependent on the proportion of convicts and ex-convicts in the population,[3] the available statistics must be considered in a wider context. Criminal statistics in general are a questionable measure of actual criminal activity. Beyond this it is necessary to consider the official crime rate in relation to the colony's apparatus for social control. The composition of New

South Wales' population must be viewed in terms not only of persons originally transported, but also broader demographic changes. International trends in crime rates for the period further suggest that the colony's criminal statistics reflect social changes which cut across national boundaries.

Figures 2 and 3 represent convictions for what in contemporary terms was "serious crime", that is, convictions before the superior courts, in New South Wales from 1831 to 1861. Convictions for offences are expressed as a rate to every 100,000 inhabitants in order to compensate for the colony's changing population. To give some indication of changing patterns of conviction for different types of crime, offences are grouped into categories introduced by Britain's criminal registrar in 1833, and which have remained basically unchanged to the present day. Offences against the person include violent crimes ranging from murder to common assaults. Some non-violent crimes are also included, notably bigamy and sodomy, but they made up only a fraction of the offences in this group. Offences against property with violence include robbery and crimes where victims were put in fear, as well as crimes committed where the offender was denied legal access such as housebreaking and burglary. Most offences against property without violence were simply denominated "larcenies", although this group also includes such offences as stock theft, embezzlement and fraud. Forgery and counterfeiting comprise a separate category, as do malicious offences against property, which almost always took the form of arson or killing and maiming livestock.[4]

The figures illustrate a sharp increase in the colony's conviction rate from 1831 to 1835, as already discussed in some detail in chapter 1. Due to an absence of returns for courts of quarter sessions from 1836 to 1838, there are no complete statistics for these years. From 1839 the conviction rate sharply declined until 1847, and then fell sharply again in the years after 1854. Convictions for offences against property exhibit the same trend, which is not surprising since they made up the vast majority of all convictions. Offences against the person reached a peak in 1833, sharply declined between 1839 and 1843, and then remained fairly stable until 1854 when the conviction rate again declined. Convictions for offences against property with violence peaked in 1834, exhibited a marked decline during the early 1840s, and thereafter decreased irregularly to the end of the period. The rate of conviction for offences against the currency and malicious offences against property remained relatively stable, although the total number of offences involved is too small to discern any meaningful trends.

Overall New South Wales' conviction rate seems to justify an emphasis on the relation between crime and convictism, especially since

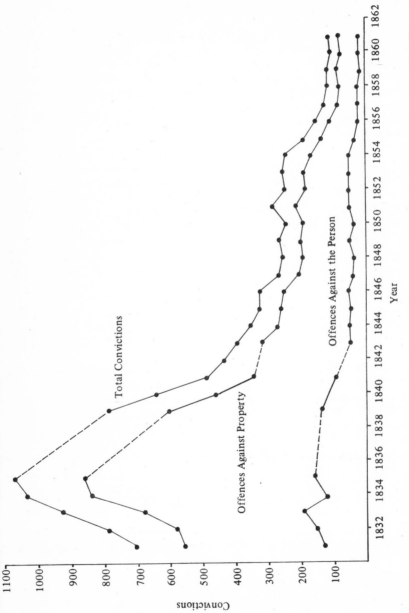

Figure 2. Total Convictions, Convictions for All Offences Against Property and Convictions for All Offences Against the Person; per 100,000 Inhabitants Before the Superior Courts of New South Wales, 1831-61.

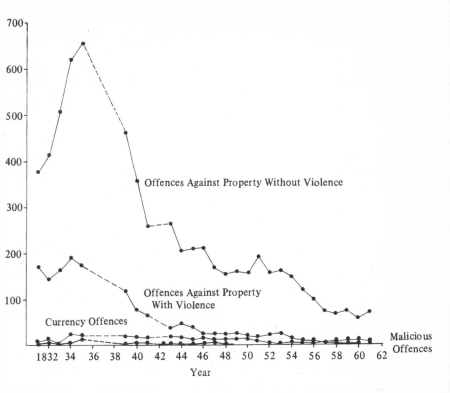

Figure 3. Convictions for Offences Against Property Without Violence, Offences Against Property With Violence, Offences Against the Currency and Malicious Offences Against Property, per 100,000 Inhabitants Before the Superior Courts of New South Wales, 1831–61.

the official crime rate plummeted once transportation ended. But the statistics are by no means an accurate measure of real crime levels.[5] The most formidable problem associated with criminal statistics is the impossibility of determining what relation officially recorded crime bears to actual criminal activity. Many crimes are never recorded, and this "dark figure" of crime makes conclusions about changing patterns of criminal statistics questionable. The statistics for New South Wales are a particularly crude index of crimes committed, since until 1858 only convictions were recorded. As a general rule criminologists argue that the further the record is removed from the commission of an offence, the less accurately it reflects the real incidence of criminal activity. For this reason, records of crimes known to the police or committals for trial would be a more accurate index of crime than a record of convictions.[6]

While many nineteenth-century observers recognized that criminal statistics did not represent all crimes committed, they circumvented the problem by assuming that undetected crimes remained a constant proportion of those recorded. Modern criminologists, as well, have often assumed that criminal statistics represent a fairly constant proportion of the real incidence of crime. Nevertheless, there are important reasons why the proportion of unrecorded criminal activity might fluctuate over time.

Whether crimes are officially recorded or not depends largely on the tendency of people to report offences. Modern victimization studies indicate that a vast number of criminal offences, in some cases over half of those committed, are never reported. It is theoretically possible for the statistics to indicate a crime wave when in fact nothing changed but reporting habits.[7] On an individual level, the likelihood of an offence being reported might vary with the victim's social group, his or her attitude toward the crime committed and the police, or the victim's relation to the offender.[8] More generally, the seriousness with which an offence is regarded might vary with time and place.

More important perhaps than reporting habits in influencing criminal statistics, is a community's machinery for law enforcement. Obviously the number of crimes detected would fluctuate with the number, efficiency and disposition of the police. The statistics are also affected by changes in the judicial system, criminal law and legal procedure. From one point of view, criminal statistics can be regarded as less a measure of criminal activity, than a reflection of the capacity and practices of a community's social control apparatus.[9] For this reason, New South Wales' criminal statistics must be considered in the light of the colony's judicial and police systems.

In relation to New South Wales, the extension of the judicial system would seem a particularly important factor influencing the rate of criminal convictions. The remoteness of superior courts was persistently complained of, largely on the grounds that many crimes went unpunished. One magistrate of Portland Bay went so far as to assert that people were reluctant to prosecute anything less than murder, for fear that their presence might be required in Melbourne to enforce a conviction.[10] Although prosecutors and witnesses were reimbursed for some travel costs, the expenses provided were often considered inadequate compensation for the time, loss of employment and inconvenience involved. The establishment of additional courts could cause an increase in recorded crime since, as the colony's chief justice noted, the greater convenience afforded might lead to a greater willingness to prosecute offences.[11]

With the New South Wales Act of 1823 the Court of Criminal Judicature, which formerly heard all criminal cases, including those originating in Van Diemen's Land, was abolished.[12] Criminal offences in New South Wales were subsequently tried by a Supreme Court and courts of quarter sessions. The Supreme Court, which opened at Sydney in May 1824, initially consisted of a chief justice. By 1827 two additional judges were appointed to the court. From that date the composition of the Supreme Court in Sydney remained the same until 1865, when a fourth judge was added to the bench.

Courts of quarter sessions, so called because justices in England were originally required to hold sessions four times a year, were also established in 1824. In New South Wales the first such courts were directed to be held at Sydney, Parramatta, Windsor and Liverpool. The courts were composed of magistrates, and presided over by an annually elected chairman. The chairman, elected from among the justices of the peace, was generally a barrister, and once elected became a salaried officer of the government. Courts of quarter sessions were authorized to try all criminal offences not punishable by death, and to try prisoners under sentence of transportation summarily without a jury.

The need for additional judges and courts, both to relieve the burden placed on judicial officers and to keep pace with settlement, was urged throughout the period under study. Yet the judicial system was only gradually expanded. In 1837 Richard Bourke proposed the creation of an additional judgeship in order that courts might be held at Port Phillip, but it was only after the Legislative Council was empowered to make provisions for the administration of justice in 1839 that steps for an appointment were taken.[13] The Council's first act relating to justice provided for the appointment of a resident judge at Port Phillip.[14] The Act also authorized the appointment of other judges which would extend the presence of the Supreme Court, but the only other addition made before 1861 was the appointment of a resident judge for Moreton Bay in January 1856.

The administration of justice was further impeded by the slow development of circuit courts. As early as 1826 Chief Justice Forbes pressed for the establishment of circuit courts, and their necessity was repeatedly urged by Governor Bourke.[15] In 1839 Governor Gipps reported that the absence of circuit courts amounted "almost to a denial of Justice". He considered both the cost of bringing prisoners and witnesses to Sydney for trial, and the consequent delay of justice "highly injurious".[16] It was also suspected that many crimes went unpunished because of the reluctance of parties and their witnesses to undertake the time and expense of travelling to Sydney in order to prosecute offences.[17]

The creation of circuit courts, also known as courts of assize, was finally authorized in 1840.[18] The courts were held before a judge of the Supreme Court, and empowered to try capital offences. Governor Gipps proclaimed three circuit districts to be visited twice a year, and in 1841 the first sittings opened at Bathurst, Berrima and Maitland. In 1847 Goulburn displaced Berrima as the site for a circuit court, on the basis that four-fifths of the cases tried at Berrima arose in the area of Goulburn, and because of the paucity of jurors at Berrima.[19] Despite the need for additional circuit courts underlined by a royal commission on law in 1849, the only court subsequently established was for the Moreton Bay district, which was held for the first time in 1850.[20]

The slow expansion of circuit courts was paralleled by that of quarter sessions. In 1831 courts of quarter sessions were held at Sydney, Parramatta, Windsor, Campbell Town and Maitland. By 1839 courts were also established in the districts of Berrima, Bathurst and Port Phillip. Courts held at Windsor and Campbell Town were discontinued from 1844, and after 1847 Goulburn displaced Berrima as the site for quarter sessions as well as circuit courts. Additional courts were not created until the District Courts Act of 1858. Under the Act the colony was divided into five districts, and a total of forty locations were designated sites where courts might be held.[21] District court judges were empowered to preside over courts of quarter sessions, and the judges were given jurisdiction over all criminal offences not punishable by death. By special commission they could also be authorized with the same powers as a Supreme Court judge for dealing with cases in remote areas.[22]

To some extent frequent protests concerning the necessity for establishing more superior courts resulted from regional rivalry. In the northern districts residents of Armidale, Tamworth and Scone all petitioned against the inconvenience of travelling to Maitland for trials, while urging the fitness of their respective towns as the site of a court of assize.[23] Similarly, residents of Windsor protested the loss of their court of quarter sessions not only on the grounds that crimes went unchecked, but also on the town's declining prosperity.[24] On the other hand, the vast distance of many settlers from courts was probably a serious obstruction to justice. Residents of Albury for example, were required to travel over 230 miles to Goulburn in order to attend a circuit court, while settlers at Tamworth were 170 miles from courts of assize and quarter sessions held at Maitland. Circuit courts were later established at Albury and Tamworth, but not until after 1868.[25]

The evidence suggests that because of the distance of many settlers from superior courts, crimes were frequently not prosecuted. For the same reason, it may be suspected that poorer members of the community were less likely to undertake prosecutions than were their wealthier neighbours. Beyond this, the impact of the judicial system on the colony's official crime rate is uncertain. It might be argued that New South Wales' declining rate of convictions from 1839 onwards reflects in part the failure of the courts to keep pace with a growing and increasingly dispersed population. On the other hand, expansion of the judicial system, most notably with the creation of circuit courts in 1841 and district courts in 1858, failed to result in any upsurge in convictions. This might suggest that in spite of greater opportunities for prosecuting offences, the colony's crime rate continued to fall.

The rate of criminal convictions would ostensibly be affected not only by the number of courts, but also by changes in legal procedure and criminal law. As discussed in chapter 1, a reduction in the number of capital offences and a curtailment of magistrates' jurisdiction in the 1830s almost certainly had a significant impact on the official crime rate. A further change of immense importance was the extension of summary jurisdiction in the 1850s to include criminal offences previously tried by the superior courts. Under the Juvenile Offenders Act of 1850 cases of simple larceny involving persons not over fourteen years of age could be tried by courts of petty sessions consisting of two or more magistrates.[26] In 1852 summary jurisdiction was extended to cases of larceny involving persons up to sixteen years of age, and in larcenies of less than five shillings to persons of all ages.[27] The jurisdiction of magistrates was again widened in 1855, to include all cases where money or property stolen did not exceed forty shillings in value.[28] There are no returns for cases tried summarily, so it is impossible to determine how many cases were diverted to courts of petty sessions. One can assume with some confidence, however, that these changes resulted in a substantial decrease in offences against property tried before the superior courts.

Changes in police numbers are more easily quantified. Nevertheless, an assessment of their influence on the statistics is complicated by the fragmented structure of New South Wales' police forces. A unified force for the colony was not permanently established until 1862, and before that date various forces were created and abolished.[29]

The backbone of New South Wales' police consisted of the metropolitan force in Sydney and the rural constabulary. Until 1810 Sydney's police operated under military control. In that year Governor Macquarie divided the town into districts, and placed the constabulary under a civilian superintendent of police. Under Governor Bourke, the administration of Sydney's police was divided between two officers, one of whom managed the constabulary, including appointments and dismissals, while the other was charged with conducting business at the police office.[30] The titles of police officials were periodically altered, but this arrangement remained basically the same throughout the period.

From 1835 onwards the colony's rural constabulary was divided into police districts. By 1847 there were forty-two police districts in New South Wales, including ten districts at Port Phillip. In that year, with the establishment of courts of petty sessions beyond the boundaries of location, the number of districts was increased to seventy-seven.[31] The constabulary of each district were entirely independent of one another. They were supervised either by a paid police magistrate appointed by the governor, or as was more often the case, by unpaid justices of the peace.

In addition to the rural constabulary and metropolitan police of Sydney, four other police forces were established in New South Wales before 1851. In 1825 a Mounted Police force, consisting of men recruited from military regiments serving in the colony, was established by Governor Thomas Brisbane. The force was formed primarily to apprehend runaway convicts, and to track down persons committing robberies and other serious offences.[32] Divisions were stationed at various posts, and small parties patrolled the main roads. The force was discontinued in December 1850, with the refusal of the Legislative Council to vote funds for their support.

In Sydney a Water Police operated alongside the regular constabulary from 1830, and in Melbourne from 1841. The force was formed primarily to prevent the escape of convicts, but later dealt principally with cases involving sailors. The administrative arrangements for the Water Police vacillated during the 1840s, but following the Police Act of 1850 Sydney's superintendent of police took charge of executive duties, while magisterial business was conducted by a Water Police magistrate.

After an unsuccessful attempt to establish a corps in 1837, a Native Police at Port Phillip was revived in 1842. The force, consisting of mounted Aborigines and European officers, was formed mainly for controlling Aborigines. In 1848 a corps of Native Police was also established in the colony's middle district. Victoria's Native Police was disbanded early in 1853, while a corps continued to operate chiefly in New South Wales' northern districts.[33]

In 1839 a Border Police force was established on the proposal of Governor Gipps, largely in response to the murder of Aborigines at Myall Creek. The force's main function was to bring some order to settler-Aboriginal relations beyond the boundaries of location. Mounted men were attached to commissioners of crown lands, who also acted as justices of the peace. The Border Police were generally men chosen from among well conducted prisoners, and received no pay. The force was disbanded in 1847 following the establishment of courts of petty sessions with attachments of police beyond the settled districts.[34]

Following the discovery of gold in 1851 two mounted forces were established in the form of a Gold Escort and Road Patrol. A Western Road Patrol operated between Sydney and Bathurst under orders of the inspector-general of police, while a smaller patrol operated in the south under the control of provincial inspectors.[35] Mounted troopers were also attached to gold commissioners. In May 1851 a chief commissioner of crown lands for the gold districts was appointed, and gold commissioners for a western and a southern district were established. For the control of every one thousand gold diggers, an establishment consisting of an assistant commissioner, a sub-commissioner, five mounted and five foot troopers was authorized by the government.[36]

To the extent that returns are available, table 3 gives a numerical breakdown of New South Wales' police. For the purpose of evaluating the impact of changing police numbers on the colony's criminal statistics, figures for the Water Police and Native Police can be excluded, since these police rarely apprehended offenders for indictable offences. The lack of returns for the Border Police also precludes the inclusion of statistics for police beyond the boundaries of location. The only comprehensive returns are for police within the settled districts, that is, the metropolitan police, rural constabulary (including Port Phillip), and Mounted Police, from 1831 to 1850.

Figure 4 represents changes in police numbers within the settled districts expressed as a rate per 1,000 inhabitants. A decline in police numbers from 1837 coincided with declining criminal convictions in New South Wales. As a result, it may be postulated that the colony's official crime rate reflected in part reductions in the police. Again, however, the evidence is ambiguous. Despite reductions in the police before 1835, the colony's conviction rate continued to rise. This might suggest that at least for the period between 1831 and 1835, the impact of changing police numbers on the crime figures was not significant. Furthermore, changes in police numbers do not necessarily reflect changes in police efficiency, and give no indication of police practices at any one time.

The complexity of variables affecting criminal statistics obviously limits their reliability as a measure of real criminal activity. The factors already discussed affected the statistics in some way, although it is difficult to delineate the influence of individual factors since they were always in interaction. All that can be stated with certainty is that New South Wales' official crime rate declined more or less steadily from 1839 onwards. Beyond this, any interpretation of the statistics must be tentative. With this in mind, however, it may be hypothesized that a combination of factors — the slow expansion of the judicial system, reductions in the police and an expansion of the magistracy's jurisdiction — were at least partially responsible for the colony's falling crime rate.

Table 3. Numerical Strength of New South Wales' Police Forces, 1831–61.

Year	Sydney	Port Phillip	Rural Police	Mounted Police	Police Beyond Settled Districts	Border Police	Water Police	Native Police	Gold Escort	Road Patrol	Gold Police
1831	76		134	104							
1832	77		148	104							
1833	94		143	104							
1834	94		165	114							
1835	98		161	111							
1836	150	4	223	124			6				
1837	150	9	263	124			6				
1838	150	10	284	146			5				
1839	150	13	280	145			6				
1840	106	28	287	127			6				
1841	117	27	289	135			19				
1842	117	42	294	146			22				
1843	96	33	262	143			15	24			
1844	95	40	255	137			15				
1845	102	47	253	156		136	13	37			
1846	102	62	252	141			13				
1847	102	112	249	138	100		13				
1848	110	126	239	130	99		19	29			
1849	110	137	248	131	95		18	59			
1850	112	150	222	35	101		16	92			
1851	151		247		87		15	50	16	36	
1852	154						15	110	22	36	
1853	177						22	112	28	57	90
1854	179						25	156	17	57	99
1855	263						27	157	20	61	85
1856	256						24	101	17	60	66
1857	187						17			59	64
1858								77			
1859	195		529								
1860											
1861	181		447				25				

Source: Returns of the Colony, "Blue Books", 1831–57 (xerox copy), ML, CY 4/262–290; Returns of Police, N.S.W, *V & PLA*, 1858, vol. 2, p. 407; 1858–60, vol. 2, pp. 558–59; 1861–62, vol. 1, p. 929.

Notes: Figures for the rural constabulary are exclusive of conveyors, and those for the Water Police are ...

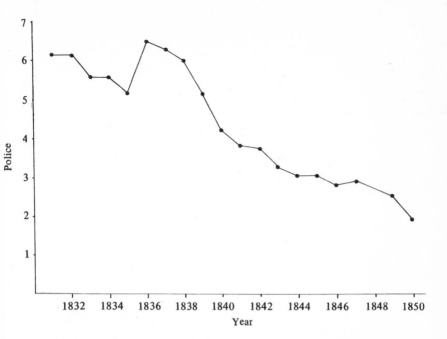

Figure 4. Police Within the Settled Districts per 1,000 Inhabitants in New South Wales, 1831–50.

New South Wales' official crime rate was affected not only by changes in the apparatus for social control, but also by the composition of the population. In this respect the declining proportion of persons transported was the most obvious change, and as already noted, the one which most contemporaries emphasized in interpreting the colony's criminal statistics. To the extent that returns are available, they indicate that a greatly disproportionate number of persons tried and convicted of criminal offences were drawn from the convict group. Judge William Burton calculated that of criminal cases tried before him between 1833 and 1838, 701 out of 853, that is eighty-two per cent, involved convicts or emancipists.[37] Returns for the early 1840s indicate that convicts under sentence and persons free by servitude together made up about seventy per cent of those tried before the superior courts.[38] Table 4, based on extant records of persons tried during 1841 and 1851, illustrates a similar trend.

These figures are incomplete, since many court records are not available, and in numerous cases the civil condition of persons tried was not recorded.[39] They do suggest that the colony's convict element, and in

Table 4. Civil Condition of Persons Tried Before the Superior Courts of New South Wales, 1841 and 1851.

Civil Condition	1841			1851		
	No. Tried	% of Tried	% of Pop.	No. Tried	% of Tried	% of Pop.
Bond	163	20.8	15.9	2	0.5	0.4
Ticket of Leave	20	2.6	4.7	7	1.9	1.1
Free by Servitude	356	45.5	14.8	181	48.7	14.2
Came Free	184	23.5	40.4	158	42.5	40.9
Born in Colony	46	5.9	22.5	21	5.6	43.5
Aborigine	13	1.7		3	0.8	
No Information	143			457		

Notes: These figures represent part of a more comprehensive analysis of persons tried during 1841 and 1851. For methods and sources employed see chapter 5. Percentages of persons tried exclude "no information" cases, so that they can be compared to population returns.

particular emancipists, made up a disproportionate number of persons tried for criminal offences. The table indicates that in 1841 convicts and ex-convicts made up seventy per cent of persons tried, while they composed only thirty-five per cent of the population. By 1851 this discrepancy was considerably reduced, but ex-convicts still accounted for fifty per cent of persons tried, while comprising only fourteen per cent of the population. In fact, the proportion of emancipists tried for offences may be understated. It was suspected that many of those persons who committed crimes after being recorded as coming to the colony free, really came free from Van Diemen's Land where they were originally transported.[40]

There are a number of reasons why convicts and ex-convicts might be expected to make up a large proportion of persons tried and convicted of criminal offences, aside from their criminal propensities. The colony's machinery for social control was directed largely toward the coercion of convicts. They were subject to more stringent regulation, kept under closer surveillance by the police, and treated differently by the courts. One may suspect that the discretion of prosecutors, constables and judges operated more favourably toward free immigrants and native-born persons than those with a criminal record.[41] Convicts and ex-convicts were apparently more likely to be convicted than were free immigrants and those born in the colony, when tried for offences.[42]

As William Bland pointed out, the fact that convicts and ex-convicts generally constituted the poorest, least educated, and lowest class in the colony, meant that they were the same class as those most prone to commit offences in any community.[43] The stigma of transportation could affect both convicts' self-image and their treatment by other members of the community. They were probably more vulnerable to economic fluctuations, since persons of convict background often faced the most limited employment opportunities. To some extent they perhaps assumed or were coerced into a role which was expected of them.

At the same time, the changing proportion of convicts and ex-convicts in the population was only one part of a broader change in New South Wales' social composition. The colony's sex ratio and age distribution had a marked impact on the crime rate, and greatly distorted the proportion of convictions involving persons originally transported. The vast majority of persons committed for offences were males. Women made up only one-fifth of those tried in both 1841 and 1851. In part this reflected their relatively small numbers in a predominantly male population. As in other communities, however, women also made up a small proportion of offenders relative to their percentage of the total population. Between 1831 and 1846, the proportion of males decreased from seventy-four per cent of the total population to about sixty per cent. Although the proportion of males fluctuated during the gold rush years, there was still a continued decline.[44] This decline in turn would have had a significant effect in lowering the colony's official crime rate. Indeed, Peter Grabosky suggests that the preponderance of males in the population was the single most important variable affecting New South Wales' crime rate during the nineteenth century.[45]

The colony's official crime rate was similarly distorted by changes in age distribution. Juveniles apparently made up only a small proportion of offenders. Only about one per cent of the persons taken into custody by the Sydney police during 1857 were under fifteen years of age.[46] Consequently a low ratio of children in the population inflated the colony's crime rate, especially during the convict era. Between 1841 and 1851 the proportion of the population aged twenty-one to forty-four dropped from fifty-six per cent to thirty-nine per cent.[47] After transportation ended as well, immigrants included a preponderance of young adults. The resulting skewed population meant that there continued to be a disproportionate number in those age groups most likely to be tried for criminal offences.

Differential sex ratios and age distribution have an important bearing on which social groups were most commonly tried for offences. Despite fears of convict contamination, especially in relation to the rising generation, the proportion of offences involving the native-born was strikingly low. To the extent that information is available, persons born in the colony made up only about six per cent of those tried during 1841, while making up over one-fifth of the colony's population. They comprised the same proportion of those tried in 1851, even though they represented over forty per cent of the population.

Ken Macnab and Russel Ward explain the relative absence of criminality among the native-born, not only in terms of Australia's environment, but also as a psychological reaction against the vicious home environment created by convict parents.[48] This appears to contradict, however, their insistence that native-born Australians closely shared the manners and outlook of convicts. It seems probable that convict parents were instead neither as vicious nor as unconcerned about their children's welfare as is commonly supposed. Edward Smith Hall and Joseph Long Innes stated their belief that ex-convict parents were generally more anxious about the education of their children than were free immigrants.[49] Caroline Chisholm similarly remarked upon emancipists' "nervous anxiety, regarding the moral and religious welfare of their children".[50]

The small proportion of native-born inhabitants tried is also partly a demographic illusion. Although census returns fail to break down the age structure of the population by civil condition, it can safely be assumed that a much larger proportion of those born in the colony, than either immigrants or convicts, were juveniles. The statistics in effect compare the criminality of five-year-olds with that of twenty-five-year-olds. The figures are also distorted because of differential sex ratios. Whereas males were over-represented among other social groups, the number of males and females was more or less equal among the native-born.

Conversely, a disproportionate number of the colony's adult males were originally transported. If it is assumed that all male convicts and ex-convicts were over fourteen years of age, they represented fifty-eight per cent of all males in the colony over this age in 1841. As late as 1851 male emancipists made up thirty-two per cent of all males in the colony over fourteen years of age.[51] Considered in this light, the number of offences involving convicts and ex-convicts seems far less dramatic.

Differences in New South Wales' law enforcement machinery and demographic patterns not only affected the crime rate over time, but made direct comparisons with other communities virtually meaningless. Nevertheless, such comparisons were made, often by implication, if not with statistical evidence. While acknowledging that such comparisons were "imperfect tests of the relative moral condition of different countries", James Macarthur cited figures from a Swedish publication indicating that the ratio of offenders to inhabitants was 1:22 in New South Wales, compared to 1:740 in England, and 1:3,500 in America.[52] Macarthur noted privately that he obtained the statistics from a newspaper extract, and that he both hoped and believed they were in error.[53] In fact, since there was no indication of the types of offences included in the different ratios, and because no national crime figures were available for America during the period, the comparison was preposterous.

While hardly approaching the statistics cited by Macarthur, the rate of conviction before the superior courts in New South Wales was much higher than in England and Wales, especially during the 1830s and early 1840s.[54] This disparity, however, can by no means be regarded as simply an effect of penal transportation, nor as a measure of real criminal activity. While the criminal law of the two communities was much the same, there were important differences in legal procedure and law enforcement. For example, if a prosecutor or witness failed to appear at a trial in Britain the case was dismissed,[55] while in New South Wales it was only postponed. In New South Wales, the attorney-general performed the function of grand juries, which may have resulted in a much higher rate of committals to trial. More importantly, the attorney-general acted as a public prosecutor in criminal cases, while in

Britain the burden of prosecution was placed entirely on private individuals until 1879.[56] By British standards New South Wales was densely policed, and one may suspect that the constabulary was more effective in detecting and apprehending suspects in small Australian communities than in Britain's urban centres. In general, a high crime rate is the expected concomitant of a community which was highly organized for coercing criminals and controlling crime.

As already indicated, New South Wales' crime rate was grossly distorted by a preponderance of males and young adults. A narrowing gap between British and colonial conviction rates from the 1840s no doubt owed much to the development of a more normalized sex ratio and age distribution. At the same time, New South Wales' smaller population meant that a relatively small change in the number of convictions could create large fluctuations in the crime rate. A similar trend was exhibited by Australia's other colonies.[57]

A detailed comparison between the crime rates of different communities would necessarily multiply the problems of assessing the influence of reporting habits, police practices, judicial changes and the composition of the population. Nevertheless, some studies of nineteenth-century criminal statistics for other communities show enough uniformity in long term trends to suggest that New South Wales' crime rate should not be considered as an isolated phenomenon. An analysis of the criminal statistics for London, Stockholm and New South Wales directed by Ted Robert Gurr reveals a similar trend in all three societies. In each community crime rates for murder and assault, and theft, showed a sharp decline from the mid-nineteenth century, followed by a more gradual decline which continued into the twentieth century.[58] This pattern is paralleled by some studies of crime rates on a national level. Work on nineteenth-century criminal statistics in England and Wales indicates a long term increase in serious crime until the mid-century, and subsequently a decline throughout the rest of the century.[59] In France major crimes against property plummeted from the early 1840s, although this trend was not followed by crimes against the person.[60] Sweden's theft rate decreased greatly between 1852 and the end of the 1880s.[61]

Precisely why the official crime rates of different communities exhibit so similar a trend during the nineteenth century is uncertain. Gurr suggests that the only simple explanation is that the statistical evidence reflects a real change in social behaviour.[62] In reference to England and Wales, V. A. C. Gatrell and T. B. Hadden also conclude that the statistics indicate a real change in criminal activity. They suggest two reasons for the declining crime rate from the mid-nineteenth century. First, there was increasing police and administrative efficiency in maintaining law and order. Second, the growing prosperity of the population during the second half of the century led to declining crime.[63]

Gurr and his colleagues reject the idea that a change in crime control was responsible for declining crime from mid-century onwards.[64] As Peter Grabosky indicates, New South Wales' crime rate showed a marked decrease before there was any marked improvement in police efficiency.[65] Aside from a short-lived attempt to implement a centralized system of police in the early 1850s, there was no major police reform before 1862. Whereas increasing police efficiency may have served to inhibit crime in the long term, however, it seems likely that a massive contraction of the police and penal system during the 1840s was partly responsible for New South Wales' falling crime rate. A change in the judicial system also had an important impact on the statistics for at least New South Wales and Britain. This was an extension of summary jurisdiction during the 1850s, which meant that a large proportion of cases previously tried before the superior courts were diverted to the magistracy.[66]

Improving economic conditions provide perhaps the most viable explanation of a long term decline in crime rates during the second half of the nineteenth century, as opposed to a sharp downturn at the mid-century. Although convictions for offences against property in New South Wales fell despite a severe economic depression during the early 1840s, prosperity may have had a more profound influence on the conviction rate from the gold rush years. Finally, it may be suggested that falling crime rates after the mid-century were indicative of declining official and public concern about crime.[67] Improved economic conditions might result in a more relaxed attitude towards the sanctity of property, and especially petty larcenies. By the 1850s fears of revolutionary violence in Europe also subsided, and this was probably translated into a general lessening of concern about crime and the "criminal class".[68] In the case of New South Wales, a decreasing crime rate after 1839 may be regarded as symptomatic of a diminishing preoccupation with crime, elicited particularly by the abolition of transportation.

In many ways the various hypotheses presented above are inter-related, and it is this interrelationship which perhaps comes closest to providing some insight into the meaning of New South Wales' criminal statistics. It may be suggested that the abolition of penal transportation to New South Wales had a profound effect on the colony's official crime rate, at least during the 1840s, but in a more indirect way than contemporaries indicated. The high proportion of convicts and ex-convicts tried for offences did not simply reflect their criminal tendencies, but their social and economic position in the community. Immigration and colonial births did not simply bring about the dilution of a vicious society, but also dramatically altered those demographic characteristics which the crime rate reflected. The ending of transportation resulted as well in diminishing public and official concern about crime, which affected policies of social control and the number of prosecutions undertaken. Reductions in police numbers, for example, while inspired largely by motives of economy, also reflected declining concern about crime. Public concern and the colony's crime rate reinforced each other, since as the crime rate fell efforts to curb crime were relaxed, which in turn might have lead to a further diminution in the crime rate. At the same time, the colony's falling conviction rate was perhaps reinforced by trends which cut across national boundaries. For this reason, and because New South Wales' crime rate continued to fall throughout the nineteenth century, the influence of convictism on the crime rate was probably confined to a fairly narrow space in time.

Notes

1. Steven Box, *Deviance, Reality and Society* (London, 1971), pp. 58–59.
2. Anon., "Transportation and Convict Colonies", *Colonial Magazine and East India Review,* vol. 18 (July-December 1849), p. 34.
3. See for example Macarthur, *New South Wales,* pp. 36, 39; Burton, "State of Society", *Colonial Magazine,* vol. 2, pp. 49, 54; Judge Stephen's Address to the Bathurst Circuit Court, *SMH,* 27 September 1844; Evidence of Lachlan Mackinnon to the Select Committee on Transportation, *PP,* 1861, vol. 13 (286), p. 85.
4. Although different modes of classification are used, the statistical trends generally conform with Peter Grabosky's analysis of "acquisitive" and "violent" crime for the period. A notable exception is for the years 1831–35, for which Grabosky's figures indicate a decrease rather than an increase. This is because Grabosky includes only convictions before the Supreme Court, whereas the following figures include convictions before courts of quarter sessions. As noted in Chapter 1 convictions both before the Supreme Court and courts of quarter sessions are a dubious measure of actual criminal trends. See Peter N. Grabosky, "Patterns of Criminality in New South Wales, 1788–1973", *Australian and New Zealand Journal of Criminology,* vol. 7, no. 4 (December 1974), pp. 220–21; Grabosky, *Sydney in Ferment,* pp. 33–34, 58; Ted Robert Gurr, Peter N. Grabosky and Richard C. Hula, *The Politics of Crime and Conflict. A Comparative History of Four Cities* (London, 1977), p. 439.
5. Concerning the application and limitations of criminal statistics see N. Howard Avison, "Criminal and Related Statistics", in Martin Wright (ed.), *Use of Criminology Literature* (London, 1974), pp. 177–93; Susan Margaret Magarey, "The Reclaimers: A Study of the Reformatory Movement in England and Wales, 1846–1893" (Ph.D. thesis, Australian National University, 1975), Appendix; V. A. C. Gatrell and T. B. Hadden, "Criminal Statistics and Their Interpretation", in E. A. Wrigley (ed.), *Nineteenth-Century Society. Essays in the Use of Quantitative Methods for the Study of Social Data* (Cambridge, 1972), pp. 336–96; Thorsten Sellin, "The Significance of Records of Crime", in Leon Radzinowicz and Marvin E. Wolfgang (eds.),

Crime and Justice, vol. 1: *The Criminal in Society* (New York, 1971), pp. 121−29; Thorsten Sellin and Marvin E. Wolfgang, *The Measurement of Delinquency* (New York, 1964), especially pp. 1−54.

6. At least in terms of general trends, however, convictions are probably comparable to committals for trial. K. K. Macnab indicates that in England and Wales during the first half of the nineteenth century committals and convictions show almost identical fluctuations. Macnab, "Crime in England and Wales", p. 61. Statistics of committals for trial in New South Wales from 1858 also conform to the pattern of conviction.

7. See Fred P. Graham, "A Contemporary History of American Crime", in Hugh Davis Graham and Ted Robert Gurr (eds.), *The History of Violence in America: Historical and Comparative Perspectives* (New York, 1969), p. 497; Richard Quinney, *Class, State and Crime. On the Theory and Practice of Criminal Justice* (New York, 1977), p. 127; P. R. Wilson and J. W. Brown, *Crime and the Community* (St Lucia, 1973), p. 85.

8. Sellin and Wolfgang, *Delinquency,* pp. 31−32; Box, *Deviance,* pp. 60−62.

9. See Charles Tilly, Louise Tilly and Richard Tilly, *The Rebellious Century 1830−1930* (London, 1975), p. 78; Erikson, *Wayward Puritans,* p. 25.

10. Evidence of Horace Flower to the Select Committee on Police, N.S.W., *V & PLC,* 1847, vol. 2, p. 72.

11. Alfred Stephen to Col. Sec., 13 March 1852, Chief Justice's Letterbook, Supreme Court, N.S.W. SA, 4/6654.

12. Concerning the organization of New South Wales' judicial system see J. M. Bennett, *A History of the Supreme Court of New South Wales* (Sydney, 1974); Alex C. Castles, *An Introduction to Australian Legal History* (Sydney, 1971); John Kennedy McLaughlin, "The Magistracy in New South Wales, 1788−1850" (LL.M. thesis, University of Sydney, 1973).

13. Normanby to Gipps, 29 August 1839, *HRA,* ser. 1, vol. 20, p. 299; 2 & 3 Vic., c. 70, sec. 2.

14. [Colony of N.S.W.] 4 Vic., No. 22, sec. 4.

15. Bennett, *Supreme Court,* pp. 75−76.

16. Gipps to Normanby, 4 September 1839, 3 October 1839, *HRA,* ser. 1, vol. 20, pp. 306−7, 360.

17. Resolutions of the Legislative Council, 25 September 1839, enclosed in Gipps to Normanby, 17 October 1839, *HRA,* ser. 1, vol. 20, p. 370.

18. [Colony of N.S.W.] 4 Vic., No. 22, sec. 16.

19. Alfred Stephen to Col. Sec., 1 October 1846, Alfred Stephen's Letterbook, ML, MSS. A 673, pp. 238−39; Alfred Stephen to Col. Sec., 29 January 1847, Chief Justice's Letterbook, Supreme Court, N.S.W. SA, 4/6653.

20. Report from Law Commission, N.S.W., *V & PLC,* 1849, vol. 1, pp. 659, 661.

21. Proclamation of 9 December 1858, *New South Wales Government Gazette,* 1858, vol. 2, pp. 2173−74.

22. [Colony of N.S.W.] 22 Vic., No. 18, sec. 25−26.

23. Petition of 161 Residents in the United Pastoral Districts of New England and McLeay, and Town of Armidale, N.S.W., *V & PLC,* 1854, vol. 2, pp. 361−62; Petition of 123 Inhabitants of Scone, N.S.W., *V & PLC,* 1855, vol. 1, pp. 707; Memorial of 126 Residents of Tamworth, N.S.W., *V & PLA,* 1856−57, vol. 1, pp. 1089−90; Petition of 1,550 Residents in the Pastoral Districts of New England, McLeay, Gwydir and Clarence, and the various Towns therein, N.S.W., *V & PLA,* 1856−57, vol. 1, p. 1093.

24. *Atlas,* 5 June 1847.

25. Petition of 70 Residents of Albury, N.S.W., *V & PLC,* 1853, vol. 1, p. 805;

Memorial of 126 Residents of Tamworth, N.S.W., *V & PLA*, 1856–57, vol. 1, p. 1089; Bennett, *Supreme Court*, p. 78.

26. [Colony of N.S.W.] 14 Vic., No. 2, sec. 1.
27. [Colony of N.S.W.] 16 Vic., No. 6, sec. 1–2.
28. [Colony of N.S.W.] 19 Vic., No. 24, sec. 11.
29. Concerning the organization of New South Wales' police see Hazel King, "Some Aspects of Police Administration in New South Wales, 1825–51", *JRAHS* vol. 42, pt 5 (1956), pp. 205–30; Hazel King, "Problems of Police Administration in New South Wales, 1825–51", *JRAHS* vol. 44, pt 2 (1958), pp. 49–70; Alice Hazel King, "Police Organization and Administration in the Middle District of New South Wales, 1825–51" (M.A. thesis, University of Sydney, 1956); G. M. O'Brien, *The Australian Police Forces* (London, 1960), chapter 2; D. Chappell and P. R. Wilson, *The Police and the Public in Australia and New Zealand* (St Lucia, 1969), pp. 4–12, 22–25, Kerry L. Milte, *Police in Australia. Development, Functions and Procedures* (Sydney, 1977), pp. 22–24. A more detailed discussion of New South Wales police is included in chapter 8.
30. Final Report of the Committee on Police and Gaols, N.S.W., *V & PLC*, 1835, pp. 418-19; Evidence of Charles Windeyer to the Select Committee on Police, N.S.W., *V & PLC*. 1847, vol. 2, p. 44.
31. Reports from Select Committees on Police, N.S.W., *V & PLC*, 1847, vol. 2, p. 23; 1850, vol. 2, p. 401.
32. Final Report of the Committee on Police and Gaols, N.S.W., *V & PLC*, 1835, p. 420; Evidence of Henry Breton to the Select Committee on Transportation, *PP* 1837 (518), vol. 19, p. 142.
33. See Gipps to Stanley, 21 March 1844, *HRA*, ser. 1, vol. 23, p. 498; C. D. Rowley, *Aboriginal Policy and Practice*, vol. 1: *The Destruction of Aboriginal Society* (Canberra, 1970), pp. 39–43; Barry Bridges, "The Native Police Corps, Port Phillip and Victoria, 1837–53", *JRAHS* vol. 57, pt 2 (June 1971), pp. 113–42; L. E. Skinner, *Police of the Pastoral Frontier. Native Police 1849–59* (St Lucia, 1975).
34. [Colony of N.S.W.] 2 Vic., No. 27; Gipps to Glenelg, 20 February, 6 April 1839, *HRA*, ser. 1, vol. 20, pp. 6, 90; Reports from Select Committees on Police, N.S.W., *V & PLC*, 1839, vol. 2, p. 150; 1850, vol. 2, p. 401.
35. Evidence of Captain Edward Battye to the Select Committee on the Police Regulation Bill, N.S.W., *V & PLC*, 1852, vol. 1, p. 933.
36. John R. Hardy to Col. Sec., 20 June 1852, N.S.W., *V & PLC*, 1852, vol. 2, p. 503.
37. Burton, "State of Society", *Colonial Magazine*, vol. 2, p. 52.
38. Percentage is based on Papers presented in Evidence of William Augustus Miles to the Select Committee on the Insecurity of Life and Property, N.S.W., *V & PLC*, 1844, vol. 2, p. 380; Appendix referred to in Evidence of J. Phelps Robinson to the Select Committee on General Grievances, N.S.W., *V & PLC*, 1844, vol. 2, p. 748; Returns cited by the Attorney-General, LC, *SMH*, 4 October 1850.
39. Whether an offender's civil condition was recorded depended largely on the committing magistrates and clerks of the bench, and it was complained that they were extremely negligent in this respect, particularly as time went on. See *SMH*, 23 August 1849; Attorney-General's Address, LC, *SMH*, 4 October 1850.
40. Burton, "State of Society", *Colonial Magazine* vol. 1, p. 436; Evidence of Stuart Alexander Donaldson to the Select Committee on Transportation, *PP*, 1861, vol. 13 (286), p. 72.

41. See Donald R. Cressey and David A. Ward (eds), *Delinquency, Crime, and Social Process* (New York, 1969), pp. 121, 123.
42. Based on an analysis of persons tried during 1841 and 1851, the conviction rate for convicts and ex-convicts was about ten per cent greater than for free immigrants and persons born in the colony who were tried for criminal offences.
43. Bland, *New South Wales*, pp. 81–82.
44. See appendix 1.
45. Grabosky makes this generalization on the basis of multiple regression analysis, which as he warns makes his findings no more than suggestive and of "questionable validity". Grabosky, "Patterns of Criminality", pp. 215, 224–25; Grabosky, *Sydney in Ferment*, pp. 165–67.
46. John McLerie to Col. Sec., 27 March 1858, N.S.W., *V & PLA*, 1858, vol. 2, p. 395.
47. Percentages are based on Census of New South Wales, 1841 and 1851.
48. Ken Macnab and Russel Ward, "The Nature and Nurture of the First Generation of Native-Born Australians", *Historical Studies*, vol. 10, no. 39 (November 1962), pp. 303–5.
49. Evidence of Edward Smith Hall and Joseph Long Innes to the Select Committee on the Renewal of Transportation, N.S.W., *V & PLC*, 1846, vol. 2, pp. 495, 497.
50. Caroline Chisholm, *Emigration and Transportation Relatively Considered; In a Letter Dedicated, by Permission, to Earl Grey* (London, 1847), p. 18.
51. Percentages are based on Census of New South Wales, 1841 and 1851.
52. Evidence of James Macarthur to the Select Committee on Transportation, *PP*, 1837, vol. 19 (518), p. 164.
53. James Macarthur to George Grey, 10 February 1837, CO 201/267, f. 511.
54. See appendix 5.
55. Philips, *Crime in Victorian England*, p. 108.
56. See ibid., pp. 96, 103–4; Currey, "Legal History of New South Wales", pp. 215–17, 418.
57. See appendix 5.
58. Ted Robert Gurr, *Rogues, Rebels, and Reformers. A Political History of Urban Crime and Conflict* (London, 1976), especially pp. 39, 45; Gurr, Grabosky and Hula, *Politics of Crime*, especially pp. 643–44.
59. Gatrell and Hadden, "Criminal Statistics", pp. 372–77.
60. Tilly, *Rebellious Century*, pp. 78–79.
61. Jan Sundin, "Theft and Penury in Sweden 1830–1920: A Comparative Study at the County Level", *Scandinavian Journal of History* vol. 1 (1976), p. 286.
62. Gurr, *Rogues, Rebels and Reformers*, p. 43; Gurr, Grabosky and Hula, *Politics of Crime*, pp. 627, 632.
63. Gatrell and Hadden, "Criminal Statistics", p. 377.
64. Gurr, Grabosky and Hula, *Politics of Crime*, pp. 643–44.
65. Grabosky, "Patterns of Criminality", p. 219.
66. See Philips, *Crime in Victorian England*, pp. 22, 48; Gatrell and Hadden, "Criminal Statistics", p. 356.
67. See Gurr, *Rogues, Rebels, and Reformers*, pp. 17, 20–21; Roger Lane, "Urbanization and Criminal Violence in the 19th Century: Massachusetts as a Test Case", in Graham and Gurr (eds.), *Violence in America*, p. 480.
68. See Philips, *Crime in Victorian England*, pp. 284, 289.

5

Offenders, Victims and Prosecuted Offences

We should ever suspect a theory of prison administration which contemplates no other end than to get rid of the transgressor, while we neglect the causes of crime . . . Tne only way of making the punishment of crime more effective, is really to raise the condition of the mass of the people, that they may have less to envy and more to lose.[1]

The official criminal statistics provide only a rough outline of offences prosecuted in New South Wales. No information is given concerning those people charged with crimes, their alleged victims, or indeed the precise form which the offences took. In order to gain a more detailed impression of offences prosecuted in the colony, it is necessary to resort to extant court records and newspaper reports. The judgment books, returns of trials and calendars of the superior courts provide information concerning the civil condition of offenders presented in chapter 4. They also record the place of trial, trial results and the court's sentence for each offence. For any information beyond this it is necessary to rely on the press.

Newspapers generally reported, in varying detail, all offences tried before specific criminal sessions. They did not, however, report all criminal sessions. In general, newspapers gave cases tried before the Supreme Court and circuit courts much fuller coverage than the quarter sessions. Reports of the quarter sessions sometimes included little more than a list of offenders and their crimes. For this reason, the information supplied is biased towards the more serious offences dealt with by judges of the Supreme Court either in Sydney or on circuit. Added to this is an inevitable journalistic bias in the selection of detail given about individual offences.

In order to provide a systematic analysis of prosecuted offences, available information was compiled on all cases tried before the superior courts during 1841 and 1851. The years 1841 and 1851 were chosen both because they bracket the most important decade in New South Wales' transition from a penal colony, and in order to make comparisons with information supplied by census returns.[2] It is arguable, too, that because of the nature of the source material, concentrating on two years provides a more viable framework for analysis than does a sample for the entire period. These "soundings", to borrow James Waldersee's term,[3] also permit a familiarity with individual cases and offenders which might be obscured in a more wide-ranging survey. Although the analysis is in the nature of a pilot study, in many respects offences tried during 1841 and 1851 may be considered characteristic of offences prosecuted during the entire period.

Data was compiled on a total of 1,754 cases, comprising 925 tried during 1841 and 829 during 1851.[4] Information for 1851 is more comprehensive both as a proportion of the total number of offences tried and in cases represented in the analysis, primarily because of the greater availability of country newspapers. The analysis includes only those cases actually brought to trial. A large number of persons (probably over ten per cent of all those committed for offences) were discharged without trial or had their cases postponed during the year. This could result from a variety of causes including a defect in the depositions taken, the attorney-general declining to proceed with a case, or the prisoner's escape, but most often because of the absence of a principal witness or prosecutor.

At the same time, cases brought to trial give an inflated picture of the number of offenders and offences prosecuted. Some persons were tried for more than one offence during the year. More importantly, two or more persons were frequently tried for their involvement in the same offence. During 1841, almost one-third of the persons brought to trial were tried with "accomplices", as were nearly one-quarter of those tried during 1851. This has an important bearing on the colony's conviction rate, since it reflected the number of persons prosecuted and not simply the number of crimes.

Information concerning the occupations of persons tried is too fragmentary to draw any firm conclusions (see table 5).[5] Several features are suggested, however, which at least deserve comment. The largest proportion of offenders could be described as either hired or domestic servants or unskilled workers. The increased proportion of free servants tried in 1851 compared with that in 1841, obviously reflects the abolition of convict assignment. Relative to census returns rural workers appear to be the most under-represented occupational group, but this is probably because they were often denominated "servants" in court reports. Offenders included a fair number of skilled workers or tradesmen as well, and more surprisingly, not a few professional and middle class people in 1851. This may reflect in part the expansion of the middle class which took place during the 1840s. Most of the cases involving middle class people were related to their particular occupation, and were often atypical of the majority of offences tried. Shopkeepers and dealers were commonly charged with receiving stolen goods. All of the four newspaper proprietors tried in 1851 were charged with libel. The only minister prosecuted was accused of performing an illegal marriage.

Table 5. Occupations of Persons Tried Before the Superior Courts of New South Wales, 1841 and 1851.

Occupation	1841		1851	
	No.	%	No.	%
Assigned Convict Servants	31	20.7		
Servants (Hired and Domestic)	18	12.0	53	28.3
Labourers	11	7.3	18	9.6
Rural Workers	5	3.3	21	11.2
Sawyers	3	2.0	3	1.6
Carriers			8	4.3
Seamen	19	12.7	17	9.1
Policemen	15	10.0	2	1.1
Soldiers	20	13.3	2	1.1
Skilled Tradesmen	9	6.0	12	6.4
Apprentices	1	0.7	2	1.1
Food Retailers (Butcher, Grocer, etc.)	2	1.3	8	4.3
Publicans and Innkeepers			5	2.7
Shopkeepers, Dealers and Brokers			6	3.2
Civil Servants (Bailiff, Postal Clerk)	3	2.0		
White-Collar Workers (Clerk, etc.)			3	1.6
Farmers and Settlers	5	3.3	7	3.7
Professionals (Newspaper Proprietor, etc.)	1	0.6	7	3.7
Other Miscellaneous Occupations	7	4.7	13	7.0
Total	150		187	

Three occupational groups in particular stand out. During 1841 large numbers of both soldiers and police were brought before the courts. The disproportionate number of soldiers owes much to the court records, which, unlike with other occupational groups, specified military offenders. Nevertheless, the frequent involvement of soldiers in criminal offences elicited comment from both judges and the press.[6]

Police were not specially recorded in judicial returns, but it is probable that newspapers put special emphasis on cases involving constables. More often than not, policemen were charged with offences related to their performance of duty. Five of the constables tried in 1841 were accused of negligence in allowing prisoners to escape, and one with perjury. That three constables were tried for manslaughter, one for murder, and one for assault, is perhaps some comment on the brutal methods allegedly employed by the police. The remaining four cases involving constables prosecuted during 1841 were for theft.

The third occupational group which appears particularly prominent is seamen, who made up a large number of those tried during both 1841 and 1851. As in the case of the police, offences were often work-related. Seven sailors tried in 1841 were charged with mutiny and insubordination, while all but one of the remainder were prosecuted for larceny. Of seamen tried in 1851, two were charged with conspiracy, nine with larceny, two with forgery, two with robbery, and one each for murder and assault. The colony's criminal statistics were thus significantly affected by Sydney's role as a port, and were further inflated by offences committed at sea or on board ship.

Newspaper reports in general give little indication of offenders' character. Persons described by such phrases as a "bad character", a "notorious thief", or an "old offender" numbered only three in 1841 and nine in 1851. This was compared with eighteen and twenty-six persons tried during 1841 and 1851 respectively given a "good", "excellent", or "very high character". During 1841 twenty-four offenders were prosecuted for more than one offence (usually of the same nature), as were forty persons in 1851. Some were no doubt established recidivists. The data hardly permit a confident assertion, as David Philips indicates in relation to England's Black Country, that most offenders were regularly employed.[7] It is worth noting, however, that few persons could be described from their occupations as members of a criminal subculture. Two persons tried were described as keepers of a disorderly house (which was not necessarily a brothel), and two other offenders were prize-fighters, both charged with manslaughter as a result of boxing matches.

Occupational information is somewhat more forthcoming about victims than offenders, but it is still too scanty to support more than some tentative generalizations (see table 6). The most apparent feature is the predominance of shopkeepers and other retailers as prosecutors. When it is considered that many skilled tradesmen had shops as well, the number seems all the more impressive. Most of those cases prosecuted were recorded as "larceny", and it seems likely that a large proportion of these involved shoplifting. Publicans formed another prominent occupational group among victims. This was perhaps because public houses had on hand two commodities always in great demand — money and liquor. The role of pubs as social centres, especially in country districts, made them an obvious place to pass bad money and forged orders, while publicans sometimes became involved in brawls with their customers. In relation to offences against the person, policemen were the most common occupational group to be reported as victims. The high proportion of assault cases involving constables in 1841 in particular, is probably some indication of their unpopularity.

Bailiffs were also favoured objects of assaults, usually as a result of executing court orders.

Table 6. Occupations of Victims in Offences Tried Before the Superior Courts of New South Wales, 1841 and 1851.

Occupation of Victim	1841 No.	1841 %	1851 No.	1851 %
Convicts Under Sentence	5	3.1		
Servants (Hired and Domestic)	2	1.2	7	2.4
Labourers	8	5.0	7	2.4
Rural Workers	2	1.2	20	6.9
Gold Diggers			3	1.0
Seamen (Including Shipmasters and Whalers)	9	5.6	19	6.6
Policemen	23	14.3	15	5.2
Soldiers			2	0.7
Skilled Tradesmen	13	8.1	35	12.1
Food Retailers	3	1.9	7	2.4
Publicans and Innkeepers	24	14.9	49	16.9
Shopkeepers, Dealers, Merchants	38	23.6	57	19.7
Civil Servants	5	3.1	8	2.8
Farmers and Settlers	15	9.3	39	13.4
Manufacturers (Mill Owner, Ship Builder, etc.)	2	1.2	3	1.0
Professionals	6	3.7	10	3.4
Other Miscellaneous Occupations	6	3.7	9	3.1
Total	161		290	

The available information for New South Wales indicates a clear class distinction between those typically prosecuted for offences and those prosecuting. Despite the large number of convicts still under sentence in 1841, only five documented cases involved prisoners as victims. This no doubt reflected in large part their non-status as property holders — all of the cases tried were for offences against the person. There were nevertheless a substantial number of prosecutions brought by working men. That many cases in 1851 were initiated by rural workers, who were comparatively isolated from police and courts, seems to suggest that there was by no means a wholesale rejection of legal channels of redress. The cost both in money and loss of time was probably the major impediment to prosecutions by working men and women, rather than anti-authoritarianism or disbelief in the sanctity of the law. As will be discussed in chapter 6, working men and women seemed more than prepared to resort to litigation before the more pervasive and less costly police courts.

Two additional groups may be singled out because of variations in their roles as offenders and prosecutors — women and Aborigines. Not only were women less likely to be prosecuted than men, but they were considerably less likely to be convicted. This further underscores the role of the colony's sex ratio in inflating the official crime rate. The defendants tried for some offences were exclusively women — notably those charged with infanticide and as "common scolds" (a blatantly sexist offence category which permitted women believed a nuisance to be tried before the superior courts). Proportionately, women were most under-represented among those tried for offences against property with violence, and offences against the currency. As in the case of men, larceny was the most common offence with which women were charged. Although women represented one-fifth of all those tried, they made up almost one-third of those prosecuted for larceny. There were also some discrepancies among the types of property men and women were accused of stealing. The greatest disparity was in cases of stock theft. About one-fifth of the men tried for property offences were charged with stealing livestock, compared with less than three per cent of the women tried. Women, on the other hand, were more likely to be tried for the theft of clothing, linen and fabric than were men. Finally, women were more often tried for committing offences against other women than men were for committing offences against women.

Both as offenders and victims, Aborigines were for the most part placed beyond the pale of the law. Between May 1824 and February 1836, only twenty-one Aborigines were tried before the Supreme Court.[8] To the extent that cases can be documented, thirteen Aborigines were tried during 1841, and only three in 1851. Even these meagre figures are overstated, since all of those prosecuted in 1841 were charged in connection with only three separate offences. Six of the offenders were tried for the robbery of flour and mutton from a station. One of those prosecuted eloquently explained that "the sheep eat the grass belonging to his kangaroo, and white fellow took kangaroo, and what not for give him sheep".[9] Five Aborigines, including three women, were charged with the murder of two whalers at Western Port, and two more were tried for another murder. The small number of Aborigines tried seems all the more striking since it was a period of increasing conflict, particularly in the Portland Bay area and Liverpool Plains. The remoteness of police and magistrates, as well as the difficulty of tracing offences to individuals and obtaining convictions, encouraged settlers to deal directly with Aborigines.

The general exclusion of Aborigines from the judicial process was equally reflected in the small number of whites prosecuted for committing offences against them. As historians have noted, the conviction and execution of seven stockmen for their role in the massacre

of Aborigines at Myall Creek in 1838 stands out as a spectacular exception arising from unique circumstances.[10] Before 1838 only three
persons were convicted for murdering Aborigines, and none of the three
were executed.[11] The prosecution of such cases was severely limited
by the disability of Aborigines as witnesses. Following the Myall Creek
massacre Governor Gipps pressed for legislation to admit the evidence
of Aborigines in criminal cases, but although an Act was passed by the
Legislative Council, it was disallowed by British law officers. The home
government later reversed its position, but subsequent attempts to
admit Aborigines as competent witnesses were defeated in the colony
until 1876.[12]

During 1841 there were eight prosecutions for offences against
Aborigines, including one for murder, two for manslaughter, and six
cases of shooting with intent. In 1851 there are no documented cases in
which Aborigines figured as victims. Because the killings of Aborigines
were usually carried out in a surreptitious manner beyond official
observation they are often difficult to document. Even so, these figures
can be compared with forty-three reported homicides committed by
whites in New South Wales' northern districts between 1838 and 1841,
and the reported killing of 113 Aborigines in the Port Phillip district
between 1836 and 1844.[13] Aborigines were widely viewed as either a
foreign enemy or as law-breakers who deserved retaliation.

One further feature of considerable significance emerges, and this is
the large proportion of offenders and their victims who were
acquainted prior to the commission of an alleged offence (see table 7).
Newspaper reports were rarely explicit about whether the person tried
and the victim were strangers or "semi-strangers" (that is, cases in
which the offender and victim met immediately before an offence,
perhaps by having a drink together in a public house). In the majority
of cases there is no information concerning the offenders' relation to
the victim, if any existed. Even so, it is apparent that in large numbers
of cases tried the offender and victim were acquainted before the crime
took place. Of the offences tried during 1841, one-seventh can be documented in which the offender and victim were previously acquainted,
and with the fuller newspaper reports available in 1851 the proportion
rises to almost one-third. This is undoubtedly an understatement, since
even if it is assumed that the vast majority of offences for which there
is no information involved strangers, the "no information" category is
grossly inflated by the skeletal reports given of many offences. A more
accurate idea of offender-victim relationships is probably given if
offences are limited to those in which the press at least mention the
victim. If this is done, the available evidence indicates that one-quarter
of those tried in 1841 were somehow acquainted with the victim prior
to the offence, and in 1851 the proportion is forty per cent. This still

probably understates the proportion of offences in which offenders and victims were previously acquainted, since newspapers frequently gave no more than the victim's name.

Table 7. Offender's Relation to Victim in Offences Tried Before the Superior Courts of New South Wales, 1841 and 1851.

Offender's Relation to Victim	1841		1851	
	No.	%	No.	%
Employee, or Former Employee	38	4.3	64	7.9
Employer	0	0.0	2	0.2
Workmate	9	1.0	12	1.5
Neighbour	2	0.2	33	4.1
Lodger	6	0.7	22	2.7
Parent	6	0.7	4	0.5
Spouse	4	0.5	4	0.5
Other Relative	1	0.1	3	0.4
Acquaintance	55	6.2	98	12.1
Stranger, or Semi-Stranger	9	1.0	2	0.2
No Information	752	85.3	555	68.6
Total	882		799	

Note: These figures exclude victimless crimes such as escaping custody or keeping a 'sorderly house.

In the largest number of these cases the offender and victim could simply be described as "acquaintances". A large proportion of offences, however, involved the prosecution of employees or former employees by employers. In 1851 there were also a substantial number of cases in which the victim and offender were neighbours, or in which the offender lodged with the prosecutor. In most of these cases the alleged offence involved some form of theft. A smaller number of prosecutions involved spouses or other relatives, and usually stemmed from some form of violence. The large proportion of offences in which offenders and victims were acquainted in some way prior to the crime may in part reflect on the efficiency of the police. For obvious reasons, offenders were much more likely to be taken into custody if the victim knew who they were. It is also revealing about the nature of offences prosecuted. It seems likely that many offences were committed as a matter of opportunity rather than as a calculated enterprise. The labourer who pilfered property from his employer, or the person who secreted some possession of a neighbour or other acquaintance were typical among those tried. In these cases at least, it is difficult to discern the omnipresent criminal class which loomed in the popular imagination.

The threat of personal violence probably instilled more fear in the community than any other form of offence. The Molesworth Committee claimed that rapes, murders and attempted murders were as common in the colony as petty larcenies were in England.[14] The statistics hardly justify this claim, although offences against the person did make up a larger proportion of prosecuted crimes than in Britain. In England and Wales between 1834 and 1856 about one-tenth of all committals were for offences against the person.[15] During roughly the same period, this offence category comprised eighteen per cent of all convictions in New South Wales.[16] Convictions for both homicide and assault declined erratically between 1831 and 1861 (see figure 5). It is worth noting, however, that violent crimes made up a higher proportion of all convictions during the gold rush decade than during the convict period.

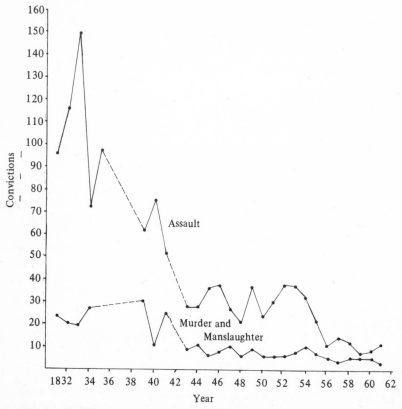

Figure 5. Convictions for Assault, Murder and Manslaughter per 100,000 Inhabitants in New South Wales, 1831–61.

A high proportion of violent offences can be explained largely in terms of the conditions of a frontier community. Although violent crime has been conventionally associated with urbanization and industrialization, this relationship has been increasingly challenged. In the United States, for example, it is the less industrialized and urbanized South which has the nation's highest violent crime rate. Recent research has placed emphasis instead on violence as a regional and cultural pattern.[17] In New South Wales conflict with Aborigines encouraged habits of both physical force and bearing weapons. This was possibly reinforced by the use of state violence in the form of floggings and executions to administer the penal system. Moreover, the high numbers of males in the population had an important bearing on the colony's violent crime rate, both because it was males who figured predominantly in such cases, and because a large adult male population increased the potential for interpersonal violence. Finally, the frequency with which offences against the person were prosecuted may have reflected in part the community's propensity for litigation. The vast majority of offences against the person tried were for common assault, and some observers believed that the populace had a particular propensity for bringing such cases before the courts.

To the extent that information is available, firearms and knives were the most common weapons used in offences against the person in 1841, with knives and "blunt instruments" gaining the ascendancy in 1851 (see table 8). These figures give a distorted impression, however, since they are biased towards more serious crimes which received fuller

Table 8. Weapons Used in Offences Against the Person Tried Before the Superior Courts of New South Wales, 1841 and 1851.

Weapons Used	1841		1851	
	No.	%	No.	%
Hands, Feet and Teeth	11	7.3	5	5.1
Firearm	24	15.9	7	7.1
Knife	24	15.9	15	15.3
Axe	3	2.0	0	0.0
Rock or Brick	3	2.0	5	5.1
Other Blunt Instrument	4	2.6	12	12.2
Poison	1	0.7	0	0.0
Drowning	1	0.7	0	0.0
Burning	1	0.7	0	0.0
Whip	1	0.7	2	2.0
Other	3	2.0	4	4.1
No Information	75	49.7	48	49.0
Total	151		98	

reportage in the press. Consequently the vast majority of offences in the "no information" category, which makes up about half of the total, were common assaults. It is probably safe to assume that the most common weapons used were fists, boots and sometimes teeth. Cornelius O'Brien, for example, was charged with biting off about half an inch of his neighbour's nose during a drunken row.[18]

The proportion of offences involving firearms is somewhat over-stated, because in cases of "shooting with intent" the weapon was known by definition. Nevertheless, the large number of cases in which guns featured in 1841 is marked. Beyond the boundaries of location in particular, firearms were often carried as a matter of course for protection against Aborigines and robbers. By 1851 fewer acts of violence involved firearms, but concern was expressed about the habit of carrying guns during the gold rush.[19] Knives were a less obvious offensive weapon, and were probably carried as a matter of convenience rather than as protection. A long-bladed knife was considered an essential tool on the diggings used in "crevicing" for gold.[20] As in the case of firearms, foreign gold seekers were accused of encouraging an "un-English resort to the knife".[21] Even before the gold rush, however, knives were commonly used in offences, and it is significant that when gold was first discovered colonists arriving at the diggings were heavily armed with guns.[22]

Michael Cannon contrasts nineteenth-century violence, when he contends most homicides were committed by strangers for the sake of gain, to modern violence in which most victims are already known to the murderer.[23] This is almost certainly a false distinction. A lack of available information prohibits the conclusion that assault cases generally involved persons already acquainted, although the proportion of offenders and victims previously acquainted is greater than for other non-violent offences. The evidence is far more persuasive in relation to the homicides to which Cannon refers, largely because they were reported in more detail in the press. Of twenty-two persons tried for murder in 1841, thirteen (about sixty per cent) can be documented as previously acquainted with their victims, as can three out of seven persons tried in 1851. In cases of manslaughter the proportion is much higher, with all but four of twenty-two persons tried during 1841 and 1851 clearly acquainted with their victims prior to the offence. As already noted in relation to offences in general, these figures are presumably an understatement because of the minimal information available about many cases. Of those people tried for murder in 1841, for example, seven were Aborigines and it is unclear whether they were acquainted with their victims.

The fact that almost one-third of the people tried for murder in 1841 were Aborigines suggests the extent to which white-Aboriginal conflict inflated the colony's violent crime rate. Even though the total number of Aborigines prosecuted was small, they significantly affected the officially recorded incidence of violence since they were usually charged in groups, and because the total number of homicides prosecuted was relatively small. This is one further way in which offences against the person were affected by frontier conditions. As for Europeans who were tried, the largest proportion of homicides can be traced to brawls, feuds and domestic arguments. Michael Cotter, who was tried for killing John Carroll after he discovered him lying with his wife in "a criminal position" behind a public house, is a fairly typical example.[24] While the frontier established a tradition of violence, the motives for its use were often much the same as in the twentieth century.

In terms of sentences passed, cases of assault were dealt with relatively lightly. About one-quarter of those convicted of assault in 1841 and 1851 were merely fined, while the largest proportion of offenders were sentenced to imprisonment for one year or less. Most persons convicted of manslaughter were awarded prison terms ranging from less than a month to two years, although two persons convicted of this offence in 1841 were sentenced to transportation. Persons convicted of "shooting with intent" or "stabbing and cutting" were usually dealt with more severely, while all persons convicted of murder in 1841 and 1851 were sentenced to death. By the 1840s, murder was the only offence in New South Wales for which persons commonly suffered the extreme penalty of the law. Of eighty-one persons executed between 1841 and 1851, sixty-five were convicted of murder, seven of wounding with intent to kill, five of rape and four of piracy.[25]

Sexual assaults made up a relatively small proportion of offences against the person tried, but those offences which actually reached the courts were, and still are, notoriously a small proportion of those committed. Women might be deterred from reporting offences through fear of the stigma which might be attached to them by the community, or even by fear of their spouse. Diana Elms, a shepherd's wife allegedly raped by an Aborigine, told the Bathurst Circuit Court that she did not inform her husband of the offence until the following day for fear he would beat her.[26] Other women probably did not wish to suffer the embarrassment of a trial, which might ruthlessly inquire into their own character. Cases could also be easily dismissed for lack of evidence, especially if the defendant was relatively respectable.

Most prosecutions for sexual assaults involved juvenile girls, a feature which was apparently paralleled in Britain.[27] This may well have been because young girls were less likely to feel the stigma which could be attached to adults, and because legal action was initiated by their parents. Of three persons committed to trial for sexual assaults on children by the Dungog bench between 1848 and 1853, two were schoolmasters. James Alexander Duff, a free immigrant, was committed to trial for the rape of a six-year-old girl.[28] The other schoolmaster, James Macbeth Gibb, was charged with a number of indecent assaults on female pupils which included putting his hands up under their petticoats and attempting to force their hands down his pants. The fact that the alleged offences took place over a substantial period of time, and that some parents, although aware of Gibb's behaviour, only came forward after others took the initiative, is some indication of the hesitancy with which such prosecutions were undertaken.[29]

Cases involving homosexuality and bestiality were even less likely to be brought before the courts than were other sexual offences. Aside from the reticence of the "victim", witnesses might have been reluctant to report such transgressions. The details of "unnatural" crimes were suppressed in the newspapers, but it is possible to gain some information from magistrates' bench books. At Parramatta, for example, Robert Goodin, born in the colony, was charged with attempting to commit an unnatural offence with a sow. The local police magistrate termed the case the most "painfully disgusting" he had ever heard, but Goodin was apparently let off with a fine for indecent exposure.[30] Charles Robinson was committed to trial at Armidale for "having unnatural connection with a bitch".[31] In another case Robert Skinner, a farm overseer, testified that when going out to the milking herd one morning he saw a man standing on a stool having intercourse with a mare belonging to Colonel Snodgrass of the Mounted Police. Through the stool used, the offence was traced to William Kelly, a free immigrant and married man.[32]

Although legally sexual offences were regarded with as much abhorrence as murder, only a small proportion of those people convicted were sentenced to death, and a smaller proportion still were actually executed. Not infrequently persons charged with rape were convicted of a lesser offence — either assault with intent or common assault. Most offenders were sentenced to imprisonment or to work in a road gang for periods of less than three years. Unnatural offences as well were punished more leniently in practice than as permitted by law. Of four persons convicted of sodomy or bestiality during 1841 and 1851, all were sentenced to prison terms of two to three years.

Aside from crimes of violence, two further offences were especially associated with lawlessness in New South Wales — bushranging and stock theft. Bushranging in particular created apprehension because it combined loss of property with the use or threat of force, and because of its social connotations. In Australian tradition robbers, convict bolters and bushrangers have often become synonymous, but it is important to draw distinctions among the three. Initially, the term "bushranger" was applied generally to prisoners illegally at large. By the 1830s, it was also applied in a more specific sense to persons living in the bush who engaged in systematic robberies.[33] Obviously not all absconding convicts turned to robbery for sustenance, although this was frequently the implication of their contemporaries. As John Richard Hardy pointed out while police magistrate for Yass, absconding did not necessarily cause more crime, nor did large numbers of convicts illegally at large necessarily produce a state of insecurity. Indeed, Hardy believed runaways were often better conducted than other servants, while they were encouraged to abscond by the indiscriminate hiring practices of settlers.[34] Bushrangers (as opposed to runaways) created apprehension not so much from their numbers, as by their ability to commit offences within a wide radius and to evade capture.

In examining the incidence of bushranging, R. B. Walker looks to convictions for armed robbery as demonstrating "the distinctive bush-ranging crime".[35] This is to confuse bushranging as a distinct phenomenon with a more generic crime. Robbery subsumed all offences which involved the taking of property by force, or the threat of violence. Even armed robbery did not necessarily imply the use of guns. Two convicts in 1844, for example, perpetrated a highway robbery armed with sticks.[36] Whereas bushranging is typically associated with the interior, robberies frequently took place in an urban setting. Among those convicted of "highway robbery" in 1846, for example, were three soldiers who knocked down and robbed a man in one of Parramatta's main streets.[37] Bushranging in the classic sense is probably best confined to robberies committed on the roads or at country residences and stores by men armed with guns, usually on horseback, and often travelling in gangs. Using this as a working definition, only seven of fifty-two cases of robbery tried in 1841 could be described from the available information as bushranging offences, as could eight of thirty-eight tried in 1851.

Historically, the importance of bushranging lies not so much in the alleged prevalence of the offence, as in its social implications. Bushranging, it has been contended, was viewed differently from other crimes, while bushrangers themselves served as heroic symbols of resistance against police, squatters and constituted authority.[38] The bushranger of Australian legend assumes the role of a "social bandit", whose victims are typically the enemies of the poor and who receives at least tacit support from the community.[39] This suggests yet another distinction which should be drawn — that is, between those who merely committed bushranging-type offences and those who could be perceived as social rebels and received some measure of popular support. There was an obvious difference, for example, between William Westwood ("Jacky Jacky"), an assigned convict who committed a series of robberies beginning with an attack on his master's home and who was later executed for his role in an attempted insurrection at Norfolk Island,[40] and Richard Seldon, a stockman accused of robbing Eliza Smith at gunpoint when she was returning home after selling a load of potatoes.[41]

The role of the bushranger as a defender of the oppressed was sometimes quite explicit, as when the overseer of one Hunter Valley station was flogged by robbers before the assigned convicts present.[42] To the extent that bushrangers expected some measure of support, there were practical reasons for them to modify their conduct in conformity with popular expectations. It was in their interests to abstain from violence, since its use usually intensified efforts for their capture. Edward Davis ("The Jewboy"), the leader of a gang tried for murder in 1841, reportedly stated "he had always opposed the shedding of blood, for he knew if they did so, they would not reign a week".[43] Victims themselves might construe bushrangers' actions in a favourable light simply because their own fears were unrealized. William Haygarth, for example, professed some sympathy for "Buchan Charley" largely because he constrained his companion, "a ruffianly-looking Irishman of the lowest grade", from doing Haygarth any physical harm.[44]

However, if some bushrangers successfully assumed the role of social bandits, the degree of support they received is easily exaggerated. Certainly contemporaries believed bushrangers were frequently aided by a network of sympathizers. Nevertheless, there are grounds for arguing that the support allegedly given to bushrangers was to a large extent an excuse for police inefficiency, and a reflection of fears of a pervasive criminal class.

Even among assigned convicts sympathy for bushrangers was by no means universal. The allegiance of convicts might be bought and paid for with rum, tea, sugar and other scarce commodities, rather than freely rendered.[45] The prospect of receiving a ticket of leave or conditional pardon was often an adequate incentive for convicts to assist in the capture of bushrangers. Since bushrangers frequently lacked discretion in who they injured or killed in their attacks, assigned servants were sometimes forced to defend their own lives, if not their master's property. A settler in 1835 described how, when bushrangers attacked three of his drays and fired on the convicts escorting them, they met heroic resistance. One of the convicts, Henry Brian, after receiving a wound in the arm, threw down his gun which had misfired, and attempted to wrestle with his assailants.[46] That the servants were armed at all is some comment on the degree to which they were trusted.

As Humphrey McQueen points out, antipathy toward the police did not necessarily mean sympathy for thieves.[47] On the contrary, animosity toward the police arose in part from their failure to control bushranging.[48] In fact, the frequent ineptitude of the police served to magnify the power of bushrangers, and made those who failed to co-operate with them appear much more vulnerable to retaliation. Bush workers, in particular, from their isolated situation, might feel at the mercy of bushrangers and more or less compelled to provide assistance.[49]

The extent to which bushrangers might rely on coercion for support rather than on sympathy has a particular relevance for the 1840s and 1850s, since there is evidence that they suffered a marked decline in social prestige during this period. There was a definite interlude between the robberies of convict bolters in the 1830s and bushranging's "golden age" in the 1860s. This was primarily because bushrangers of the 1840s and 1850s were not perceived as part of a social struggle.

Bushranging in the 1830s emerged as the most coherent form of resistance to an oppressive penal system, and assumed an obvious significance for convicts who felt victimized. The convict bushranger was typically viewed as an unfortunate driven to the bush by ill-treatment, and to crime by desperation.[50] Through his actions other convicts might vicariously experience the taste of freedom and rebellion. With the abolition of assignment and the consequent decline of convicts in private service during the early 1840s, bushrangers largely lost their *raison d'etre* as social bandits. Charles Cozens asserted in 1848 that bushranging was almost unknown in New South Wales because the number of prisoners had so greatly declined, and because conditional freedom was so easily obtained.[51] Another observer noted at the mid-century that while bushrangers had once possessed a certain dignity, they were no longer romantic figures. Instead, they committed petty and cowardly robberies of the poor and defenceless.[52] When bush-rangers were extolled in the 1840s and 1850s, it was still the archetypal convict rebel Bold Jack Donahoe who was spoken of, rather than con-temporaneous robbers.[53]

The resurgence of bushrangers as social bandits in the 1860s repre-sented a new and different phase. Whereas bushranging had been wedded to the penal system in the 1830s, in the 1860s conflict centred around land and the land regulations. Some observers continued to trace support for bushrangers to the colony's convict origins. Chief Justice Alfred Stephen, at the trial of the Clarke brothers in 1867, attributed sympathy for bushrangers to "the old leaven of convictism not yet worked out".[54] As was often the case, convictism served to mask more fundamental social issues. The end of the bushranging era in the 1880s resulted not from the old convict leaven being worked out but probably from a redistribution of land and the growth of rural trade unionism which displaced bushrangers in reflecting class interests.[55]

The seriousness with which robbery was regarded was reflected in the penalties awarded to those convicted of the offence. Under the Bushranging Act as originally passed in 1834, persons sentenced to death for robbery or for plundering a house with violence were to be executed within twenty-four hours of their conviction.[56] This section of the Act was repealed in 1838, and the last executions for robbery took place the following year.[57] The majority of persons convicted in 1841 were sentenced to transportation, usually for ten years. In 1851 the standard punishment for persons convicted of robbery was four or more years hard labour on the roads or public works. Bushrangers tended to receive much harsher punishments than other robbers. All of those persons convicted of bushranging-style offences in 1841 were sentenced to transportation, while in 1851 all were sentenced to hard labour for seven to fifteen years.

In terms of the penalties awarded, stock theft was placed on a par with robbery. Until 1833 cattle, horse and sheep stealing were capital offences, and after that date punishments remained harsh. In 1841, seventy-five per cent of the offenders convicted of horse and cattle stealing were sentenced to transportation. By 1851 punishments were more lenient, although still severe relative to other property offences. The majority of those convicted of stock theft were sentenced to hard labour on the roads or public works for four to five years.

Chief Justice James Dowling insisted that such "dread examples" of punishment were necessary, since stock theft posed an obvious threat to a pastoral country.[58] The offence seemed all the more dangerous because it was assumed that it was systematically perpetrated by professional thieves. According to Judge Roger Therry, cattle stealing made up the staple business of New South Wales' criminal sessions, and "was reduced to a sort of science by the criminal class in the Colony".[59] Similarly, magistrate Charles Lockhart asserted that animals were stolen not in scores, but in hundreds by "well-organized bands".[60] At least in relation to those offences actually prosecuted, however, stock theft appears to have been neither systematic nor the work of professionals.

Most persons tried for stock theft were accused of stealing only one or two animals. Of nineteen prosecutions for cattle stealing in 1841 in which the number of animals allegedly stolen is known, only two cases involved the theft of five or more cattle, and in 1851 only two out of twenty-seven documented cases involved the stealing of five or more animals. The largest number of cattle stolen by any one offender prosecuted in 1841 and 1851 was nine head. In cases of horse stealing, almost inevitably only one animal was allegedly stolen. The large number of prosecutions for the theft of single animals seems all the more striking in the light of the apparent difficulties in bringing rural offenders before the courts.

This does not, of course, prove that stock theft was not engaged in systematically or on a large scale. Prosecutors were only compelled to substantiate the theft of one animal to secure a conviction. Some persons also figured in more than one case. George Brown, for example, was acquitted on a charge of stealing a horse from William Oakenfell at Maitland's circuit court, but convicted of stealing a horse from Timothy McCarthy.[61] In one 1842 case George Oakes and Daniel McGane were convicted of stealing twenty-five head of cattle belonging to Sydney merchant Charles Campbell. But it is significant that Chief Justice Dowling considered that this case exceeded in enormity any case of cattle stealing tried before him during the past fifteen years.[62] Police magistrate John Richard Hardy asserted as well that although there was a great deal of cattle stealing, it was practised in a small rather than a wholesale manner.[63]

There is virtually no information concerning the relations between offenders and victims for stock theft cases tried in 1841, although at least five persons tried the following year were current or former employees of the prosecutor.[64] Among those tried in 1851 were six persons who were employees of the victim, two neighbours, and seven persons otherwise acquainted with the prosecutor prior to the alleged offence. Known defendants in stock theft cases ranged from John Burns, described as "an old man of about seventy" charged with stealing a cow near Hartley, to Robert Myers, a young boy tried at Berrima for slaughtering a heifer, to James McMahon, given testimonials of the "highest respectability", and who was accused of stealing cattle by a servant after he refused his wages.[65] While far from conclusive, the available evidence casts doubt upon contemporary notions that stock theft was principally the work of organized criminal bands. It is probable that most animal thefts were committed by amateurs on a minor scale, either to supplement their diet or an income.

As in the case of other property offences, convictions for stock theft increased during the early 1830s, although at a much more rapid rate than other crimes (see figure 6). This was no doubt due largely to the repeal of the death penalty for cattle, horse and sheep stealing in 1833, which facilitated prosecutions and probably meant that juries were more likely to convict offenders. Convictions for stock theft declined during the 1840s, but exhibited an increase during the gold rush years. Two other features also stand out. The first is the small number of convictions for sheep stealing. The second is an increase in convictions for horse stealing relative to cattle stealing from the mid-1840s.

The slaughter of sheep for food, often with the owner's tacit approval, was believed to be a widely practised outback custom. Russel

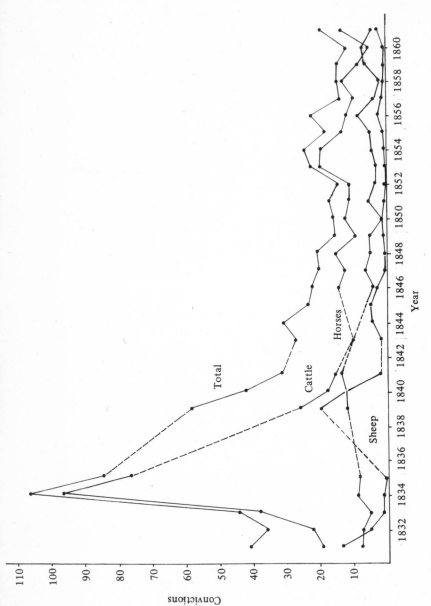

Figure 6. Convictions for Stock Theft per 100,000 Inhabitants in New South Wales, 1831–61.

Ward goes so far as to suggest that "every honest bushman, more or less, was a thief upon occasion".[66] This might explain in part why stock owners were reluctant to prosecute offenders for sheep stealing. Whether in fact all bushmen indulged in the practice, however, is questionable. At least occasionally, fellow shepherds acted as principal witnesses against workmates accused of killing sheep.[67] The small number of convictions for sheep stealing may well have resulted more from the fact that they were less valuable than other animals and much more difficult to identify as stolen.

Reasons for an increasing number of convictions for horse stealing relative to other stock is equally difficult to discern. There is some evidence that the statistics reflect a real increase in horse theft. In the Bathurst district, for example, the crime allegedly became so prevalent by 1848 that one newspaper urged the formation of a vigilante association for its suppression.[68] An increasing incidence of horse theft may have stemmed in part simply from a larger number of horses which could be stolen. The number of horses in the colony tripled between 1842 and 1856, increasing at a faster rate than either cattle or sheep.[69] At the same time there was a great demand for horses. William Fox, writing from the Major's Creek diggings in 1852, reported that any person who could scrape together the requisite cash immediately purchased a steed.

> The great staple for talk apart from gold is horses. There they come out in a manner to me perfectly astounding — appelations, to me many of them quite new, are bestowed in sweet confusion — I hear a running fire of mares, foals, fillies, hacks, cobs, screws, bays, blacks, roans, piebalds, skewbalds, silver manes and tails, shakes in the near forelegs, brands in the off shoulders . . .[70]

Horses derived importance in the community not only as valuable economic commodities, but also as symbols of social status.

Relative to other forms of property allegedly stolen in 1841 and 1851, livestock featured in about ten per cent of the offences against property prosecuted (see table 9). The most common items stolen, however, were money and clothing.[71] Money was obviously an attractive item for theft, since it could be easily used and was difficult to trace. Clothing was another commodity easily put to use or disposed of, although the large proportion of offences involving wearing apparel is also indicative of the limited range of consumer goods available. A substantial number of cases involved the theft of food and drink, more especially in 1841. This probably reflected both the larger number of convicts under sentence in 1841 wishing to supplement their rations and recreation, and the more depressed state of the economy. A fair number of cases, particularly in 1851, involved the taking of several miscellaneous items during the course of an offence. Other items commonly stolen included watches, fabric, linen, household goods, tools and building materials.

Table 9. Property Stolen in Offences Against Property Tried Before the Superior Courts of New South Wales, 1841 and 1851.

Property Stolen	1841		1851	
	No.	%	No.	%
Money	79	11.8	102	16.2
Clothing	57	8.5	102	16.2
Watch	19	2.8	15	2.4
Jewellery	6	0.9	3	0.5
Other Personal Item	4	0.6	0	0.0
Food	38	5.7	14	2.2
Drink	23	3.4	8	1.3
Cattle	30	4.5	28	4.4
Horses	28	4.2	35	5.6
Sheep	6	0.9	1	0.2
Small Animal	5	0.7	11	1.7
Farm Produce	3	0.4	9	1.4
Saddlery	6	0.9	10	1.6
Tools	4	0.6	17	2.7
Building Material	7	1.0	11	1.7
Rope or Wire	2	0.3	2	0.3
Bags	2	0.3	2	0.3
Fabric	16	2.4	19	3.0
Linen	8	1.2	12	1.9
Silver or Plate	2	0.3	1	0.2
Gold	1	0.2	1	0.2
Cooking Utensils	8	1.2	4	0.6
Glassware	6	0.9	10	1.4
Furniture	0	0.0	5	0.8
Ship's Equipment	3	0.4	5	0.8
Books	3	0.4	4	0.6
Stationery or Letters	3	0.4	2	0.3
Miscellaneous Items	9	1.3	33	5.2
Other	4	0.6	17	2.7
No Information	285	42.7	157	24.9
Total	667		640	

Notes: These figures include all offences against property with or without violence, and exclude offences against the currency, malicious offences against property, and miscellaneous offences where no loss of property was involved. The proportion of cases involving livestock are overstated relative to other forms of property, since the property stolen was known by definition in cases of cattle, horse and sheep stealing.

As in Britain, simple larceny was statistically the colony's most important offence. There was no distinction between petty and grand larceny, and items allegedly stolen were often of quite small value. Property stolen by persons prosecuted for theft in 1842 included a pair of stays, a quart of ale valued at one shilling, a tumbler, a glass of brandy and a brush. Four persons tried during 1841 and 1851 were accused of stealing ordinary bags. Some other cases can only be described as bizarre. John Kenny, for instance, a convict, was tried before the Sydney Quarter Sessions in 1841 for stealing two volumes of *Ivanhoe*. He was acquitted on this charge, but was convicted of "stealing a note in the receiving watch-house, which he afterwards concealed by swallowing it". For this offence he was sentenced to be worked in irons for three years.[72]

To the extent that information is known about offenders' relation to their victims, the largest proportion of larceny cases involved employees or former employees charged with stealing from their employers. One observer in the 1850s believed young servant girls in particular were tempted to theft by "those unbecoming unservantlike innovations in dress and tawdry ornaments so much indulged in at present".[73] Thefts by employees in general can probably be more aptly attributed to the particular opportunities they had for pilfering, and the fact that they were likely suspects if property was missed by their master. In some cases employees may have considered the pilfering of property as a justifiable perquisite. It was also believed that those thefts actually prosecuted made up only a small proportion of those committed by servants, since employers were frequently too apathetic to initiate court proceedings and simply dismissed the offending employee instead.[74] The attitudes of various employees and employers toward property further underscores the fallibility of the official statistics as a measure of crime.

Aside from offences involving servants, there were other work-related prosecutions for larceny as well. David Wilson, for example, a bookbinder, was tried for stealing some printed sheets entrusted to him for binding. The theft was only detected when the sheets were discovered at a butter stall in the market where Wilson had sold them as waste paper.[75] Similarly, Thomas Bodenhaim was accused of stealing a watch left with him for repair.[76] Tradesmen might also occasionally be victimized by their competitors. James Turner, a Bathurst shoe-maker, was charged with snatching a couple of boots from the counter while visiting the shop of another boot and shoemaker.[77]

Shoplifting was another prevalent form of larceny. The display of goods outside shops and in doorways in particular was criticized by law enforcement officials as offering especial temptations to potential thieves. During 1857 alone, 390 persons were taken into custody by the

Sydney police for shoplifting or stealing show goods, representing over one-quarter of all persons arrested on charges other than drunkenness or petty misdemeanours.[78] Over half of these cases were summarily dealt with by the magistracy, but before an expansion of the magistracy's jurisdiction in the mid-1850s, all such cases were tried before the superior courts.

The most common penalty awarded to persons convicted of larceny during both 1841 and 1851 was a prison term of six months or less. As in the case of other offences, however, there was a marked reduction in sentences passed during the decade. About one-third of those convicted of larceny in 1841 received sentences of six months or less, compared to almost sixty per cent of those convicted in 1851. Of those convicted in 1841, twelve per cent were sentenced to transportation (usually for seven years), while there were no transportations for larceny in 1851. The largest proportion of other offenders convicted in 1841 and 1851 were sentenced to work on the roads or public works for terms ranging from six months to eight years. In general, convicts and ex-convicts convicted of larceny were more harshly punished than those persons without a criminal record.

As representing the single most common offence, larceny cases had a substantial impact on the overall conviction rate. Convictions for larceny made up about forty per cent of the total convictions before the superior courts between 1831 and 1861.[79] One might also expect that the incidence of larceny convictions would be strongly influenced by economic conditions. As in the case of all offences against property, however, there is no consistent correlation with economic trends. While there was a sharp increase in convictions during the depressed year of 1843, there were similar peaks during the more prosperous years of 1846 and 1851 (see figure 7). A marked decline in convictions during the mid-1850s probably reflected most of all changes in summary jurisdiction.

This contrasts with the apparent trend in Britain. Analysis of England and Wales' criminal statistics for the first half of the nineteenth century indicates that property offences consistently increased in times of economic adversity, and diminished in periods of prosperity.[80] Regional studies in England illustrate the same trend.[81] This does not necessarily imply that property offences were the direct result of want. But while thefts were probably not simply a means of fighting starvation, poverty and unemployment were the conditions under which property offences increased.

Of perhaps greater significance in relation to New South Wales, is the fact that the correlation between adverse economic conditions and crime in Britain was limited to the first half of the nineteenth century. As the century progressed, the incidence of property offences ceased to

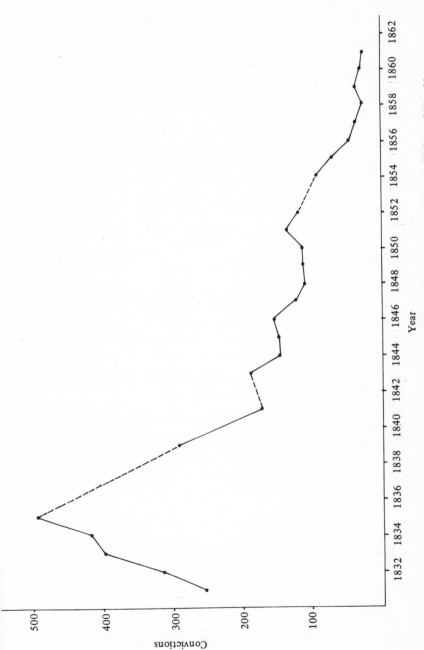

Figure 7. Convictions for Larceny per 100,000 Inhabitants in New South Wales, 1831–61.

be positively associated with economic depression. It appears that there was a transition from poverty-based crime to prosperity-based crime, so that by the twentieth century property offences tended to diminish in periods of depression and increase in periods of affluence.[82] This general trend in modern western communities is explained largely in terms of relative deprivation, increased opportunities for crime and materialist values associated with the affluent society.[83]

While there are obvious problems in comparing modern industrialized society with a pastoral and pre-industrial community, the correlation between affluence and property offences suggests some insight concerning crime in New South Wales. Contemporaries were prone to view crime in a land of plenty as confirmation that the colony was corrupted by convictism and victimized by a parasitic criminal class. The Molesworth Committee reported in 1838 that:

> In old communities, where there is a comparative want of employment, and profits are low, the amount of crime is not a perfectly sure test of the moral state of society, as the general uneasiness of the population gives birth to innumerable offences against property; but in these new communities, where there is a pressing demand for labour, and great facilities for acquiring wealth, crimes so numerous and so atrocious as those, perpetrated in New South Wales and Van Diemen's Land, truly indicate the depth of their moral depravity.[84]

But prosperity itself could influence the incidence of property offences in a positive as well as a negative way. The "acquisitive competitiveness"[85] of immigrants fostered a culture conducive to acquisitive crime. A high degree of social and economic mobility also served to contrast the position of those who failed to improve their material condition, and could create a sense of deprivation and envy among the more depressed segments of the community.

The theme of colonial materialism, so frequently harped on by contemporaries, in part betrayed alarm caused by New South Wales' social and economic mobility. Most colonists, however, immigrated with expectations of improving their material circumstances, and as such the community was largely preoccupied with personal gain. After overcoming a period of initial deprivation in New South Wales, a recently arrived Henry Parkes pronounced his aspirations clearly. "I am now anxious about getting money, not being at all content to come here for no purpose ... Nothing like getting money; nothing can be done without it. I know the value of money now! Money! money! money! is my watchword for the future!"[86] The colony's convict population, if not imbued with petit-bourgeois values, demonstrated a similar interest in accumulating property. Port Phillip squatter Edward M. Curr noted that the "work and burst" philosophy of old hands was substantially modified by their investment in livestock, dogs, guns and other possess-ions.[87] Material advancement was one way of easing the social stigma of convictism. While hardly legitimizing crime, New South Wales' materialist outlook and acquisitive values could encourage the commission of property offences. The high premium placed on property also explains in part the extent to which prosecutions for theft were undertaken.

Thefts motivated by immediate need were apparently few in New South Wales, but not unknown. John Marshall, an ex-convict tried in Melbourne for stealing a cheese in 1841, contended that he stole the food out of sheer starvation after he was discharged from his job without payment of his wages. The court was convinced enough by this defence to let him off with the time he had already spent in custody awaiting trial.[88] More often, property offences were probably related to the relative deprivation felt by those who failed to share in the colony's prosperity, rather than to people suffering total destitution.

Characterizations of New South Wales' affluent working classes over-looked the fact that for many years convicts under sentence formed a large and propertyless segment of the population. Employment opportunities for ex-convicts were also more circumscribed than most observers suggested. Stories of fortunes made by ex-convicts were widely circulated as criticism of the transportation system's leniency. Those achieving some measure of wealth were relatively few, while the richest and best known of the emancipist merchants, Samuel Terry, died the same year the Molesworth Committee issued its report. By the 1830s opportunities for ex-convicts were contracted considerably by the greater availability of free labour and immigrants with capital.[89] Although exiles were snapped up by squatters to work in the interior, they could face grave difficulties in finding work in their proper trades. James Johnston, a hatter by occupation exiled to Port Phillip, asserted that there was little opportunity for those of his kind to work except as shepherds, because prejudice against them was so "exceedingly violent". He considered he was able to find employment dressing hats only because no other tradesmen were available.[90] Employers reported-ly had a general objection to hiring ex-convict servants, and those with a convict taint were the first to lose their jobs in periods of economic distress.[91] Considered in this context, the proportion of offences involving those free by servitude seems far from surprising.

While materialism and relative deprivation suggest conditions which are conducive to crime, thefts might result largely as a matter of oppor-tunity. Chief Justice Francis Forbes believed that the frequency of burglaries and robberies was due partly to the insecurity of houses, and "a great looseness with respect to the keeping of property in New South Wales".[92] The *Herald* reported that thefts were facilitated by the workmen's practice of leaving their tools in unfinished buildings where they could be easily pilfered.[93] As already noted, the open display of goods for sale was considered another invitation to stealing. The colony's relative prosperity possibly led to a greater casualness in protecting property. It was further believed that thieving was encouraged by the ease with which property could be disposed of with numerous brokers and dealers.[94]

As important in contributing toward opportunities for crime was the pattern of settlement and pastoral expansion. This was most apparent in relation to stock theft. The theft and concealment of animals was greatly facilitated by the size and isolation of stations, absentee owners, large numbers of unbranded livestock, the broken and relatively inaccessible terrain of some districts, and a general absence of enclosures. Horses might be stolen not only when turned out to forage, but when left tied outside a store or public house. The ease with which horses could be sold with little inquiry about their origin was believed to be a further inducement to theft.

A dispersed population and poor communications provided particular opportunities for the commission of other types of offences as well. Travellers coming from the country with recently paid wages or finances for a stay in the metropolis were easy targets for robbers.[95] The conveyance of large quantities of stores in the interior led to dray robberies, particularly towards the end of the year when goods were laid in for the shearing season.[96] As in the case of stock theft, the topography of certain regions was also thought particularly attractive for the operations of bushrangers.

A shortage of coin and bank notes in country districts, and a consequent reliance on orders, greatly widened the scope for forgery. Governor Gipps was inclined to attribute the prevalent use of orders to New South Wales' convict character, which made it unsafe to carry or keep cash. A similar system, however, failed to develop in Tasmania, and it was distance which principally led to the widespread use of orders.[97] The ease with which such orders could be drawn or altered was believed a major incentive to forgeries while the transmission of orders (often without specifying the payee) encouraged robbery of the mails.[98]

Overall, the impression which emerges of prosecuted offences is of casual and fairly petty affairs, springing from opportunity rather than from a criminal conspiracy. Cases prosecuted in New South Wales were better typified by shoplifting than by bushranging. Often the evidence is too fragmentary to draw definite conclusions. But there are strong grounds for challenging some conventional stereotypes and assumptions about crime and criminals, such as the relation between offenders and victims in cases of violence, the degree to which livestock was stolen by organized rustlers, and the pervasive presence of a criminal underworld and professional gangs which featured so largely in popular perceptions of crime.

There are also grounds for at least modifying the standard view of the transportation system. The supposed advantage of transportation was that it not only rid Britain of its criminal population, but placed offenders in a setting where there were greater opportunities for gaining an honest livelihood. As both contemporaries and historians have emphasized, it seems indisputable that New South Wales' economic climate and the chance to make a fresh start encouraged many convicts to abstain from the commission of subsequent crimes. But this does not mean that those convicts who failed to "reform" were necessarily hardened or professional criminals. In some respects conditions in New South Wales were no less conducive to crime than in Britain. The proximity of the frontier and a predominantly male population promoted violence, most apparent in relations with Aborigines. The frontier also provided special opportunities for property offences. More importantly, the acquisitive aspirations of those immigrating to New South Wales fostered a culture which stimulated both the commission and prosecution of acquisitive crimes. Finally, portrayals of offenders as habitual and professional criminals fail to show the extent to which offences were work-related, or otherwise involved persons who previously had some contact with one another. Convicts and ex-convicts were the most vulnerable to the pressures of a new and relvatively affluent community because they were generally the most economically deprived, because they experienced the stigmatizing effect of the penal system, and because they were often expected to behave as criminals.

Notes

1. *SMH*, 20 June 1861. *Herald*'s emphasis.
2. Census returns before 1841 and after 1851 lack essential information concerning the civil condition of inhabitants. Returns taken during the 1830s fail to distinguish emancipists from those born in the colony, or ticket of leave holders from convicts under sentence. The 1851 census was the last return to include reference to residents' civil condition. See T. A. Coghlan, *General Report on the Eleventh Census of New South Wales* (Sydney, 1894), pp. 74, 76.
3. James Waldersee, *Catholic Society in New South Wales 1788–1860* (Sydney, 1974), p. 48.
4. This mode of analysis was suggested by David Philips's study of crime in England's Black Country between 1835 and 1860, although there are substantial variations in the type of data employed and analyzed. The sources used are extant judgment books, returns of trials and court calendars listed under "Superior Court Records" in the Bibliography; criminal sessions and

committals to trial reported in *SMH*, 1841, 1851; *Port Phillip Patriot*, 1841; *Empire*, 1851; *Bathurst Free Press*, 1851; *Goulburn Herald*, 1851; *Maitland Mercury*, 1851. Unless otherwise noted the statistics cited in this chapter are based on the analysis of these sources. For greater statistical detail relative to the analysis see Michael Sturma, "Vice in a Vicious Society: Crime and the Community in Mid-Nineteenth-Century New South Wales" (Ph.D. thesis, Australian National University, 1980), pp. 157–218, 401–3.

5. Occupational information is available for sixteen per cent of those persons tried in 1841, and twenty-three per cent of those tried in 1851.

6. See for example *SMH*, 14 October 1844; *Bell's Life*, 19 September 1846.

7. Philips, *Crime in Victorian England*, p. 287.

8. Reece, *Aborigines and Colonists*, p. 225.

9. *Port Phillip Patriot*, 7 January 1841.

10. See Gipps to Glenelg, 19 December 1838, *HRA*, ser. 1, vol. 19, pp. 701–2; Molony, *Architect of Freedom*, pp. 140–7; Reece, *Aborigines and Colonists*, pp. 34–42, 145–58; Rowley, *Destruction of Aboriginal Society*, pp. 35–37.

11. Reece, *Aborigines and Colonists*, p. 105.

12. Gipps to Normanby, 14 October 1839, *HRA*, ser. 1, vol. 20, p. 368; Gipps to Russel, 7 April 1841, vol. 21, p. 313; Stanley to Gipps, 6 July 1843, vol. 23, p. 9; Clark, *History of Australia*, vol. 3, pp. 428–29; Molony, *Architect of Freedom*, pp. 149–56.

13. *SMH*, 20 February 1844; Reece, *Aborigines and Colonists*, pp. 220–23.

14. Report from the Select Committee on Transportation, *PP*, 1837–38, vol. 22 (669), p. 27.

15. Gatrell and Hadden, "Criminal Statistics", p. 369.

16. Percentage is based on Returns of the Colony, "Blue Books", 1831–57 (xerox copy), ML, CY 4/262–290; N.S.W., Registrar General's Office, *Statistical Register of New South Wales*, 1858–61. The percentage refers to convictions for offences against the person from 1831 to 1861, with the exception of the years 1836–38, and 1842 when returns are unavailable. Part of the disparity between convictions in New South Wales and committals in Britain may be due to a higher conviction rate for offences against the person than other types of offences.

17. Sheldon Hackney, "Southern Violence", in Graham and Gurr (eds.), *Violence in America*, p. 516, 518; Tilly, *Rebellious Century*, p. 80; Howard Zehr, "The Modernization of Crime in Germany and France, 1830–1913", *Journal of Social History*, vol. 8 (Summer 1975), p. 129.

18. *SMH*, 3 February 1841.

19. See for example Fitzroy to Pakington, 5 February 1853, *PP*, 1852–53, vol. 64, [1684], p. 496.

20. Evidence of John Richard Hardy and Henry Harper to the Select Committee on the Management of Gold Fields, N.S.W., *V & PLC*, 1852, vol. 2, pp. 682, 703.

21. Chief Justice Alfred Stephen's Address to the Central Criminal Court, *People's Advocate*, 8 October 1853.

22. See *SMH*, 20 June 1851.

23. Michael Cannon, "Violence: The Australian Heritage", *National Times Magazine*, 12–17 March 1973, p. 28.

24. *Goulburn Herald*, 9 August 1851; *Empire*, 11 August 1851.

25. Compiled from Returns of the Colony, "Blue Books", 1841–51 (xerox copy), ML, CY 4/273–4/284.

26. *Bathurst Free Press*, 22 February 1851.

27. See Philips, *Crime in Victorian England*, p. 269.

28. Dungog Bench Book, 16 June 1849, N.S.W. SA, 4/5537.

29. Ibid., 18 August 1853.

30. Parramatta Bench Book, 3, 12 May 1849, N.S.W. SA, 4/5613; *SMH*, 5 May 1849.

31. Armidale Bench Book, 17 July 1848, N.S.W. SA, 4/5489.

32. Dungog Bench Book, 2, 5 August 1843, N.S.W. SA, 4/5536.

33. See Gipps to Stanley, 29 March 1845, *HRA*, ser. 1, vol. 24, pp. 308–9; Evidence of James Macarthur to the Select Committee on Transportation, *PP*, 1837, vol. 19 (518), p. 202; Charles Cozens, *Adventures of a Guardsman* (London, 1848), p. 148; Mundy, *Our Antipodes*, p. 71; R. B. Walker, "Bushranging in Fact and Legend", *Historical Studies* vol. 11, no. 42 (April 1964), p. 206.

34. Evidence of John Richard Hardy to the Committee on Police and Gaols, N.S.W., *V & PLC*, 1839, vol. 2, pp. 276–77.

35. Walker, "Bushranging", p. 206.

36. *SMH*, 3 April 1844.

37. *Bell's Life*, 11, 18 April 1846.

38. Ward, *Australian Legend*, chapter 6; Walker, "Bushranging", pp. 218–19.

39. E. J. Hobsbawn, *Primitive Rebels. Studies in Archaic Forms of Social Movement in the 19th and 20th Centuries* (Manchester, 1959), chapter 2. See also Pat O'Malley, "Class Conflict, Land, and Social Banditry: Bushranging in Nineteenth Century Australia", *Social Problems* vol. 26, no. 3 (February 1979), pp. 271–83; John McQuilton, *The Kelly Outbreak 1878–1880. The Geographical Dimension of Social Banditry* (Melbourne, 1979), especially pp. 2, 187.

40. *SMH*, 8 April, 5, 21 May, 19, 20 July 1841; Return of Prisoners Tried and Convicted at the Circuit Court held at Berrima, 1841–47, Supreme Court, N.S.W. SA, X884.

41. *Bathurst Free Press*, 22 February 1851.

42. "E.E." to Editor, *Sydney Gazette*, 9 October 1841.

43. *SMH*, 25 February 1841.

44. Henry William Haygarth, *Recollections of Bush Life in Australia, during a Residence of Eight Years in the Interior* (London, 1848), pp. 37–42.

45. See *Sydney Gazette*, 22 December 1838.

46. Unsigned Letter to Editor, *Sydney Herald*, 1 October 1835.

47. McQueen, *New Britannia*, p. 139.

48. See Chappell and Wilson, *Police and Public*, p. 31.

49. See Harris, *Settlers and Convicts*, p. 35.

50. See for example Alexander Harris, *The Emigrant Family: or, The Story of an Australian Settler*, edited by W. S. Ramson (London, 1849; reprint ed., Canberra, 1967), p. 188; Charles MacAlister, *Old Pioneering Days in the Sunny South* (Goulburn, 1907; facsimile ed., Sydney, 1977), p. 81.

51. Cozens, *Guardsman*, p. 155.

52. Mundy, *Our Antipodes*, p. 72.

53. See for example Ibid., p. 70; Cozens, *Guardsman*, pp. 149–54; Henry Thomas Fox, Diary, 28 March 1852, ML, MSS. 1045/3, pp. 145–47.

54. Quoted in Inglis, *Australian Colonists*, p. 267.

55. O'Malley, "Bushranging", pp. 279–80.

56. [Colony of NSW] 5 Wm. IV, No. 9, sec. 6.

57. [Colony of NSW] 1 Vic., No. 2: Returns of the Colony, "Blue Books", 1839 (xerox copy), ML, CY 4/271.

58. *SMH*, 19 March 1842.

59. Therry, *Reminiscences*, p. 213.

60. Charles George Norman Lockhart, "Sketch of a Proposed System of Police

for the Colony of New South Wales", 1851, Police, N.S.W. SA, 2/674. 15, pp. 12–13.

61. *Maitland Mercury,* 5 March 1851; *SMH,* 6 March 1851.
62. *SMH,* 26 March 1842.
63. Evidence of John Richard Hardy to the Committee on Police and Gaols, N.S.W., *V & PLC,* 1839, vol. 2, p. 272.
64. *SMH,* 2 February, 10, 13 September, 11 October 1842.
65. *SMH,* 1 April 1842, 9, 11 September 1844; *Atlas,* 15 March 1845.
66. Ward, *Australian Legend,* p. 161.
67. See for example *SMH,* 10 September 1842, 27 September 1849.
68. P. J. Vaile, "Free Society and the Range of Crime in the Bathurst District before the Gold Rush", *JRAHS* vol. 64, pt 3 (December 1978), p. 197.
69. N.S.W., Registrar General's Office, *Statistical Register of New South Wales,* 1861.
70. Fox, Diary, 10, 11 April 1852, ML, 1045/3, pp. 157–58.
71. This was also the case in larcenies tried before the Supreme Court of Western Australia between 1830 and 1855. Compare with Judith Fall, "Crime and Criminal Records in Western Australia 1830–55", *Studies in Western Australian History* no. 3 (November 1978), p. 22.
72. *SMH,* 19, 23, 24 February 1841; Register of Criminal Cases Tried at the Sydney Quarter Sessions, 1841, Clerk of the Peace, N.S.W. SA, 2916.
73. "J.F.C." to Editor, *SMH,* 5 March 1853.
74. Crown Prosecutor's Address to the Sydney Quarter Sessions, *Empire,* 10 February 1851.
75. *SMH,* 29 December 1849.
76. *SMH,* 19 November 1841; Register of Criminal Cases Tried at the Sydney Quarter Sessions, 1841, Clerk of the Peace, N.S.W. SA, 2916.
77. *SMH,* 8 October 1849.
78. John McLerie to Col. Sec., 27 March 1858, N.S.W., *V & PLA,* 1858, vol. 2, pp. 395–96.
79. Percentage is based on Returns of the Colony, "Blue Books", 1831–57 (xerox copy), ML, CY 4/270–4/290; N.S.W., Registrar General's Office, *Statistical Register of New South Wales,* 1858–61. Information is incomplete for the years 1836–38, 1842 and 1853.
80. Macnab, "Crime in England and Wales", especially pp, 311–12, 394; Gatrell and Hadden, "Criminal Statistics", especially p. 368.
81. Philips, *Crime in Victorian England,* p. 145; Gurr, Grabosky and Hula, *Politics of Crime,* p. 209.
82. Gatrell and Hadden, "Criminal Statistics", p. 385.
83. See Gurr, Grabosky and Hula, *Politics of Crime,* pp. 209–12; Jackson Toby, "Affluence and Adolescent Crime", in Cressey and Ward (eds.), *Delinquency,* pp. 286, 309; Howard Zehr, *Crime and the Development of Modern Society. Patterns of Criminality in Nineteenth Century Germany and France* (London, 1976), pp. 82–83.
84. Report from the Select Committee on Transportation, *PP,* 1837–38, vol. 22, (669), p. 27.
85. McQueen, *New Britannia,* pp. 124–25.
86. Henry Parkes to Sister, 21 May, 8 August 1841, in Henry Parkes, *An Emigrant's Home Letters* (Sydney, 1896), pp. 109, 112.
87. Curr, *Recollections of Squatting,* pp. 439–40.
88. *Port Phillip Patriot,* 16 September 1841; Session Returns of Prisoners Tried and Convicted at the Port Phillip Supreme Court, 1841–45, Col. Sec., N.S.W. SA, X46A.

89. See Priestly, "Molesworth Committee", p. 178.
90. Quoted in Evans and Nicholls, *Convicts and Colonial Society*, p. 205.
91. Evidence of Charles Windeyer and Joseph Long Innes to the Select Committee on the Insecurity of Life and Property, N.S.W., *V & PLC*, 1844, vol. 2, pp. 403, 419; Colonial Secretary's Address, LC, *SMH*, 2 October 1844; Evidence of Stuart Alexander Donaldson to the Select Committee on Transportation, *PP*, 1861, vol. 13 (286), p. 73.
92. Evidence of Francis Forbes to the Select Committee on Transportation, *PP*, 1837, vol. 19 (518), p. 78.
93. *SMH*, 5 December 1842.
94. See for example *Bell's Life*, 3 November 1849; *People's Advocate*, 12 October 1850.
95. See for example *SMH*, 18 October 1844; Mundy, *Our Antipodes*, p. 71.
96. Unsigned Letter to Editor, *Sydney Herald*, 1 October 1835; William Burrows, *Adventures of A Mounted Trooper in The Australian Constabulary: being Recollections of Seven Years' Experience of Life in Victoria, and New South Wales* (London, 1859), pp. 122–23.
97. S. J. Butlin, *Foundations of the Australian Monetary System* (Melbourne, 1853), pp. 288–90.
98. Judge Stephen's Address to the Maitland Circuit Court, *SMH*, 11 September 1841; *Empire*, 4 February 1851; Vaile, "Crime in Bathurst", pp. 194–95.

6

The Magistracy and Petty Offences

Magistrates, who are accustomed to sit at Petty Sessions, are men of all others, who see and who know most of the characters and dispositions of the lower orders of society; the amount of capital crime may be known in the Superior Courts, but the *real amount of moral depravity* can be better ascertained in the inferior Courts of Justice.[1]

The vast majority of offences were not adjudicated before the superior courts, but were heard by magistrates sitting alone, or by courts of petty sessions consisting of two or more magistrates. The available statistical evidence indicates that only about five per cent of those persons taken into custody by the police were committed for trial, while the remainder were either discharged or dealt with summarily.[2] The fact that such a large proportion of judicial business was left in the hands of men who often appeared to lack ability and impartiality, led to widespread criticism. At least among those who articulated their grievances, however, the magistracy's bias and incompetence was considered less of a problem than their neglect of duty. The focal point of complaints against magistrates was the obstruction they posed to court proceedings through their failure to attend the bench regularly.

Concern about the magistracy's non-attendance at local courts was in turn indicative of the colonists' penchant for undertaking prosecutions. Before transportation and assignment ceased, the bulk of magisterial business involved minor infractions of penal discipline. Despite numerous impediments to bringing convicts before the courts, assigned servants were commonly tried for relatively innocuous offences. After transportation ended, the triviality of much magisterial business was again a striking feature. In large part, petty offences tried before the lower courts were less indicative of the community's "moral depravity" than of its machinery for social control and its litigiousness. In this context, the penal code by the 1840s was giving way to a code of respectability, which embodied not only new standards of behaviour, but also a new competitiveness for social prestige.

Magistrates, also known as justices of the peace or JPs, were initially appointed and removed by the governor. With the introduction of responsible government, magistrates continued to be nominally appointed by the governor, but in reality they were selected by the ministry in power. Within their respective districts, magistrates exercised summary jurisdiction over minor offences, and carried out various administrative duties including supervision of the police, licensing public houses, and preparing jury lists. In addition to unpaid JPs, magisterial functions were performed by stipendiary, or as they were more commonly known, police magistrates. Their duties were essentially the same as those of other magistrates, but they served as paid officials of the government. In general, police magistrates were appointed only in populous districts where there was a great deal of judicial business, or where the unpaid magistracy appeared inadequate.

In unsettled districts, beyond the boundaries of location, magisterial powers were vested in commissioners of crown lands. As itinerant JPs, they were required to visit stations within their districts at least twice a year. They were also charged with preventing the unauthorized occupation of crown lands, settling boundary disputes, and collecting licence fees and stock assessments. Commissioners on the goldfields, first appointed in 1851, served in an analogous capacity. Aside from exercising summary jurisdiction, they supervized gold escorts, settled disputed claims, and collected licence fees from diggers.

The administration of justice by the magistracy was a matter of continual complaint. Much of the criticism directed at JPs can be attributed to dissatisfied prosecutors and defendants, who vented their anger in anonymous letters to the press. But there is also evidence of a more general dissatisfaction with the magistracy. Since magistrates required no legal training, their competence to perform judicial duties was frequently attacked. The *Atlas,* probably reflecting the opinion of lawyer Robert Lowe, asserted that "in ninety-nine cases out of every one hundred, Justices of the Peace *know absolutely nothing* of the laws which they are called upon to administer".[3] If in more moderate language, the same sentiment was often echoed by other colonial observers.

The absence of any legal requirements was a result of following the example of Britain, where the only qualification for admission to the bench was based on property. Nevertheless, there are social and geographical reasons why the system was less satisfactory in the colony than in England.[4] The colonial magistracy largely lacked the habit of authority, personal bonds and the tradition of deference which characterized relationships in much of the English countryside.[5] New South Wales' limited population ostensibly meant that JPs could not be selected with as great a discretion. Because of the colony's dispersed population, JPs in the interior were also exempt from some of the checks on magisterial abuses which existed in England. In many districts there was no local press to report legal irregularities. Nor were lawyers scattered enough to influence the judicial proceedings of remote benches. Furthermore, distance and impediments to communication made it difficult to appeal against the decisions of rural magistrates.[6]

The relative autonomy of many magistrates made their impartiality all the more questionable. Although JPs were prohibited from acting in cases involving their own servants, most were employers of labour. In cases involving convicts, there were obvious reasons why magistrates would be expected to show great sympathy towards their fellow landholders. As one justice of the peace observed: "It is the feeling of doing as you would be done by — of punishing another man's servant in the way in which you would wish him to punish yours; that is with the severity with which every man regards an offence against himself."[7] This same feeling could affect the magistracy's dealings with other workers. Whether by intention or not, contemporaries often noted, magistrates were prejudiced in favour of their own class and interested parties in dispensing justice.

Criticism of the magistracy's objectivity was most vocal in relation to their administration of the Masters and Servants Act. As initially passed in 1828, servants summarily convicted under the Act of offences such as neglect of work or absenting themselves before fulfilling a contract, could be imprisoned for up to six months. In addition, they could be compelled to forfeit all wages due. Servants who destroyed or lost any property entrusted to them were required to pay double the value of the property or in default spend up to six months in prison.[8] These provisions applied only to servants employed on farms and estates, and engagements for time, but a new Act in 1840 was expanded to encompass servants under engagements generally. At the same time, the maximum penalties servants were liable to were reduced from six to three months imprisonment.[9] Although the Act was further amended in 1845 and 1847, the penal clauses remained substantially the same until 1857.[10] The administration of the Act appeared prejudicial not only because most JPs were drawn from the ranks of employers, but also because servants had little recourse against their decisions. The high costs of an appeal, the time and expense of travelling to a superior court, and the frequent necessity of obtaining a lawyer's services, virtually prohibited the less affluent from seeking another hearing.[11]

The magistracy's impartiality was questioned on more general grounds as well. Leaving aside cases involving labour relations, their connections in small communities often meant that their judgments might easily be swayed by associates, family, or business ties. The supervisory capacity they exercised over the police, and hence their role in apprehending suspects, was calculated to give them more than a passing interest in the outcome of prosecutions. Since they heard one party's story before issuing a summons or warrant, they might become prejudiced against the defendant. They were also susceptible to political influences, especially since their duties included revision of the electoral rolls. Within two years after the introduction of responsible government the commission of the peace was increased by fifty per cent, and it was alleged that many appointments were based on political considerations.[12]

In general, however, censure of the magistracy focused less on their incompetence and prejudices, than on their inaccessibility and neglect of duties. As in the case of the superior courts, colonists frequently protested that the distance between benches placed them virtually beyond the pale of the law. Although new courts were periodically created, the pattern of settlement and slow transport precluded easy access to JPs in many areas. Courts of petty sessions were not established beyond the boundaries of location until 1847. Before that date settlers were compelled to travel to the nearest bench within the settled districts, or await the irregular visits of commissioners of crown lands. Even after the introduction of petty sessions, settlers were still often required to travel immense distances.

Still more galling was the fact that after travelling great distances, persons often had their cases postponed because the local JPs failed to appear at court. Attorney-General Plunkett stated his belief that "parties have come a distance of thirty or forty miles, not only once, but twice or three times, to get their cases decided, and found no Bench. They lose their time, they lose their money, and probably the loss is so great that they do not ask a decision at all."[13] In some districts an insufficient number of magistrates served to prevent cases being heard. The commission of the peace was not significantly expanded until the advent of responsible government, when under Charles Cowper's ministry tradition was broken by including professionals and tradesmen as well as large landholders.[14] Even so, in 1861 it was asserted that while magistrates in the cities had increased, their numbers in country areas had actually declined through resignations and departures.[15]

More often, judicial efficiency was hindered not so much by a scarcity of magistrates, as by an apparent abdication of responsibility on the part of those appointed. Complaints that local JPs ignored their judicial duties were legion. Magistrate's bench books and newspaper reports suggest that in most districts only one or two justices of the peace regularly attended court. The non-attendance of magistrates meant that courts were often held at infrequent and irregular intervals. Even when court was convened, cases requiring the presence of two JPs, such as those under the Masters and Servants Act, were frequently postponed for want of a second magistrate. As table 10, based on bench books in which the JPs attending were recorded, suggests, the presence of a second magistrate in country districts was often uncommon.

Table 10. Magisterial Attendance at Various Country Benches During 1831, 1841, 1851 and 1861.

	Number of Magistrates present on Days Which Cases were Heard				
Bench	One JP	Two JPs	Three or More JPs	No Information	Total Days Court was Convened
Picton 1831	64	6		1	71
Port Macquarie 1831	86	12	4	2	104
Muswellbrook 1841	66	26	5	3	100
Picton 1841	8	22		3	33
Yass 1841	45	8	2		55
Armidale 1851	49	5	1		56
Mudgee 1851	36	8	1		44
Warialda 1851	11	6	2	1	20
Balranald 1861	20	5	3		28
Kiama 1861	7	7	33		44
Tenterfield 1861	18	8			26

Source: Armidale Bench Book, January-December 1851, N.S.W. SA, 4/5489; Balranald Bench Book, January-December 1861, N.S.W. SA, 4/5505; Kiama Bench Book, January-December 1861, N.S.W. SA, 4/5577; Mudgee Bench Book, January-December 1851, N.S.W. SA, 4/5591; Muswellbrook (Merton) Bench Books, January-December 1841, N.S.W. SA, 4/5601; Picton (Stonequarry) Bench Books, January-December 1831, N.S.W. SA, 4/7572–7573; Picton Bench Book, January-December 1841, N.S.W. SA, 4/5627; Port Macquarie Bench Book, January-December 1831, N.S.W. SA, 4/5637; Tenterfield Bench Book, January-December 1861, N.S.W. SA, 7/74; Warialda Bench Book, January-December 1851, N.S.W. SA, 4/5679; Yass Bench Book, January-December 1841, N.S.W. SA, 4/5703.

One reason cited for the magistracy's lethargy, and one which further distinguished them from their English counterparts, was the absence of a leisured squirearchy with a tradition of public service. A select committee of the Legislative Council concluded in 1839 that:

> There is a marked distinction between a newly found Society, thinly scattered over a wild and unimproved Country and all necessarily engaged in the active pursuits of life, and the mother-country possessing in great numbers men of wealth, and leisure, and ready to devote their time and talents to Public objects. In this Colony, as in all new Countries, there are no men of leisure.[16]

The same distinction was drawn by Judge Roger Therry twenty years later. He believed the greatest impediment to the administration of justice by the magistracy was the absence of a county gentry "having nothing to do, as in England".[17]

To some extent magisterial neglect can also be attributed to the distance many justices of the peace resided from the courts. At Bathurst, for example, it was reported that all but one of the district's magistrates lived too far away from the settlement to make the journey conveniently.[18] But even in Sydney the inactivity of men appointed to the commission of the peace was a matter of incessant comment. During the year ending September 1852, forty of the district's sixty-eight magistrates never appeared at the Police Office.[19] Although the press persistently expressed views to the contrary, many justices of the peace apparently regarded their appointment primarily as a titular honour.

The most common means urged for improving the day-to-day administration of justice was the appointment of salaried police magistrates. During 1860 alone a dozen locations forwarded petitions or applications to the colonial secretary requesting the appointment of a stipendiary magistrate.[20] New South Wales' first police magistrate was appointed at Parramatta in 1825 by Governor Brisbane, and by 1840 there were twenty-six stipendiary magistrates in the colony.[21] Following the introduction of a partially elected Legislative Council, however, their numbers were radically reduced. By 1846 only seven of the colony's forty-one benches had stipendiary magistrates.[22] The Council refused to vote funds for the support of most police magistrates both as a measure of economy, and in opposition to Governor Gipps.[23] It seems likely as well that country gentlemen resented their superintendence and impingement on their authority.[24] Only under public pressure were their numbers gradually increased during the 1850s, and the displacement of unpaid JPs by stipendiary magistrates continued into the twentieth century.[25] The appointment of police magistrates alleviated the most pressing problem associated with the magistracy by ensuring that someone regularly attended the bench. This was especially the case from 1850, when police magistrates were empowered to act alone in cases formerly requiring the presence of two or more justices of the peace.[26]

Magisterial attendance and the accessibility of the courts in various districts no doubt exercised a profound influence on the number and type of cases brought before the bench. The magistracy's composition might affect the character of prosecutions, particularly since judicial business was often left in the hands of one or two men. Thus at Penrith the administration of justice was allegedly dominated by the "religious fanaticism" and "straight-laced notions of morality" entertained by the town's leading JP.[27] Much more than in relation to "serious" crime, changes in police numbers and practices might significantly alter the pattern of cases summarily tried. For these reasons, the offences brought before the lower courts reflected in large part the colony's machinery for social control.

Since returns of offences tried summarily in New South Wales were not systematically compiled until 1879, difficulties are posed in determining precisely what types of cases were brought before the magistracy. The only comprehensive statistics available are for the early 1840s and irregular periods at mid-century. The limited time span for which statistics were recorded, as well as the amorphous system of categorization used, makes it difficult to gain more than some general impressions. Those offence categories (out of the total of sixty-two categories recorded) which comprised one per cent or more of the total cases dealt with summarily during the periods for which statistics are available are set out in table 11, as well as "all other offences". The most marked trend was a decline in cases of drunkenness during the early 1840s, which is discussed in chapter 7. There was also a decline in offences aggregated as "disobedience, abusive language and disorderly conduct",[28] which presumably reflected a decline in convict cases, as did a decrease in persons illegally at large. As a proportion of all offences, cases under the Masters and Servants Act, threatening language, common assault and "unspecified" offences showed the clearest increase following the cessation of transportation.

More detailed information concerning offences tried before the magistracy is provided by newspapers and magistrate's bench books, although neither source is entirely satisfactory. The press reported in detail only a small portion of the cases brought before the police courts. The emphasis was often on cases which offered a moral message for the lower classes. Alternatively, a tone of trivialization was frequently adopted. Testimony was recorded replete with Jewish, Irish and Chinese accents. The antics of drunkards received special attention, and were often reported in a mock-heroic style epitomized by *Bell's Life in Sydney*. William a'Beckett, a leading temperance proponent later to become Victoria's first chief justice, complained of such facetious reportage, noting that the press would do better to analyze the moral decline of persons brought before the bench "instead of winding up with a jest or something worse".[29] In one sense the press was interested in providing mass entertainment, but since gossip and ridicule were an effective deterrent to misbehaviour in a small community, the press was also a potent instrument of social control.[30]

Magistrates' bench books provide a more comprehensive view of offences summarily dealt with, but there are serious gaps in the surviving records. There are no bench books available for Sydney and many other populous districts for the period under study. Extant bench books usually cover only short periods of time, and vary widely in the amount of detail recorded about cases. It is possible that many cases

Table 11. Offences Tried Summarily by the Magistracy in New South Wales, 1841–45, 1 January 1848 to 31 March 1849, and 1 January 1850 to 30 September 1851.

	1841		1842		1843		1844		1845		Jan. 1848-Mar. 1849		Jan. 1850-Sept. 1851	
	No.	%	No.	%	No.	%	No.	%	No.	%	No.	%	No.	%
Drunkenness	15,691	61.3	9,630	59.7	6,187	52.8	4,293	46.8	4,471	49.6	7,142	58.8	6,302	37.2
Other Offences Unspecified	2,441	9.5	1,520	9.4	1,212	10.4	1,042	11.4	1,261	14.0	1,843	15.2	4,765	28.2
Disobedience, Abusive Language and Disorderly Conduct	2,262	8.8	1,283	8.0	1,129	9.6	721	7.9	492	5.5	240	2.0	1,129	6.7
Illegally at Large	1,469	5.7	528	3.3	332	2.8	237	2.6	186	2.1	218	1.8	342	2.0
Masters and Servants Act	533	2.1	627	3.9	696	5.9	788	8.6	543	6.0	600	4.9	1,114	6.6
Common Assaults	955	3.7	693	4.3	730	6.2	672	7.3	790	8.8	1,010	8.3	1,004	5.9
Neglect of Work	490	1.9	414	2.6	226	1.9	95	1.0	107	1.2	43	0.4	184	1.1
Rogues and Vagabonds	365	1.4	478	3.0	233	2.0	376	4.1	187	2.1	381	3.1	411	2.4
Riot and Breach of the Peace	269	1.1	160	1.0	273	2.3	417	4.5	479	5.3	72	0.6	135	0.8
Thefts and Larcenies	262	1.0	146	0.9	132	1.1	101	1.1	65	0.7	101	0.8	77	0.5
Threatening Language	105	0.4	95	0.6	107	0.9	86	0.9	89	1.0	157	1.3	611	3.6
Wilful Damage to Property	32	0.1	51	0.3	46	0.4	49	0.5	37	0.4	51	0.4	183	1.1
All Other Offences	708	2.8	493	3.1	417	3.6	297	3.3	308	3.5	289	2.4	663	4.0
Total	25,582		16,118		11,720		9,174		9,015		12,147		16,920	

Source: Returns of Criminal Statistics, N.S.W., V & PLC, 1847, vol. 1, p. 1111; 1849, vol. 1, p. 632; 1849, vol. 1, p. 1111; 1852, vol. 1, p. 944.

went unrecorded, either through neglect or because they might prove embarrassing to the local JPs. Generally, the bench books include only a summary of the prosecutions brought before the bench and the court's judgment. Nevertheless, they provide some broad impressions, as well as some rare glimpses of the community and the law in practice.

A survey of the bench records makes it clear that offences involving assigned servants dominated the judicial business of the magistrates' courts during the 1830s. The defendants in about ninety per cent of the cases brought before the benches at Port Macquarie and Stone-quarry during 1831, for example, were convicts under sentence.[31] Although this proportion later declined, extant bench books complete for the year 1841 indicate that convicts still made up the largest pro-portion of offenders, both in total numbers and relative to their pro-portion of the population. Over sixty per cent of the defendants in cases brought before the magistracy at Patrick's Plains, Picton (as Stonequarry was known from 1841) and Yass during 1841 were convicts in assigned service or on road gangs, although they comprised less than twenty per cent of the population in all of these districts.[32] As noted in relation to offences tried before the superior courts, this owed much to differences in the sex and age composition of those originally transported and other colonists. More importantly, the large number of convict cases was indicative of the stringent and pervasive standards of discipline to which they were subjected.

While convict cases brought before the magistracy were overwhelm-ingly minor breaches of discipline, there were local variations in the types of misconduct most frequently prosecuted. Convicts charged with neglect of work made up one-quarter of all cases brought before the Port Macquarie bench in 1831, for example, but only ten per cent of the cases at Stonequarry, where persons tried for absconding or being absent without leave predominated. At Queanbeyan, thirty-one per cent of the convict cases dealt with during 1841 were for disobedience. During the same year one-tenth of all cases brought before the Yass bench were for losing or neglecting sheep, while such cases made up five per cent or less of those tried at Patrick's Plains, Muswellbrook and Picton.[33] These regional differences in offences prosecuted presumably reflected not only differences in population, but also conditions of labour, settlers' attitudes and the composition of the magistracy.

The number of petty offences prosecuted showed a marked decline during the early 1840s. The *Australian* boldly announced in 1842 that the declining number of minor offences was "a striking proof that the general tone of moral and social feeling is rapidly improving, and that we may now justly claim to be considered not only a shrewd and intelli-gent community, but a well-conducted community."[34] In reality, the decrease in petty offences largely reflected a decline in the number of convicts under sentence, and consequently a decline in cases resulting from infractions of convict discipline. The assignment of convicts to private settlers was ended in July 1841. Although convicts already assigned remained in private service until they became eligible for a ticket of leave or gained their freedom, all convicts were to be removed from service within the period prescribed by their original sentence. This measure prevented the possibility of masters forestalling their servants' freedom by charging them with subsequent offences.[35] At the same time, a massive reduction in police numbers following the cessation of transportation would be expected to cause a marked decline in the detection of petty offences.

While the number of cases summarily tried fell sharply during the 1840s, the abolition of transportation by no means created a vacuum in judicial business before the lower courts. Newspaper reports and magistrates' records suggest, instead, two features which were to become increasingly apparent by mid-century. First, as attention was diverted from the regulation of convicts, there was evidence of a growing concern with the community's moral standards in general. The *Herald* lamented in 1841 that it was "really disgraceful" to see the number of young tradesmen who went parrot shooting on Sunday instead of attending church services, while others "accompanied by numbers of dissolute females, betake themselves to boating, and sail up and down the harbour, singing lewd and obscene songs".[36] The same year toll fees were doubled for Sunday travelling, and this measure was followed by the appointment of a select committee to investigate the observance of the Sabbath.[37] Although the committee's attempt to implement a general Sunday Observance Act was unsuccessful, a new Act prohibited shooting on Sunday for pleasure or profit.[38] Sabbatarian legislation was symptomatic of a more diffuse effort to impose stricter standards of personal behaviour. *Bell's Life* went so far as to assert in 1846 that while proportionately there was less "real crime" than in the United Kingdom, offences overlooked in Britain were in the colony "tortured into crime".[39] Following the discovery of gold, drunkenness, sly-grog selling, gambling, prize fighting, desecration of the Sabbath, and other evidence of "immoraltiy", rather than more serious offences, were the focal points of widespread anxiety.[40]

A second feature which emerges is the community's litigiousness. Judge Burton's image of the population continually moving to and from the courts, if less than apt in relation to the higher tribunals, often seems relevant to the petty sessions. Despite regional variations in the types of convict misconduct most frequently brought before the bench, in all districts prosecutions often arose out of petty altercations or fits of pique. Thus John Hazel received seven days solitary confinement for allegedly making "a noise like breaking wind" when his overseer chastized him about the speed of his ploughing.[41] In another case, John Morris was sentenced to twelve months in an iron gang for rashly threatening his master, who had criticized the dimensions of a haystack he was making.[42] The colony's free inhabitants showed a similar disposition to prosecute one another when their sensitivities were offended or when minor disputes arose. The alacrity with which apparently petty offences were prosecuted seems all the more striking in light of the incessant complaints made about the difficulties of initiating cases and the magistracy's conduction of business. In this context, it is significant that colonists appeared vexed more by the magistrates' non-attendance than by their incompetence.

Prosecutions for obscenity in New South Wales provide a case in point of both the enforcement of more stringent standards of personal behaviour, and the community's litigiousness. During 1843 and 1844 the first legal proceedings were instituted against obscene publications with the suppression of three Sydney tattle sheets, the *Satirist*, *Omnibus*, and *Paddy Kelly's Budget*.[43] There were also occasional complaints made against the display for sale of indecent engravings and prints.[44] In general, however, efforts to suppress obscenity were directed less against printed matter than against offensive public conduct. One of the more striking features of offences summarily tried during the early 1840s was the large number of cases for indecent exposure. Still more striking was an upsurge in obscene language cases at the mid-century.

During 1841 there were 252 apprehensions by the police for "exposure of person" in Sydney alone.[45] Although there was a decline in such cases during the early 1840s, as in most petty offences, they remained common throughout the mid-nineteenth century. The large number of arrests for indecent exposure can be attributed in part to police practices. Since constables received a portion of the fines for convictions before 1850, it was in their direct interests to make as many apprehensions as possible. For the same reason doubts were sometimes raised as to whether the offence was actually committed. The incidence of arrests also owed much to the broad definition of indecent exposure, which ranged from "having connection" in a public place to bathing in Sydney Harbour within view of the government Domain.

Persons guilty of indecent exposure were usually liable to a fine, although harsher punishments were sometimes awarded, depending on the nature of the offence.[46] Andrew Gannon, a labourer, was sentenced to twelve months imprisonment at hard labour for allegedly following Anne Barker through the tap room of a public house with his pants down, while making lewd suggestions.[47] At Maitland, a tailor named Michael Lester testified that he watched a man urinate on the verandah of the *Mercury* newspaper office, and then walk out into the street exposing himself, asking "where is the bloody woman that will take six inches of this". The offender, Owen Crusacle, was sentenced to three months hard labour in Maitland Gaol.[48] These incidents serve to underline the crudity of some colonists, but they were by no means typical of the offences prosecuted.

More often than not arrests for indecent exposure involved persons charged with "making water in the street". Some defendants were apparently too intoxicated to realize or care that they were committing an offence. Edward McCormick, for example, was found lying drunk in one of Mudgee's streets with his trousers down. The arresting constable testified that "he seemed to be easing himself, and then fell into it". McCormick pleaded in his defence that he did not remember any part of the circumstances.[49] Other defendants "pleaded necessity". Although public houses were required by law to provide toilet facilities, their failure in this respect was believed largely responsible for offences against decency.[50] One Sydney resident in 1860 lamenting the want of public urinals noted both the severe fines inflicted for "alleged public indecencies", and that there were "few towns in the old country unprovided with these indispensable places".[51] As was often the case, this particular form of colonial "immorality" was related to more fundamental social conditions.

At least in some quarters, the prevalence of obscene labguage was a matter of greater concern. The *Sydney Gazette* reported in 1839 that:

> It is a matter of doubt which is the greatest evil in Sydney, the vice of drunkenness or the custom of vile swearing in the streets. Great as is the former evil it is in some respects less objectionable than the horrid oaths and obscene language which is current in our streets among the lower orders, and so disgusting to all respectable persons, but more particularly so to those newly arrived in the colony.[52]

Similarly, C. Rudston Read later remarked that the habit of swearing and use of "coarse low-life language" was the "greatest vice" practised at the gold diggings.[53] While most observers regarded drunkenness as a more serious social problem, the use of obscene language was commonly mentioned as being one of the most palpable signs of widespread moral depravity in New South Wales.

Magistrates' bench books suggest that public concern about obscene language reached a peak in the years immediately following the discovery of gold. At Parramatta there were fifty-five prosecutions for obscene language during 1852, ninety-five the following year and over two hundred in 1854. Cases involving obscene language made up over ten per cent of all cases brought before the Parramatta bench during these years.[54] This phenomenon was not apparent in all districts, but it was far from uncommon. Prosecutions for obscene language at Mudgee, for example, began to escalate at the end of 1853, increasing in number from five in 1851 to thirty-two in 1854.[55] In the "chaste village" of Camden, where there were only three obscene language cases between 1847 and 1851, the number increased to sixteen in 1852, twenty-five in 1853, and then declined to nineteen in 1854. Almost one-fifth of the cases heard before the Camden bench in 1853 involved charges of obscene language.[56]

While there are no extant bench books for many of the colony's larger population centres, the prevalence of obscene language cases is suggested by other evidence. Obscene language cases figured prominently in the police business reported by most local newspapers in the 1850s. A similar trend is suggested by returns of police apprehensions in Sydney for 1857 and 1859 (the only years available which distinguish obscene language as a separate offence category). During 1857 Sydney's police took 519 persons into custody for using obscene language, and 581 persons during 1859. In both years apprehensions for obscene language made up over seven per cent of all arrests, and in 1859 obscene language was Sydney's most common offence after drunkenness.[57]

The proliferation of obscene language cases at the mid-century owed much to a new Vagrancy Act passed in 1849.[58] Following the Act's passage, magistrates in many districts expressed their intention of acting more vigorously to suppress obscene language.[59] At the same time, police were encouraged to charge suspected drunkards with obscene language, since they could be subjected to more severe penalties under the Act. For instance, Mary Innis was arrested for a breach of the Vagrancy Act at Parramatta by a constable who overheard her say "I don't care a Bugger", while she stood drunk at a street corner.[60] Not infrequently, the obscene language in question was addressed to policemen by suspects after they were apprehended. Thus Mary Salsbury was charged with using obscene language to Mudgee's chief constable, who deposed that he found her lying drunk in front of a public house, and that when he lifted her up she told him "to kiss her arse".[61]

As in the case of indecent exposure, the large number of apprehensions for obscene language can be attributed in part to the use of police discretion, or rather to the lack of it. Under the Vagrancy Act persons convicted of using profane or obscene language "to the annoyance of the inhabitants or passengers in any public street or place" were liable to a fine not exceeding five pounds, or in default, imprisonment for up to three months.[62] The letter of the law was often enforced with what now seems undue vigour. Prosecutions sometimes resulted from policemen overhearing domestic endearments. Mary Ann Fleming was charged with calling her husband a "bloody bugger" in a public house,[63] while Joseph Parfitt was accused of calling his wife a "bloody leech" or "wretch" (the arresting constable wasn't sure which) in a public street.[64] Cases also arose of persons charged with using objectionable language in private homes, although the legality of such prosecutions was questioned.[65] William and Margaret Bourke, for example, were fined twenty shillings each or a week in gaol for calling each other "a bloody old bitch" and "a bloody old bugger" as a constable passed their house.[66] Although less numerous, "obscene" language cases included blasphemies as well. For instance, Thomas Dowan, an ex-convict, was sentenced to four days in Parramatta Gaol for using the expression "Holy Jesus",[67] and Elizabeth Sicwood was fined three pounds for swearing "By the Bloody Holy Ghost" at Braidwood.[68] In many cases the offensive language prosecuted was used in an idiomatic sense, rather than with any obscene or blasphemous intent. It seems that persons were commonly convicted for using words which were a normal part of their speech and an acceptable mode of expression among certain groups.[69]

Not only the police and magistracy, but also private citizens were active in regulating this particular aspect of social behaviour. At Parramatta about half of the cases involving obscene language prosecuted between 1852 and 1854 were initiated by civilians.[70] At other benches the proportion could be much higher. The available records further suggest that the proportion of prosecutions initiated by private citizens was increasing during the period.

Prosecutions for obscene language were generally precipitated by minor disputes. Business transactions figured occasionally in cases. John Coulter, a free immigrant, was charged by Andrew Payton, a publican, with calling him a "bloody liar" in an altercation over Coulter's bar bill.[71] In another case William Wright, a carpenter, accused an ex-convict named Michael Dagherty of using indecent language to himself and his wife when they approached him in the street concerning the length of time he was taking to repair an umbrella. Wright deposed that when asked when he intended to return the umbrella, Dagherty told him to bugger himself, slapped his bottom a dozen times, and told him to kiss it. When Wright's wife interjected that this was some language to use after keeping the umbrella so long, he retorted that "she might go and fuck herself".[72]

More commonly, the prosecutor and defendant were neighbours. For instance, Mary Delaney informed magistrates at Parramatta that when she went out on her verandah her neighbour, Sarah Ward, said to her in a loud voice that "I was a whore from my cradle and that I had my belly up to my chin with a bastard". Her testimony was confirmed by another neighbour, a watchmaker named William Dodd-

Turner, who deposed that Ward also called him a "humpy back wretch".[73] In another case involving two women who lived next door to each other and who both kept small shops, Sarah Crump was summonsed to the Maitland bench by Mary Glen for calling her "a bloody whore and a bloody bitch" from her back gate.[74] In some cases the offensive language was not even directly addressed to the prosecutor. Henry Sheriff Potter, a Braidwood innkeeper, charged a neighbour, Eleanor Holder, with repeatedly saying to her husband during a quarrel outside his house, "why don't you go into the Bloody Melbourne Whore Mrs Potter".[75]

The number of men and women involved in cases of obscene language, both as prosecutors and defendants, was fairly evenly divided. The civil condition and occupation of parties were only irregularly recorded, but the social status of both prosecutors and defendants apparently cut across class lines. The large number of cases involving neighbours suggests that the social standing of the prosecutor and defendant was often comparable. At the same time, those involved in prosecutions ranged from members of the working class to justices of the peace.

The avidity with which colonists prosecuted obscene language cases was indicative of a more general litigiousness which extended to other types of offences. The *Australian* observed that:

> It really is surprising the spirit of litigation which prevails amongst the lower classes of Sydney. The same faces appear time after time to make their complaint of grievous and fancied injuries, which if passed by with a little forbearance, would soon be put a stop to; . . . Nor have people when excited by those feelings any regard for that saving wisdom, by which alone they can improve their condition, but they eagerly throw away their money to the lawyers to manage their cases for them, and to the already tedious and heavy business of the Court is added the grandiloquent speeches and sparkling witticism of attorneys, who strive to make a case, appear of the most aggravated description, which a soft answer or a little forbearance might have altogether averted.[76]

The "trumpery" nature of theatening language cases, assaults and similar breaches of the peace in particular was frequently commented upon by the Sydney press. On the grounds that frivolous cases arising from domestic squabbles and neighbourly quarrels were unduly numerous, the *Herald* went so far as to suggest that complainants failing to substantiate their charges should be subjected to punitive costs.[77]

In country districts prosecutions for threatening language were fewer than those for obscenity, but almost all were initiated by private citizens rather than by the police. As with obscene language cases, prosecutions for threatening language showed a marked increase from the early 1850s. Again as with obscene language cases, prosecutions for threatening language often appeared to be the outcome of minor disputes which assumed a seriousness out of proportion to the actual offence. Following a dispute over cutting timber, for example, Margaret Faye was bound over to keep the peace towards George Colebrook, a boat builder, who charged her with threatening to "dash his brains out".[78] In another case precipitated by a straying horse, Elizabeth Howe had Mary Belcher bound over to keep the peace for allegedly saying "she would wring Howe's neck off".[79]

Even in cases of assault, the resort to criminal prosecutions sometimes seems surprising. In a case accorded special seriousness by the *Herald*, John Corrigan, about ten years of age, was charged by Mrs Riley, described as "a respectable looking female", with assault. Corrigan and Riley lived near each other, and on the morning of the alleged assault the boy entered the Riley's verandah while they were at breakfast. Mr Riley told the boy to go away and then bodily removed him from the house. Corrigan then threw some stones at the door, and later at Mr Riley when he left for work. Mrs Riley went outside to prevent her children from being pelted too. She deposed, "the little rascal then went up to her, kicked her, and said he would kick her guts out". Corrigan admitted kicking her clothes, but denied touching her person, which is not improbable considering female costume of the period.[80] In another case Mr Strettles charged Mrs West with assault when her only offence consisted of spitting at him, and saying "take that".[81]

The upsurge in prosecutions for obscene language and similar offences may be explained partly in terms of a demand for greater order. In dealing with nineteenth century crime in Massachusetts, Roger Lane offers this explanation to account for a statistical increase in drunkenness and similar misdemeanours which accompanied a decline in serious crime. According to Lane, a fall in "real crime" permitted condoned standards of conduct to rise. As definitions of order changed, the machinery of social control was extended to deal with offences previously overlooked. Urbanization also meant that behaviour which was acceptable in a more independent community required greater regulation. As a result, there was a "progressive heightening of standards of propriety", and an "increasing reliance on official law enforcement".[82]

This interpretation seems to adapt itself neatly to the case of New South Wales. From 1839 the colony's serious crime rate, that is, offences tried before the superior courts, sharply declined. Although the number of police relative to the population declined during the same period, the cessation of transportation meant that their activities could be diverted from regulating the behaviour of convicts to that of the community in general. The colony's falling crime rate, the diminishing proportion of convicts in the population, and closer settlement, all interacted to create a greater sensitivity to offensive public conduct. Within this context, growing concern with obscenity was symptomatic of changing definitions of acceptable behaviour.

On the other hand, a "heightening of standards of propriety" may only partly explain a phenomenon which is related to more complex social relations. Lane's interpretation refers to the widening ambit of police activities. But in New South Wales the number of obscene language and similar cases initiated by private citizens as opposed to the constabulary is particularly striking, and suggests that perhaps in New South Wales there was more involved than simply a greater demand for order.

The offending language used in some obscene language cases suggests that tensions between social and national groups at least occasionally underlaid apparently minor disputes. For example, John Yeats prosecuted Mrs Dick for using obscene language following a neighbourly quarrel. Yeats deposed that when he complained to Mrs Dick about her daughter taking a piece of wood out of his closet, she replied that her daughter was a decent child and not a bastard like his children. When Yeats's wife then ordered her away from their door, Mrs Dick called her "a blindeyed convicted bitch" and said "she was not sent out here by the expense of the Government and while she and her daughter were in bed my wife and Bastards were whoring about the Town".[83] In an analogous case, Norah Cahill charged Judith Hyder with calling her a "bloody Irish Immigrant Bugger" from her verandah.[84] At Maitland the Campbell and Foran families figured in a series of obscene language and minor assault cases. Significantly, the first recorded altercation took place at the Catholic burial ground when John Foran reportedly called William Campbell "a north of Ireland paleface bugger".[85]

Colonial prejudices obviously provide only a partial explanation of prosecutions. It is probable that the colony's convict origins exercised a more profound influence. In part, the penal system provided an infrastructure for widespread litigation. Despite complaints concerning the inaccessibility of courts and JPs, the exigency of regulating convict labour resulted in a more developed legal system. The Reverend John Dunmore Lang, who was inclined to attribute the colony's pervasive spirit of litigation to the encouragement of the legal profession, also thought that ex-convicts were particularly likely to patronize lawyers in view of their past experience.[86] A more satisfactory explanation is that the practice of taking assigned servants to court for the most minor infractions may have instilled a habit of resorting to the courts for settling personal and work-related disputes.

At the same time, colonial litigiousness may have reflected the absence of a tradition for handling matters of inter-personal conflict. Large influxes of newcomers, especially after the discovery of gold, meant that many persons were relatively unacquainted with both their neighbours and local sanctions for settling differences. The fact that magistrates were willing to take cognizance of often highly personal cases provided further encouragement to litigation.

Perhaps most importantly, colonial litigiousness was indicative of concern with respectability. In part, this was related to more rigid standards of behaviour and a heightened sensitivity to disorder in the sense that Roger Lane denotes. But respectability also emerges as a product of social relationships. It is in relation to a "competitive struggle" for social status that the prevalence of obscene language cases and similar offences seems most significant.[87] The courts provided a means of settling quarrels and "getting even". They also afforded an official and public means of asserting one's own moral worth and status. By morally downgrading others before the magistracy, persons might increase their own chances of being regarded as respectable.

Another characteristic attributed to New South Wales society, an inordinate passion for scandal and gossip, might be viewed in a similar light. This feature, like the colony's litigiousness, no doubt owed much to the community's small size and a lack of intellectual amusements. But gossip was also an obvious means, if an unconscious one, for asserting one's own morality, while undermining that of others. Sydney's scandal sheets, for which there was an apparent market, were probably rendered objectionable as much from their assault on upstanding citizens as by their vulgarity. The *Satirist's* aspersions ranged from characterizing James Macarthur as "the concentrated essence of 'humbug'", to innuendo concerning the sobriety of temperance leaders.[88] The suppression of *Paddy Kelly's Budget* was called for on the grounds that its insinuations "against the character of women whose reputations stand high" caused a great deal of mischief.[89] There was also the omnipresent concern about the colony's image. The *Herald* insisted that such papers were sent back to England to prove New South Wales' depravity.[90]

The quest for respectability was heightened by New South Wales' convict background. Governor Gipps noted that the fear of being suspected of convict taint acted "in a wholesome manner as a restraint".[91] The same fear could inspire attempts to assert visibly one's moral superiority, and helps explain why some observers believed that social rivalry and apeing of Britain's middle classes reached almost absurd proportions.[92] By far the most common offensive language prosecuted were the words "bugger" and "whore", which were perhaps all the more objectionable because of the association of homosexuality and prostitution with convictism.

Perhaps more important in contributing to the scramble for respectability was the similar background of most immigrants, and the degree of social fluidity within the colony. The relatively even distribution of financial resources among immigrants, along with opportunities for social advancement, fostered competition for social status. That prosecutions for obscene language frequently involved neighbours is perhaps not surprising, since competition was presumably most intense between persons of comparable social position. That prosecutors ranged from magistrates to labourers may be some indication of the pervasiveness of the concern with respectability. The upsurge in obscene language cases following the discovery of gold in particular, suggests a rush for respectability coincident with the new prosperity of many immigrants.

With reference to Sydney's Police Office, the *Herald* observed in 1853 that:

> Perhaps there are few things that would strike the new comer in this colony more forcibly than the number of the cases daily tried, the nature of them, and the interest manifested in them by a large concourse of idle people, who, in these busy times, ought to have something better to do.[93]

The *Herald's* implication was not the degree to which immorality prevailed in the colony, but the community's propensity for legal proceedings. As other newspapers, it expressed both bewilderment and bemusement at the readiness with which those from humbler walks of life squandered their time and money on court proceedings. In contrast to the supposed prevalence of anti-authoritarianism, the working classes appeared far from inhibited in resorting to the police and courts, at least when it served their self-interest. Thus in spite of magisterial bias, clauses under the Masters and Servants Act for the recovery of wages were widely used by labourers.[94] Legislation ostensibly intended to improve morality could also be manipulated to serve other purposes, just as prosecutions for obscene language were frequently used to carry out private vendettas.

At the same time, the community's litigiousness reflected deep-seated social rivalry, and a preoccupation with social status. The frequent trivialization by the press of petty prosecutions brought before the magistracy overlooked the same litigious tendency of the upper classes who glutted the civil courts with law suits from early settlement,[95] and who could afford to stage their wranglings in a more dramatic manner before the superior courts. Even more emphatically than cases of obscene language, threatening language and minor assaults, numerous prosecutions before the Supreme Court for libel and analogous offences indicated an intense concern with publicly demonstrating one's prestige and moral worth. The courts served as a principal forum for delineating and reinforcing the boundaries of respectability and social status which so much preoccupied the community.

Notes

1. *Sydney Gazette,* 31 October 1840. *Gazette's* emphasis.
2. Percentage is based on Papers referred to in Evidence of H. C. Wilson to the Committee on Police and Gaols, N.S.W., *V & PLC,* 1839, vol. 2, p. 371; Return of Criminal Statistics, N.S.W., *V & PLC,* 1847, vol. 1, p. 632.
3. *Atlas,* 22 March 1845, The *Atlas's* emphasis.
4. John Kennedy McLaughlin, "The Magistracy and the Supreme Court of New South Wales, 1824–1850: A Sesqui-Centenary Study", *JRAHS,* vol. 62, pt 2 (September 1976), p. 108.
5. See Douglas Hay, "Property, Authority and the Criminal Law", in Douglas Hay, Peter Linebaugh and E. P. Thompson (eds.), *Albion's Fatal Tree. Crime and Society in Eighteenth-Century England* (London, 1975), pp. 54–55.
6. See *Atlas,* 22 March 1845, 5 June 1847; *People's Advocate,* 30 June 1849, 14 July 1850; *Bathurst Free Press,* 22 March 1851; *Bell's Life,* 16 September 1854; Evidence of Alfred Stephen to the Select Committee on the State of the Magistracy, N.S.W., *V & PLA,* 1858, vol. 2, p. 121; Harris, *Settlers and Convicts,* p. 228.
7. Evidence of Henry Fysche Gisborne to the Committee on Police and Gaols, N.S.W., *V & PLC,* 1839, vol. 2, pp. 298–99.
8. [Colony of N.S.W.] 9 Geo. 4, No. 9, sec. 1, 3.
9. [Colony of N.S.W.] 4 Vic., No. 23, sec. 2, 4, 7.
10. [Colony of N.S.W.] 9 Vic., No. 27; 11 Vic., No. 9; 20 Vic., No. 28,
11. See final Report of the Select Committee on the State of the Magistracy, N.S.W., *V & PLA,* 1858, vol. 2, p. 93; Evidence of Alfred Stephen and Daniel Henry Deniehy to the Committee, pp. 122, 143; Evidence of Justice Wise to the Select Committee on the Management of the Central Police Office, N.S.W., *V & PLA,* 1862, vol. 2, p. 526.
12. Final Report of the Select Committee on the State of the Magistracy, N.S.W., *V & PLA,* 1858, vol. 2, pp. 91–93; Evidence of Robert Owen and Edward Deas Thomson to the Committee, pp. 115, 171, 175; H. M. Oxley to T. A. Murray, 6 June 1858, Appendix to the Report, p. 190.
13. Evidence of John Hubert Plunkett to the Select Committee on the State of the Magistracy, N.S.W., *V & PLA,* 1858, vol. 2, p. 141.
14. Powell, *Patrician Democrat,* p. 133.
15. Report of the Select Committee in Reference to the Unpaid Magistracy, N.S.W., *V & PLA,* 1861, vol. 1, p. 897.
16. Report of the Committee on Police and Gaols, N.S.W., *V & PLC,* 1839, vol. 2, p. 192. See also McLaughlin, "Magistracy", LL.M. thesis, p. 287.
17. Evidence of Justice Therry to the Select Committee on the State of the Magistracy, N.S.W., *V & PLA,* 1858, vol. 2, p. 110.
18. Evidence of John Street to the Committee on Police and Gaols, N.S.W., *V & PLC,* 1839, vol. 2, pp. 284-85; *SMH,* 25 June, 5 July 1850.
19. Return of Magistrates' Attendance at the Sydney Police Office, N.S.W., *V & PLC,* 1852, vol. 1, p. 912.

20. Report from the Select Committee in Reference to the Unpaid Magistracy, N.S.W. *V & PLA*, 1861, vol. 1, p. 898.

21. Currey, "Legal History of New South Wales", p. 262; King, "Problems of Police Administration", p. 58.

22. Gipps to Stanley, 9 July 1844, *HRA*, ser. 1, vol. 23, p. 672; Gipps to Gladstone, 11 June 1846, vol. 24, p. 89.

23. King, "Problems of Police Administration", p. 58; McLaughlin, "Magistracy", LL.M. thesis, pp. 321, 455–56.

24. See for example Mr Windeyer's Address, LC, *SMH*, 25 October 1843; Evidence of Robert Owen to the Select Committee on the State of the Magistracy, N.S.W., *V & PLA*, 1858, vol. 2, p. 118.

25. D. J. Macdougall, "Law", in A. C. McLeod (ed.), *The Pattern of Australian Culture* (New York, 1963), p. 269.

26. [Colony of N.S.W.] 14 Vic., No. 43, sec. 29.

27. "Vox Legis" to Editor, *Bell's Life*, 20 June 1846.

28. Since returns for 1841–45 do not include cases dealt with at Hyde Park Barracks the number of convict cases is understated. An increase in this offence category in the 1850–51 period might be attributable to the arrival of exiles, an increase in disorderly conduct cases, or the inclusion of obscene language cases which showed a marked increase in the 1850s.

29. *Australian Temperance Magazine*, 1 July 1838.

30. See Berger, *Invitation to Sociology*, p. 72.

31. Percentages and figures are based on Port Macquarie Bench Book, January-December 1831, N.S.W. SA, 4/5637; Picton (Stonequarry) Bench Books, January-December 1831, N.S.W. SA, 4/7552–7573.

32. Percentages are based on Singleton (Patrick's Plains) Bench Books, January-December 1841, N.S.W. SA, 4/5662, 7686; Picton Bench Book, January-December 1841, N.S.W. SA, 4/5627; Yass Bench Book, January-December 1841, N.S.W. SA, 4/5703; Census of New South Wales, 1841. These percentages exclude cases in which the defendant's civil condition was unknown in order to compare them with population figures. Since for some benches the number of "no information" cases was substantial, the figures must be regarded as tentative.

33. Percentages are based on Port Macquarie Bench Book, January-December 1831, N.S.W. SA, 4/5637; Picton (Stonequarry) Bench Books, January-December 1831 and 1841, N.S.W. SA, 4/7572–7573, 4/5627; Queanbeyan Deposition Book for Assigned Servants, January-December 1841, N.S.W. SA, 4/5650; Yass Bench Book, January-December 1841, N.S.W. SA, 4/5703; Patrick's Plains Bench Books, January-December 1841, N.S.W. SA, 4/5662, 7686; Muswellbrook Bench Book, January-December 1841, N.S.W. SA, 4/5601–5602.

34. *Australian*, 16 November 1842.

35. Gipps to Russell, 21 July 1841, *HRA*, ser. 1, vol. 21, p. 442; Gipps to Stanley, 1 January 1843, vol. 22, p. 456; Gipps to Glenelg, 8 October 1838, vol. 19, p. 604.

36. *SMH*, 5 May 1841.

37. LC, *SMH*, 17, 24 June 1841; Report from the Committee on the Shooting on Sunday Prevention Bill, N.S.W., *V & PLC*, 1841, pp. 269–72.

38. [Colony of N.S.W.] 5 Vic., No. 6.

39. *Bell's Life*, 31 October 1846.

40. See for example *Bathurst Free Press*, 15 October 1851; *Goulburn Herald*, 1 November 1851; *Empire*, 24 August 1852.

41. Singleton (Patrick's Plains) Bench Book, 4 March 1841, N.S.W. SA, 4/5562.

42. Picton Bench Book, 30 October 1841, N.S.W. SA, 4/5627.

43. Roe, *Quest for Authority*, pp. 191–92; Molony, *Architect of Freedom*, pp. 45–46.
44. See for example *SMH*, 5 June 1844; *Atlas*, 14 December 1844.
45. Appendix to Report from the Select Committee on the Insecurity of Life and Property, N.S.W., *V & PLC*, 1844, vol. 2, p. 387. This return excludes convict cases tried at the Hyde Park Barracks.
46. [Colony of N.S.W.] 4 Wm. IV, No. 7, sec. 22; 2 Vic., No. 2, sec. 22.
47. Camden Bench Book, 2 May 1854, N.S.W. SA, 4/5528.
48. Maitland Bench Book, 27 October 1853, N.S.W. SA, 4/5541.
49. Mudgee Bench Book, 26 May 1854, N.S.W. SA, 4/5591.
50. See for example *Sydney Illustrated News*, 11 November 1854.
51. "Constant Reader" to Editor, *SMH*, 1 February 1860.
52. *Sydney Gazette*, 29 August 1839.
53. C. Rudston Read, *What I Heard, Saw, and Did at the Australian Gold Fields* (London, 1853), p. 43.
54. Compiled from Parramatta Bench Books, 1852–54, N.S.W. SA, 4/5613–5615.
55. Compiled from Mudgee Bench Book, 1851–54, N.S.W. SA, 4/5591.
56. Compiled from Camden Bench Books, 1847–54, N.S.W. SA, 4/5527–5528.
57. Metropolitan Police Returns, N.S.W., *V & PLA*, 1858, vol. 2, p. 397; Appendix referred to in evidence of John McLerie to the Select Committee on the Condition of the Working Classes of the Metropolis, N.S.W., *V & PLA*, 1859–60, vol. 4, p. 1452.
58. [Colony of N.S.W.] 13 Vic., No. 46.
59. See for example *People's Advocate*, 5 January, 9 February 1850; *SMH*, 23 March, 17 August, 23 September 1850 (supplement); *Maitland Mercury*, 31 December 1851. Although opposition to obscene language was most vocal immediately following the Act, the bench books suggest that the movement for its suppression spread gradually, affecting different districts at different times.
60. Parramatta Bench Book, 1 June 1852, N.S.W. SA, 4/5614.
61. Mudgee Bench Book, 13 September 1850, N.S.W. SA, 4/5591.
62. [Colony of N.S.W.] 13 Vic., No. 46, sec. 7.
63. Parramatta Bench Book, 8 August 1853, N.S.W. SA, 4/5614.
64. Mudgee Bench Book, 8 December 1853, N.S.W. SA, 4/5591.
65. See *Bell's Life*, 7 September 1850; *SMH*, 4 September 1850; "Lex." to Editor, *SMH*, 12 March 1861.
66. Parramatta Bench Book, 20 May 1854, N.S.W. SA, 4/5615.
67. Parramatta Bench Book, 2 November 1852, N.S.W. SA, 4/5614.
68. Braidwood Bench Book, 7 February 1856, N.S.W. SA, 4/5517.
69. See Edward Sagarin, *The Anatomy of Dirty Words* (New York, 1962), pp. 33, 37; Paul R. Wilson, "What is Deviant Language?", in Wilson and Braithwaite (eds.), *Two Faces of Deviance*, p. 47.
70. Compiled from Parramatta Bench Book, January 1852–December 1854, N.S.W. SA, 4/5614–5615.
71. Parramatta Bench Book, 4 January 1853, N.S.W. SA, 4/5614.
72. Parramatta Bench Book, 31 January 1852, N.S.W. SA, 4/5613.
73. Parramatta Bench Book, 17 April 1852, N.S.W. SA, 4/5614.
74. Maitland Bench Book, 7 March 1854, N.S.W. SA, 4/5541.
75. Braidwood Bench Book, 12 October 1854, N.S.W. SA, 4/5517.
76. *Australian*, 26 September 1842.
77. *SMH*, 15 October 1853.
78. Parramatta Bench Book, 20 May 1850, N.S.W. SA, 4/5613.
79. *Sydney Gazette*, 2 April 1840.

80. *SMH*, 6 November 1851.
81. *SMH*, 4 June 1851.
82. Roger Lane, "Crime and Criminal Statistics in Nineteenth-Century Massachusetts", *Journal of Social History*, vol. 2 (Winter 1968), especially pp. 160–63; Lane, "Urbanization and Criminal Violence", pp. 474–76, 482–83.
83. Braidwood Bench Book, 27 January 1853, N.S.W. SA, 4/5517.
84. Parramatta Bench Book, 20 October 1853, N.S.W. SA, 4/5614.
85. Maitland Bench Book, 2 September 1853, 17 January 1854, N.S.W. SA, 4/5541.
86. Lang, *Historical Account*, vol. 2, pp. 230–31.
87. See Douglas, "Deviance and Respectability", especially p. 6.
88. *Satirist*, 11 February, 11 March 1843.
89. *SMH*, 27 February 1844.
90. *SMH*, 19 April 1843.
91. Report on the General State of the Colony, enclosed in Gipps to Russell, 14 September 1841, *HRA*, ser. 1, vol. 21, p. 510.
92. See for example Louisa Ann Meredith, *Notes and Sketches of New South Wales during A Residence in that Colony from 1839 to 1844* (London, 1844), pp. 52–53; Marjoribanks, *Travels*, pp. 22–23.
93. *SMH*, 15 October 1853.
94. See Crowley, "Working Class Conditions", pp. 296, 300; Adrian Merritt, "The Development and Application of Masters and Servants Legislation in New South Wales – 1845 to 1930" (Ph.D. thesis, Australian National University, 1981), especially pp. 208, 411–13.
95. See M. Roe, "Colonial Society in Embryo", *Historical Studies* vol. 7, no. 26 (May 1956), p. 153.

7

Drunkenness

> The question of drunkenness, so far as the mere discussion of it is concerned, is sufficiently easy. The thing is to be regarded in two aspects — as a vice, and also as a crime. If a man gets drunk quietly in his own home, he is simply vicious; if he appears drunk in the public streets, he is criminal too.[1]

As New South Wales' most common crime and "prevailing vice", drunkenness evoked more intense and persistent concern than any other offence brought before the magistracy. Few accounts of the colony written during the first half of the nineteenth century fail to comment on the prevalence of intemperance. "Drink, drink, drink", one writer concluded, was New South Wales' "universal motto".[2] Yet another temporary resident, drawing on the motif of Australia as a land of contrarieties, asserted that, "In fact, not to drink is considered a crime".[3]

While contemporaries perhaps exaggerated the extent of intemperance in New South Wales, there is little doubt that it posed a genuine social problem. A high incidence of drunkenness probably resulted from relatively favourable economic conditions and a frontier environment, rather than from a vicious population. Perceptions of intemperance as the colony's greatest social evil did not, however, rest simply on its alleged prevalence or on moral principle. Opponents of drunkenness were more inclined to emphasize its social costs in terms of the colony's economic progress, public health and criminality. In these respects, drunkenness appeared to threaten the community. At the same time, the temperance cause played a largely symbolic role in reinforcing the respectability of its adherents.

In delineating the causes of intemperance, contemporaries frequently noted the relatively prosperous condition of the working classes. In 1839 Edward Lockyer, a Parramatta magistrate, was typical in attributing drunkenness to "the abundance of money, and the ease with which it is obtained".[4] The correlation between intemperance and economic conditions was more emphatically pronounced following the discovery of gold in New South Wales. Despite initial praise of the diggers' sobriety, drunkenness and its

attendant evils was soon a staple topic of newspaper correspond-
ents.[5] Fears that drunkenness was rapidly increasing in part
stimulated the appointment of a select committee on intemperance
in 1854. Witness after witness testifying before the committee stated
their opinion that drunkenness was primarily due to the large
quantities of money in the hands of diggers, the increased rate of
wages, and the improved condition of workers.[6]

The facility with which many contemporaries connected
drunkenness with high wages is to some extent suspect. An assumption that workers squandered their money on drink was related in
some minds to notions of the moral inferiority of the lower orders.
The supposed intemperance of the working classes was also a
convenient whipping boy for frustrations concerning the difficulty
of obtaining cheap and docile labour.[7] Nevertheless, the correlation
between drunkenness and economic conditions gains support from
other evidence.

The available statistics indicate that during the depression of the
early 1840s, arrests for drunkenness, both in the district of Sydney
and in the colony as a whole declined sharply (see table 12). During
the same period apprehensions for drunkenness also made up a
diminishing proportion of all arrests by the police. Arrests for
drunkenness both numerically and proportionately reached their
lowest level in 1844, when wages fell to their lowest rate during the
period.[8] Apprehensions for drunkenness also showed a marked
increase following the discovery of gold in New South Wales, although
the upsurge in arrests was less striking than the decline which took
place during the early 1840s. A decline in arrests at the end of the
decade also coincided with the colony's waning economic fortunes.

As with criminal statistics generally, statistics for arrests of drunks
are of questionable validity. Rates of arrest were affected by changes in
the composition of New South Wales' population, as already outlined in
chapter 4. Even more than in the case of "serious" crime, the number
of arrests for drunkenness may reflect public concern more than the
actual incidence of the offence. Declining apprehensions between 1841
and 1845 were almost certainly affected by two changes in the police.
The first was a substantial reduction in the constabulary between 1841
and 1845. A second change was the appointment of a new superintendent for Sydney's police in 1841. Whereas constables previously
interfered with suspected drunkards indiscriminately, the new superintendent, William Augustus Miles, instructed constables not to take
persons into custody unless they were unable to take care of themselves
or were creating a nuisance. As Miles noted in 1844, a declining number
of arrests did not prove there was less drunkenness, although he did
consider that there was "decidedly less".[9]

Table 12. Arrests for Drunkenness in the District of Sydney and New South Wales.

| Year | Sydney | | New South Wales | | |
	Arrests	% all Arrests	Arrests	% all Arrests	Arrests per 1,000 pop.
1841	7,710	60.4	16,501	51.5	110.3
1842	4,240	49.1	10,381	47.5	64.9
1843	3,289	45.7	6,865	39.4	41.5
1844	2,443	38.7	5,179	35.2	29.9
1845	2,786	40.1	6,007	38.7	33.1
1851	3,993		6,684		33.9
1852	4,842		8,036		38.6
1853	6,018		10,307		44.6
1857	4,012	55.7			
1859	4,386	56.8	9,419		28.0
1860	5,742		10,166		28.2
1861	2,903		6,195		17.3

Source: Appendix referred to in Evidence of William Augustus Miles to the Select Committee on Police, N.S.W., *V & PLC,* 1847, vol. 2, p. 60; Criminal Statistics, N.S.W., *V & PLC,* 1847, vol. 1, p. 632; Intemperance (Criminal and Other Statistics), N.S.W., *V & PLC,* 1854, vol. 2, pp. 514–15; Metropolitan Police Returns, N.S.W., *V & PLA,* 1858, vol. 2, p. 397; Appendix referred to in evidence of John McLerie to the Select Committee on the Condition of the Working Classes of the Metropolis, N.S.W., *V & PLA,* 1859–60, vol. 2, p. 1452; N.S.W., Registrar General's Office, *Statistical Register of New South Wales,* 1859–61.

Following the gold discoveries, arrest statistics were an even more inadequate measure of the actual incidence of drunkenness. The relatively small number of arrests after 1850 compared to the early 1840s can be attributed largely to a further change in the police. Constables no longer received a portion of the fines for drunkenness, so there was less incentive to make arrests. On the goldfields a lack of prison accommodation and the distance of public houses from police offices also meant that most drunkards went unapprehended. In some cases where persons were found drunk in and around public houses, the publican was simply compelled to provide beds for them.[10]

In addition to police practices, the number of apprehensions for drunkenness depended largely on the visibility of the offence. Changes in public drinking habits might radically affect the pattern of arrests. Sydney's police magistrate, James Sheen Dowling, thought that on the basis of men charged with ill-using their wives, many men never brought before the bench for drunkenness might be "perfect sots at home".[11] It was suspected that drinking in private houses increased during the

1850s, which offers another possible explanation for the relatively small number of arrests then compared to the early 1840s.

At the same time, there is no means of determining the actual number of persons arrested for drunkenness, since one person might be apprehended a number of times. What evidence is available suggests that the statistics are swollen by multiple arrests of the same people. James Dowling estimated that there were about fifty people apprehended on charges of drunkenness as often as once a month in Sydney, and some who were dealt with sixteen or seventeen times a year.[12] Similarly, at Bathurst between 1850 and 1856, twenty people accounted for a total of 131 arrests for drunkenness.[13]

Statistics for alcohol consumption are perhaps a more adequate measure of drinking habits, and they reflect even more dramatically the colony's economic fortunes (see figure 8).[14] The amount of spirits on which duties were collected in New South Wales, both in terms of total gallons and gallons per head of population, sharply declined in the early 1840s. As in the case of arrests for drunkenness, per capita consumption of alcohol appears to have reached the lowest level in 1844. Rising spirit consumption to 1847, a decline at the end of the decade, and then a large upsurge during the gold rushes, also coincides with fluctuations in wage levels. In 1855, as wage levels began to fall, consumption sharply declined. Furthermore, comparison between spirit consumption in New South Wales and the United Kingdom gives some credence to the colony's reputation for intemperance.

Again, however, these figures are open to criticism. Increasing consumption of alcohol does not necessarily indicate increasing drunkennes. Since the figures include only spirits on which duties were collected, they take no account of spirits smuggled into the colony or illicitly distilled. Especially in the early 1840s, changes in the duties imposed on spirits may have radically affected the consumption figures. Following an increase of duties in 1840 and 1841, Governor Gipps attributed declining revenues collected on spirits largely to an increase in smuggling and illicit distillation, although he also considered drunkenness to be declining.[15] Towards the end of 1845 duties on spirits were substantially reduced, which might account for a consequent increase in spirits on which duties were paid.[16] There is also the possibility that spirits were not consumed at the time duties were collected.

Comparison between consumption figures for New South Wales and the United Kingdom raises further problems. Rates of consumption would obviously be affected by differences in population composition, and in particular by the disproportionate number of adult males in New South Wales. When consumption rates are expressed as a ratio to males, the disparity between spirit consumption in New South Wales and

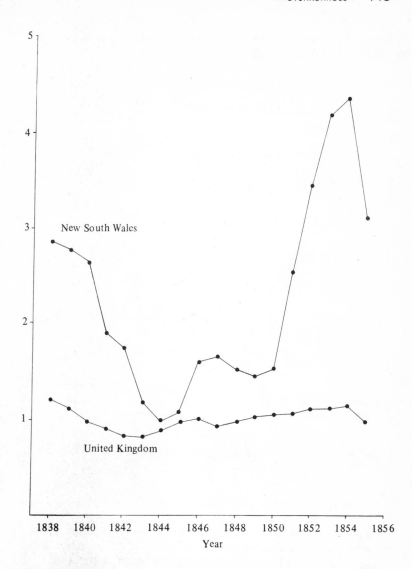

Figure 8. Per Capita Consumption of Spirits in New South Wales and the United Kingdom, 1838–55.

the United Kingdom is considerably reduced (see figure 9). During the depression years of 1844 and 1845 per capita consumption in the colony even dipped below that of Britain. The gap would probably be narrowed even more if there was sufficient information to compare statistics for marriage and age distribution.

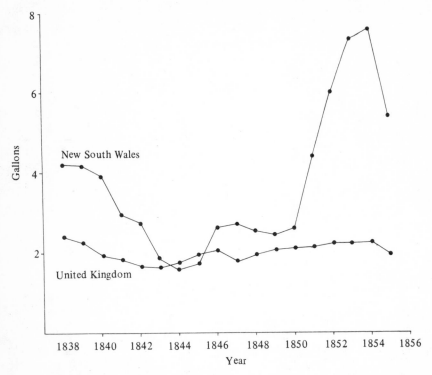

Figure 9. Per Capita Consumption of Spirits by Males in New South Wales and the United Kingdom, 1838–55.

The high level of spirit consumption in New South Wales might also be attributed in part to the relative scarcity of beer. James Macarthur considered New South Wales one of the most drunken communities in the world, but he also noted that the amount of spirit drinking was due largely to a want of beer, cider, wine and "other refreshing liquors".[17] Considered as a ratio of proof alcohol to volume, it was much more expensive to import beer than spirits. Imported beer retailed at about twice the price of the colonial product,[18] while beer brewed in the colony was for many years limited both in quantity and quality.[19] One observer in the 1850s claimed that colonial ale was not only inferior to imports, but also "decidedly unwholesome", producing unpleasant side-effects such as dysentery.[20] The distance of many localities from breweries also meant that beer was more difficult and expensive to transport than spirits.[21] More and better beer only gradually became available with improved transport, technological advances in brewing, the establishment of breweries in country towns, and the development of large urban markets.[22] In later years consumption of spirits decreased dramatically as beer consumption increased, a trend which was paralleled in the United States.[23]

Despite these objections, the close correspondence between economic conditions and statistics for arrests and alcohol consumption, supported by literary evidence, suggests a definite pattern. Indeed it appears that the relationship between economic conditions and apprehensions for drunkenness in New South Wales persists to the present.[24] The correlation between increasing drunkenness in periods of prosperity and declining intemperance in times of depression is further supported by studies of other communities.[25] Assuming that drunkenness was directly related to economic conditions, the prevalence of intemperance in New South Wales was perhaps most of all a reflection of the relative prosperity of workers.

The *Sydney Morning Herald* concluded in 1851 that thousands had "too much money", and because they did not know how to use it, they spent it on drink.[26] This was no doubt an over-simplification, but it perhaps contained an element of truth. As Brian Harrison notes, drunkenness may result not only "from squalor, overwork and underpay, but sometimes also from the possession of funds without an accompanying tradition which assures their constructive application".[27]

The relation between drinking habits and prosperity was reinforced by the conditions of a frontier community. The preponderance of males in Australia, particularly those without families placing demands on their wages, contributed to intemperance. Edward Willis, a magistrate at Geelong, considered that because of the scarcity of marriageable women in the district, "the labourers have little inducement to settle or save money; but so soon as they receive their wages, in nine cases out of ten, they gather in public houses, and there spend their earnings".[28] Another observer suggested that a lack of savings banks in the interior, and hence a means of safely keeping money, encouraged many persons to dissipate their wages on drink.[29] The lack of opportunity for labourers to acquire land was cited as a further reason why so much money was spent on alcohol.[30] More generally, there was only a limited range of alternative consumer goods within the reach of working class incomes to compete with alcoholic beverages, and few alternative places of amusement which could compete with the public house in occupying the leisure time of workers.

In part, drunkenness might be viewed as a response to the rigours of colonial life. Alcohol was in one sense an obvious and available means of escapism. Among bush workers in particular, the isolation and monotony of their employment, as well as a lack of dependants, encouraged a tradition of "work and burst".[31] In urban centres as well, the pub provided not only a focal point of social life, but often also a refuge from crude housing. The *Herald,* during the same month in which it asserted labourers had too much money, noted that because of a housing shortage five or six persons were frequently forced to share a small room intended for one person.[32] On the goldfields, public houses offered a similar resort for diggers who mainly camped in tents.[33]

At least one observer believed it was in the interest of squatters to encourage excessive drinking in order to ensure a cheap labour supply. The faster labourers wasted their money, the sooner they would return to work, and the longer they would remain servants.[34] More generally, however, the apparent correlation between drunkenness and wage levels added grist to arguments that drunkenness undermined labour discipline. Employers were urged to support the temperance cause on the grounds that sober servants were more efficient and conscientious. Governor Gipps, patron to the New South Wales Temperance Society, explained that:

> The want of labour is the cry throughout the land . . . but not withstanding this great demand for labour, how much of it is lost through drunkenness? If a man gets drunk one day in a week he does not lose one day's work only, for, in addition to the operation of getting drunk, there is the operation of getting sober, and, if in addition to the actual loss of labour in this way, they took into further consideration the loss of persons to look after drunkards — the constables, the gaolers, and the scourgers — he thought he was justified in saying that at least one-third, probably one-half, of the productive energy of the Colony is destroyed by drunkenness.[35]

Aside from its impact on the labour market, drunkenness appeared to threaten the colony's economic progress in other ways. The huge expenditure on foreign spirits, it was asserted, "swallowed down" the colony's wealth and sapped its commercial interests. Emphasis was placed on the higher taxes necessitated as support for police and prisons for dealing with drunkards. It was feared that respectable immigrants might be discouraged by colonial intemperance, while those who arrived might be rendered useless. Because of the allowance of spirit rations on board ship and the monotony of the voyage, it was believed many immigrants became drunkards at sea. Those who arrived safely might be "contaminated" by the colony's dissipated population.[36] In view of the colony's large investment in immigrants, Judge Alfred Stephen informed the New South Wales Temperance Society that it was important that they should be kept sober not only to form a virtuous population, but because "the consequences produced by the spirit trade had too frequently been the premature death of numbers of these immigrants, while others were punished for crime".[37]

As Judge Stephen's remark suggests, economic arguments against intemperance were further related to its impact on public health and the colony's crime rate. Contrary to popular notions that drink, at least in moderate quantities, was essential for health and stamina, opponents of drink emphasized its harmful physical effects. The temperance press argued that alcohol was unnecessary for strenuous labour, afforded no protection against the weather, and in fact made the body more susceptible to injury. Under a column entitled "Medical Testimony", the *Australian Temperance Magazine* provided a steady flow of extracts from medical journals, physicians' reports and other testimonials illustrating the injurious properties of alcohol. To further underscore the point, a Sydney Total Abstinence Benefit Society, formed in 1841, claimed its members were healthier than any comparable group of men who were not teetotallers.[38] Disease and insanity were among the consequences widely attributed to over-indulgence in spirits, while more oblique references were made to sexual impotence.[39]

Still more dramatic evidence concerning the deadly effects of alcohol was found in coroners' inquests, which provided the subject matter for another column in the *Australian Temperance Magazine.* According to the *Temperance Advocate,* which superseded the *Magazine* in 1840, the statistics of inquests furnished "undeniable proofs" that eight-tenths of the deaths were caused by drunkenness.[40] The statistics were a far cry from the *Advocate's* claim, but not unimpressive. Of coroners' inquests held in the district of Sydney during 1840, fifteen per cent of the deaths examined were attributed to intemperance, as were eleven per cent the following year.[41] During 1853 alone coroners' inquests and magisterial inquiries determined that 205 persons in New South Wales died from drink.[42] It was further claimed that these figures understated the proportion of deaths attributable to intemperance, since they did not include unknown deaths in distant parts of the colony, and because the juries at inquests sometimes leaned "towards the morality and good points of deceased persons".[43] Nevertheless, the figures owed much to the imprecision with which causes of death were determined. Men who fell from their drays in a drunken stupor could be legitimately claimed as victims of drunkenness, but deaths "occasioned by drink" also included a substantial proportion of suicides, and persons who died from diseases supposedly aggravated by intemperate habits.

Such drastic effects were attributed not only to excessive consumption of alcohol, but also to the types of alcohol consumed. Female convicts were believed to have a penchant for drinking their mistresses' cologne,[44] and one may suspect that more injurious substances were sometimes resorted to when liquor was unavailable. It was further believed that drinkers were sometimes drugged or "hocussed" by would-be robbers. According to one Melbourne physician, thieves had only to blow tobacco oil from a pipe into the glass of their victim in order to render them insensible, and not infrequently permanently disabled.[45] There was an even greater danger of being poisoned by a publican. It was allegedly common practice for publicans to doctor their stock in order to give it pungency after watering it down, or to stimulate the thirst of their customers. The suspected agents used to accomplish this ranged from tobacco juice to sulphuric acid.[46] Judging from the number of lunatics he met on the gold fields, Charles Henry Green, gold commissioner for New South Wales' western district, concluded that only adulterated spirits could produce "such frequent and fearful prostration of the powers of the mind".[47] There was, however, virtually no check on the practice. The law against adulterating spirits and beer was inoperative since there was no official either in Sydney or on the goldfields capable of analyzing the stock of publicans.[48]

If drink seemed to take a frightful toll on the colony's health, still greater emphasis was placed on its relation to crime. Although contemporaries demonstrated a striking lack of consistency in delineating the sources of criminality, intemperance was widely acclaimed the "parent of crime". Public houses were generally thought to be the resort of criminals, while publicans and sly-grog sellers were frequently suspected of acting as receivers for stolen goods. More importantly, it was assumed that most offenders were either intoxicated when they perpetrated crimes, or that they committed offences in order to satisfy their appetite for liquor. Highway robberies, it was claimed, were usually perpetrated either to procure the means of purchasing rum, or to steal alcohol being conveyed to the interior on drays. Burglaries were inspired by spirits, while forgeries were committed by "habitual drunkards of the more educated class". Drunkenness was believed to be the exciting cause of murders, while stimulating prostitution and sexual assaults.[49] A continuous stream of exemplary cases linking drunkenness to crime was provided by temperance newspapers. The connection between intemperance and more serious offences also provided the staple topic of addresses by judges from the bench.

The prominent role judicial officers played in the temperance movement served to reinforce the relationship between alcohol and crime. Before departing the colony in 1836, Chief Justice Francis Forbes chaired the first public meetings of the New South Wales Temperance Society.[50] Other leading proponents of temperance included Supreme Court judges James Dowling, William Burton, Alfred Stephen, William a'Beckett and Roger Therry, as well as Attorney-General John Plunkett and Sydney police magistrate Charles Windeyer. Involvement with the temperance cause may explain their preoccupation with drink as a source of crime, or it may be that their judicial experience impressed upon them the need for reform. In either case, law enforcement officials vied with each other in estimating the proportion of offences which could be attributed to drink. Chief Justice Alfred Stephen believed that three-fourths of the crimes committed sprang from drunkenness, while Attorney-General Plunkett considered the proportion to be four-fifths. John McLerie, as Sydney's superintendent of police, estimated that intemperance was the source of five-sixths of all crimes.[51]

The tendency of contemporaries to attribute almost every form of crime to drink suggests that their generalizations should be regarded with scepticism. Their beliefs were frequently reinforced by prisoners who blamed alcohol for their downfall, but such professions are also suspect. Many persons tried for offences probably pleaded they were drunk for lack of a better defence, or in order to protect their self-image.[52] Others may have believed that they would be dealt with more leniently, either by telling judges what they wanted to hear, or because they would not be considered responsible for their actions. Although legally drunkenness was not considered an excuse for crime, in instances where a defendant's intent was in question, such as cases of intent to murder or do grievous bodily harm, intoxication was taken into account as to whether persons were capable of forming any specific intent.[53] Juries might also recommend prisoners to mercy or acquit them on the grounds that they were intoxicated when they committed an offence.

While contemporaries probably over-emphasized intemperance as the "parent of crime", their observations cannot simply be dismissed. Modern research continues to suggest a strong connection, if not necessarily a causal relationship, between drunkenness and more serious offences. This was particularly the case in relation to violent crime.[54] The possible correlation between alcohol and crime suggests another way in which economic conditions may have affected New South Wales' crime rate, and in particular the incidence of violence. An analysis of Britain's criminal statistics for the nineteenth century indicates that arrests for drunkenness and assaults fluctuated in direct proportion to one another. It has been suggested that high wages and high employment led to a greater consumption of alcohol, which in turn contributed to a higher rate of violent crime.[55]

Convictions for serious assaults tried before the superior courts exhibit a trend similar to that for alcohol consumption during the mid-1840s and early 1850s, but the absence of a similar pattern for other periods makes any correlation extremely tenuous. Apprehensions for all assaults during the early 1840s, the only years for which comprehensive statistics are available, do show a trend similar to that noted in nineteenth-century Britain. Between 1841 and 1845 arrests for assault sharply declined, and as in the case of drunkenness, reached the lowest level in 1844 (see table 13). The correlation between declining arrests for drunkenness and assaults, however, is rather dubious since arrests for most offences declined during the period. Furthermore, at least in relation to Sydney, this pattern must be qualified. While there was a sharp decline in arrests for assault between 1841 and 1843, the decline was due entirely to decreasing assaults on policemen. Apprehensions for common assault actually increased during the period. The implication of the statistics is that declining arrests for drunkenness simply meant that there were fewer assaults provoked on the police.

Table 13. Arrests for Assault in New South Wales and the District of Sydney, 1841–45.

| Year | New South Wales | | Sydney | |
	Arrests for Assault	Arrests per 100,000 Pop.	Arrests for Common Assault	Arrests for Assault on Police
1841	1,688	1127.8	276	708
1842	1,302	814.3	362	289
1843	1,407	849.9	412	264
1844	1,301	750.3		
1845	1,591	876.3		

Source: Criminal Statistics, N.S.W., *V & PLC,* 1847, vol. 1, p. 632; Appendix to Select Committee on the Insecurity of Life and Property, N.S.W. *V & PLC,* 1844, vol. 2, pp. 387, 391, 395.

The frequency with which assaults were precipitated by seemingly trivial disputes is perhaps the most suggestive evidence of some correlation between drunkenness and the incidence of violence. In one case, for example, James Barlow, a labourer at Parramatta, and his wife Catherine, were accused of attacking George Ringnose with a pen knife, tongs, a bar of iron and a tomahawk. Both Ringnose and the Barlows were drunk, and the attack was apparently motivated by the victim's refusal to toss for half a pint of rum.[56] In another case, a Goulburn woman was accused of shooting her husband during an argument over a bottle of brandy.[57] Offences in which drink was actually the central issue in arguments were comparatively few, but court reports furnish abundant examples of cases in which alcohol apparently served to break down inhibitions to violence.

Drunkenness almost certainly affected the incidence of crime in another way. As Chief Justice Stephen noted, the drunkenness of victims frequently presented opportunities for crime which would not have otherwise existed.[58] One man in Sydney for example, described as "a respectably dressed tailor", was so drunk when walking along Sussex Street that he lay down, only to discover after coming to his senses that his watch was stolen.[59] In a similar case, Charles Baker was observed walking around drunk before falling against a wall with enough force to knock him unconscious. A passer-by was later seen rifling his pockets, although Baker's impression was that he had been attacked before being robbed.[60] According to the colony's attorney-general, the most frequent victims of robberies were drunken sailors or others "reeling along the street", and intoxicated settlers coming from the country with their pockets full of money.[61]

As the preceding discussion suggests, the campaign to curb drunkenness in New South Wales consisted largely of publicizing the "baneful" effects of drink. More direct, if rather fitful, approaches to suppressing intemperance were used as well. In 1839 a select committee of the Legislative Council, chaired by Anglican Bishop William Grant Broughton, recommended the prohibition of distillation in the colony. The committee considered that distillers did not make a substantial contribution to colonial agriculture, while from "a moral point of view" such a measure was desirable as a first step towards the repression of drunkenness.[62] This measure was never adopted, although as already noted, duties on spirits were increased in 1840 and 1841. Further legislation was passed to encourage the production of wine, largely with the hope that it might displace spirits as the colony's favoured beverage.[63] For the same reason, colonial breweries received official encouragement from the early 1800s.[64]

Official limitations on the number of public houses licensed was another means periodically urged for inhibiting intemperance. It was believed that a large number of pubs not only increased the temptation to drink, but also that intense competition led to nefarious practices such as selling at unlawful hours and adulterating spirits. The *Sydney Morning Herald* went so far as to claim that liberal licensing tended to drive the "more respectable" publicans out of business.[65] Nevertheless, there were few constraints on the licensing of pubs. It was thought that strict limitations on licensing encouraged sly-grog selling, and from 1830 licences were granted more or less on the "free trade" system.[66] Some observers considered that even provisions requiring applicants to furnish character references were of doubtful consequence. Chief Justice Alfred Stephen called the system "a farce", asserting that the ease with which certificates of character were obtained could "almost be termed a national vice".[67]

While some colonists emphasized the necessity of limiting the number of public houses, others pointed to the need for counter-attractions to the pub. Although disassociating itself from total abstinence societies "or any other foolery of the kind", *Bell's Life* admitted that drunkenness was "the crying evil of the day". This it believed was due largely to a lack of facilities for popular recreation, and recommended the establishment of mechanics' institutes.[68] Similarly, the *People's Advocate* stressed the need for "amusement and recreation of an innocent, intellectual, and healthful nature", such as reading rooms, libraries and other social and intellectual societies. This, it asserted, would do far more to suppress intemperance than "all the penal legislation that can be devised", while the establishment of a debating society would do more to guarantee a town's morality than twenty constables.[69] Yet another suggestion for attacking the drink problem was the improvement of housing, so that working men and women might take pride in their homes.[70]

The temperance movement itself provided an important counter-attraction to public houses, as well as a concerted campaign against drunkenness.[71] The New South Wales Temperance Society held its first public meeting in 1834, and Sydney's first Catholic temperance society was founded the following year. In 1838 a Total Abstinence Society was established. It is difficult to assess the movement in terms of its following. Statistics of membership in the societies are few, and even when available are of questionable value. Membership fluctuated wildly, while many abstainers might not be affiliated with the movement.[72] Since membership was often on a family basis, it is impossible to determine how many potential drinkers were involved.

It is equally impossible to determine what impact temperance societies had on colonial drinking habits. Although some observers attributed declining drunkenness during the early 1840s partly to the influence of the temperance movement, their views may have been over-optimistic. The fortunes of the temperance movement, like that of publicans, apparently followed economic trends. By 1841 the New South Wales Temperance Society was heavily in debt, and the following year the society's newspaper was discontinued due to its increasing insolvency and general lack of support.[73] This newspaper was followed by the *Teetotaller*, organ of the Total Abstinence Society, but it also proved a financial liability and managed to survive until September 1843 only through the gratuitous services of its editor.[74] The temperance movement seemingly began to lose momentum at the same time that drunkenness appeared to decline.

The movement's fiscal difficulties were not the only problems which limited its effectiveness. Although temperance enthusiasts claimed that they embraced all sections of the community without political or religious distinctions, the movement was torn by divisions. Some societies were accused of aggravating community antagonisms. At Illawarra the use of Irish colours and insignias by the Teetotal Society was objected to as giving offence to Protestants and endangering the public peace.[75] Temperance activities were often viewed with scepticism and jealousy by members of the clergy. Church of England minister Alfred H. Stephen told the select committee on intemperance in 1854 that he objected to temperance and teetotal societies on the grounds that if religious bodies failed to promote temperance, other societies were of little use.[76] Despite frequent protests to the contrary, there was also tension among constituents of the movement. Although a staunch supporter of the temperance cause, the *Sydney Morning Herald* on occasion ruthlessly attacked total abstainers.[77] Teetotallers themselves were divided in April 1843, when members of the Australian Total Abstinence Society seceded to form a separate society.[78]

The temperance movement frequently seemed less concerned with the reform of drunkards than with confirming the morality of its members. As in Britain and America, drinking habits served as an important indicator of social status, and it was largely through the concept of respectability that the movement made its appeal.[79] Leading light of the New South Wales Temperance Society, Reverend John Saunders, denied that it was in any sense a "drunkards' Society". Although drunkards might be reclaimed "if opportunity offered", its main purpose was to keep sober men sober.[80] There was in fact generally a sharp distinction between those brought before the police court on charges of drunkenness, and the membership of temperance societies. Their meetings were almost inevitably described in terms of "a dense mass of respectably dressed people", "well-dressed tradesmen", the "respectability" and "moral worth" of the colony, with special attention to the large proportion of ladies present. Reverend W. B. Boyce, superintendent of the Wesleyan Church in New South Wales from 1846, thought that the majority of members in temperance societies were "persons not likely to be intemperate under any circumstances".[81] The emphasis was primarily on setting an example, rather than on actual participation in reclaiming victims of drink. "Are not the labouring classes of every country", Reverend D. J. Dryer rhetorically asked a Bathurst temperance meeting, "most powerfully influenced by the example of their superiors?"[82]

One can probably assume that the drunkard was far less likely to come in contact with the temperance enthusiast than with the police. The constabulary formed the real front line against drunkenness, while the most consistent approach to intemperance was punitive. Convicts under sentence who were convicted of drunkenness could receive up to fifty lashes for a first offence, and ticket of leave holders could have their ticket revoked. For free persons the standard penalty was a fine of from five shillings to one pound, or in default of payment, a short term of solitary confinement, work on the treadmill, or imprisonment in the stocks.[83] In 1849 the maximum fine for drunkards was increased to two pounds, while the alternative sentence of solitary confinement was increased from twenty-four to forty-eight hours.[84] In the case of recidivists, the penalties could be multiplied by the number of their previous convictions. Still more stringent penalties could be awarded under the Vagrancy Act, which permitted magistrates to imprison "habitual drunkards" for up to three months.[85]

The failure of such penalties to reform drunkards was frequently admitted. Some contemporaries believed that incarceration only made offenders more hardened towards their indiscretions. In its opening number, the *Temperance Advocate* noted that compulsion and punishment seldom seemed successful, "whilst persuasion, evidence, and especially *example,* operate with a force and efficacy calculated alike to reclaim and reform".[86] Attitudes toward the punishment of drunkards, however, even among temperance supporters, were equivocal. When asked if provisions for alternative recreations might not attract persons from the public house, Chief Justice Stephen, the most vocal temperance advocate on the New South Wales bench, believed such alternatives would prove useless. He suggested instead that persons convicted of drunkenness twice within six months should serve a long prison sentence at hard labour, while women convicted of a third offence within that time should have their heads shaved.[87] The *Teetotaller* asserted that although penalties inflicted for drunkenness were more severe than anywhere else in the world, no amount of punishment would induce reform. But it recommended the still more punitive measure of total prohibition.[88]

At least during the 1830s, the necessity of treating drunkenness primarily as a crime was linked with the colony's convict origins. When two women were accused of causing the death of their children through habits of intemperance in 1839, the *Sydney Gazette* editorialized that:

> In other countries there exists a moral influence arising from the force of public opinion, which operates powerfully in restraining the spread of this devouring crime; but here the tone of society is hopelessly low, and nothing but the dread of punishment the law awards to the offender operates to prevent its regular indulgence.[89]

Long after transportation ended, however, a coercive approach to drunkenness was related to notions that a significant portion of the community was hostile to, or at least refused to accept, the ideals of temperance and abstinence. This was probably even more the case as the temperance movement lost momentum.

Both the belief that drunkenness was mainly a moral failure, and an absence of alternative medical and welfare facilities, ensured that drunkards became primarily a police problem. The idea that drunkards should be punished also owed much to perceptions of who the victims of drunkenness were. James Sheen Dowling, as Sydney's police magistrate, characterized chronic alcohol offenders as "the lowest of the low — women of the town, barrowmen, and men with no fixed abodes or habitations, who get their livings casually; many of them weak and debilitated, and who get drunk with one or a couple of glasses of spirits."[90] A similar view of drunkards was given by *Bell's Life* in its descriptions of the Police Office.

> The morning of Monday presented a more formidable array of the devotees of the bottle than ordinary. Some thirty lugubriously looking bipedal specimens of both sexes, "ranked all in a row" . . . Bleared and besotted brutes, some with noses all awry, and dim oculars, set in rainbow tinted frames; some shirtless, shoeless; some struggling to ape the garb of respectability, but all bearing the foul stamp of degradation . . . [91]

One observer later recommended that such cases should be disposed of at the Police Office before nine o'clock in the morning, so that citizens might be spared the sight of them being escorted from the watch-house to face sentencing.[92]

Perceptions of drunkards as drawn from the lowest segments of the community were in fact reinforced by discriminatory police practices. As Dowling informed the select committee on intemperance in 1854, persons who could pay the forty shilling fine for drunkenness were released from custody when sober, while others were charged publicly before the police court.[93] This effectively excluded from the public's gaze those "whose social position was above the common" and those who would be "disgraced if called before the bench".[94] Before this practice was adopted, the arrest of otherwise "respectable" citizens on charges of drunkenness was a major factor generating hostility toward the police.

As with other aspects of New South Wales' moral character, it is questionable whether the colony deserved its reputation for drunkenness. At least some persons, if the exception, believed that drunkenness was no more visible than in English towns.[95] Observers were often more impressed by the number of public houses in the colony than by the number of drunkards.[96] In this respect, however, New South Wales does not compare unfavourably with other communities. In 1821 there was one public house for every 349 inhabitants in New South Wales, while in the newly incorporated American city of Boston in 1823 there was a liquor licence for every 65 persons, excluding a large number of illegal sellers.[97] In 1841 the ratio of pubs to population in Sydney was 1:255, compared to 1:117 in Glasgow, and 1:108 in the English country town of Banbury.[98] This is not to suggest that New South Wales was particularly temperate, but simply that the number of public houses in a community, like statistics of arrests and alcohol consumption, is a dubious index of its drinking habits. In Britain, after the Beer Act of 1830, the figures were bloated by a huge number of beer houses, while in New South Wales many pubs depended on the seasonal business of bush workers.

It is likely that relatively high wages and frontier conditions in New South Wales did make drunkenness a more glaring social problem than in Britain. At the same time, concern about intemperance in the colony was heightened by fears concerning the availability and social mobility of labour, which became most apparent following the discovery of gold. More than any other crime or vice, drunkenness appeared to threaten colonists' two great obsessions — moral and material progress.

Contemporaries were by no means oblivious to the deeper implications of colonial drinking patterns in terms of New South Wales' social environment. A select committee appointed in 1859 reported that many witnesses considered intemperance to be largely an effect rather than a cause of misery and discomfort, and recommended improvements in public education, sanitation, housing, recreational facilities and more active sympathy from the upper classes. The committee could not refrain, however, from stating its belief that drunkenness was a prime source of the distress complained of, and recommending a more stringent licensing system.[99] In general, it was expedient to attribute drunkenness to personal failure or the depravity of the "lower orders". While there was an increasing awareness that treating drunkenness primarily as a crime failed to make men moral, a punitive approach continued to reflect the paucity of alternatives for ameliorating both individual drinking habits and fundamental social conditions.

Notes

1. *Illustrated Sydney News*, 25 February 1854.
2. Byrne, *Wanderings*, vol. 1, p. 136.
3. Frank Fowler, *Southern Lights and Shadows: Being Brief Notes of Three Years' Experience of Social, Literary and Political Life in Australia* (London, 1859; facsimile ed., Sydney, 1975), p. 52.
4. Evidence of Edward Lockyer to the Committee on Police and Gaols, N.S.W., *V & PLC*, 1839, vol. 2, p. 281.
5. See for example *Bathurst Free Press*, 29 July 1851; *Empire*, 23 July 1851; *Bell's Life*, 2 August 1851.
6. See for example Evidence of James Sheen Dowling, John McLerie, and

Charles Henry Green to the Select Committee on Intemperance, N.S.W., *V & PLC*, 1854, vol. 2, pp. 537, 556, 639.

7. See A. W. Martin, "Drink and Deviance in Sydney: Investigating Intemperance, 1854–5", *Historical Studies* vol. 17, no. 68 (April 1977), pp. 358–60.

8. For fluctuations in wage levels see Crowley, "Working Class Conditions", p. 243.

9. Evidence of William Augustus Miles to the Select Committee on the Insecurity of Life and Property, N.S.W., *V & PLC*, 1844, vol. 2, p. 380.

10. Evidence of Charles Henry Green to the Select Committee on the Gold Fields Management Bill, N.S.W., *V & PLC*, 1853, vol. 2, p. 450; and to the Select Committee on Intemperance, N.S.W., *V & PLC*, 1854, vol. 2, pp. 640–41.

11. Evidence of James Sheen Dowling to the Select Committee on Intemperance, N.S.W., *V & PLC*, 1854, vol. 2, p. 538.

12. Ibid., p. 537. See also Annexure referred to in Evidence of Alfred Stephen, p. 608.

13. Compiled from Bathurst Register of Convictions, 1848–77, N.S.W. SA, 7/91.

14. Analysis of spirit consumption figures for New South Wales by A. E. Dingle indicates a similar correspondence with economic conditions. There are, however, substantial variations in the consumption statistics, presumably because Dingle's figures for the period do not include domestically produced spirits. See A. E. Dingle, " 'The Truly Magnificent Thirst': An Historical Survey of Australian Drinking Habits", *Historical Studies* vol. 19, no. 75 (October 1980), especially pp. 234, 247–48.

15. Gipps to Stanley, 15 June, 23 November 1845, *HRA*, ser. 1, vol. 24, pp. 372, 627–28; Gipps to Stanley, 7 March 1842, vol. 21, p. 720.

16. [Colony of N.S.W.] 9 Vic., No. 20, sec. 1. See also *SMH*, 15 November 1849, 7 June 1851.

17. Macarthur, *New South Wales*, p. 62.

18. Prices of Provisions and Clothing, 1847–56, Returns of the Colony, "Blue Book", 1856, CO 206/98.

19. T. A. Coghlan, *Labour and Industry in Australia from the First Settlement in 1788 to the Establishment of the Commonwealth in 1901* (London, 1918; reprint ed., Melbourne, 1969), vol. 1, p. 511; T. G. Parsons, "The Limits of Technology or Why Didn't Australians Drink Colonial Beer in 1838?" *Push from the Bush* no. 4 (September 1979), especially pp. 24–26; A. E. Dingle, "Drink and Drinking in Nineteenth Century Australia: A Statistical Commentary", *Monash Papers in Economic History* no. 6 (1978), p. 9.

20. Lancelott, *Australia*, vol. 2, p. 84.

21. Dingle, " 'Truly Magnificent Thirst' ", p. 235.

22. Ibid., p. 236; Dingle, "Drink and Drinking", p. 32; Parsons, "Colonial Beer", p. 26.

23. See Joseph R. Gusfield, *Symbolic Crusade. Status Politics and the American Temperance Movement* (Urbana, 1963), p. 132.

24. Grabosky, *Sydney in Ferment*, pp. 71, 118–19, 136.

25. See Gatrell and Hadden, "Criminal Statistics", p. 365, 371; Gurr, Grabosky and Hula, *Politics of Crime*, pp. 237, 260.

26. *SMH*, 22 March 1851.

27. Brian Harrison, *Drink and the Victorians. The Temperance Question in England 1815–1872* (London, 1971), p. 393.

28. Evidence of Edward Willis to the Select Committee on Police, N.S.W., *V & PLC*, 1847, vol. 2, p. 42. See also Geoffrey Blainey, *The Tyranny of*

Distance. How Distance Shaped Australia's History (Melbourne, 1966; reprint ed., 1970), p. 171; Dingle, " 'Truly Magnificent Thirst' ", p. 240.

29. Lockhart, "Proposed System of Police", Police, N.S.W. SA, 2/674.15, pp. 10–11.
30. Byrne, *Wanderings,* vol. 1, p. 285; Harris, *Settlers and Convicts,* pp. 164, 225; Evidence of John Robertson to the Select Committee on the Condition of the Working Classes of the Metropolis, N.S.W. *V & PLA*, 1859-60, vol. 3, p. 1437.
31. Ward, *Australian Legend,* p. 100; Dingle, " 'Truly Magnificent Thirst' ", pp. 237–38.
32. *SMH,* 8 March 1851.
33. See Reverend H. A. Palmer to Col. Sec., 31 July 1854, N.S.W., *V & PLC,* 1854, vol. 2, p. 511; J. Buchanan to Under Secretary for Lands and Public Works, 1 July 1857, Copies of Letters Sent to Officers and Private Individuals from Assistant Gold Commissioner, New England, Gold Commissioners, N.S.W. SA, 4/5475.
34. James Lang, cited in Paul Edwin Leroy, "The Emancipists from Prison to Freedom: The Story of the Australian Convicts and their Descendants" (Ph.D. thesis, Ohio State University, 1960), p. 372.
35. *SMH,* 19 April 1841.
36. See for example *Australian Temperance Magazine,* 1 September 1837; *Teetotaller,* 11 January 1842; Evidence of Ernest Augustus Slade to the Select Committee on Transportation, *PP* 1837 (518), pp. 63–64; Evidence of Reverend W. M. Cowper to the Select Committee on the Condition of the Working Classes of the Metropolis, N.S.W., *V & PLA,* 1859-60, vol. 4, p. 1384; Melville, *Australia,* pp. 100–1.
37. *SMH,* 17 July 1841.
38. *Teetotaller,* 29 January, 12 March 1842.
39. See for example Lang, *Historical Account,* vol. 2, p. 157; Evidence of Richard Greenup, MD, and Francis Campbell, MD, to the Select Committee on Intemperance, N.S.W., *V & PLC,* 1854, vol. 2, pp. 545-46, 548, 551; Report from the Commissioners of Inquiry on the Lunatic Asylums of New South Wales, N.S.W., *V & PLC,* 1855, vol. 3, p. 769.
40. *Temperance Advocate,* 11 November 1840.
41. *SMH,* 17 August 1842.
42. Magisterial Inquiries and Coroners' Inquests, N.S.W., *V & PLC,* 1854, vol. 2, p. 378.
43. *Temperance Advocate,* 9 December 1840.
44. Meredith, *Notes,* p. 77; Byrne, *Wanderings,* vol. 1, p. 144.
45. *Port Phillip Gazette,* quoted in *Atlas,* 25 March 1848.
46. See for example Evidence of Francis Campbell, John McLerie, Archdeacon McEncroe and John Rutter to the Select Committee on Intemperance, N.S.W., *V & PLC,* 1854, vol. 2, pp. 552, 556, 565, 595.
47. Charles Henry Green to Col. Sec., 17 May 1854, enclosed in Fitzroy to Newcastle, 12 June 1854, *PP,* 1854–55, vol. 38, [1859], p. 185.
48. Ibid.; Evidence of John McLerie to the Select Committee on Intemperance, N.S.W., *V & PLC,* 1854, vol. 2, pp. 556, 558.
49. See for example Report from the Select Committee on Transportation *PP,* 1837–38, vol. 22 (669), p. 31; Evidence of Joseph Long Innes to the Committee on Police and Gaols, N.S.W., *V & PLC,* 1839, vol. 2, p. 418; Backhouse, *Narrative,* pp. 156–57; Evidence of Alfred Stephen to the Select Committee on Destitute Children, N.S.W., *V & PLC,* 1854, vol. 2, p. 200.
50. *Australian Temperance Magazine,* 1 July 1837. See also Roe, *Quest for Authority,* p. 168.

51. Evidence of Alfred Stephen to the Select Committee on Destitute Children, N.S.W., *V & PLC*, 1854, vol. 2, p. 200; *Temperance Advocate*, 24 March 1841; Evidence of John McLerie to the Select Committee on Intemperance, N.S.W., *V & PLC*, 1854, vol. 2, p. 560.
52. See Box, *Deviance*, pp. 230–31.
53. See J. Gordon Legge, *A Selection of Supreme Court Cases in New South Wales, from 1825 to 1862* (Sydney, 1896), vol. 1, pp. 797–99.
54. See Allen A. Bartholomew, "Alcoholism and Crime", *Australian and New Zealand Journal of Criminology* vol. 1 (1968), pp. 76–77, 82, 93–94; Timothy Cook and Celia Hensman, "Alcoholism and Crime – An Introductory Bibliography", in Wright (ed.), *Criminology Literature*, p. 86; Howard Jones, *Alcoholic Addiction. A Psycho-Social Approach to Abnormal Drinking* (London, 1963), pp. 10–11.
55. Gatrell and Hadden, "Criminal Statistics", p. 371.
56. *SMH*, 16 January 1844.
57. *SMH*, 15 January 1850 (Supplement).
58. Evidence of Alfred Stephen to the Select Committee on Destitute Children, N.S.W., *V & PLC*, 1854, vol. 2, p. 200.
59. *SMH*, 28 February 1844.
60. *SMH*, 15 April 1851.
61. LC, *Sydney Herald*, 6 July 1838.
62. Report from the Committee on Colonial Distillation, N.S.W., *V & PLC*, 1839, vol. 2, pp. 492, 494.
63. [Colony of N.S.W.] 7 Vic., No. 7; Gipps to Stanley, 1 January 1844, *HRA*, ser. 1, vol. 23, p. 284.
64. Walter S. Campbell, "The Use and Abuse of Stimulants in the Early Days of Settlement in New South Wales", *JRAHS* vol. 18, pt 2 (1932), pp. 95–96; J. M. Freeland, *The Australian Pub* (Melbourne, 1966), p. 28.
65. *SMH*, 24 April 1849.
66. See Evidence of Charles Windeyer to the Committee on Police and Gaols, N.S.W., *V & PLC*, 1839, vol. 2, p. 403; Bourke to Glenelg, 18 December 1835, *HRA*, ser. 1, vol. 18, p. 231; Evidence of Joseph Long Innes and Gilbert Elliot to the Select Committee on Police, N.S.W., *V & PLC*, 1847, vol. 2, pp. 50, 80; Evidence of Edward Deas Thomson to the Select Committee on the State of the Magistracy, N.S.W., *V & PLC*, 1858, vol. 2, p. 176.
67. Evidence of Alfred Stephen to the Select Committee on Intemperance, N.S.W., *V & PLC*, 1854, vol. 2, p. 605.
68. *Bell's Life*, 29 July 1854.
69. *People's Advocate*, 21 July 1850.
70. *SMH*, 22 March 1851.
71. See Roe, *Quest for Authority*, especially pp. 165–74, 187–90.
72. See Brian Harrison, "Drink and Sobriety in England 1815–1872: A Critical Bibliography", *International Review of Social History* vol. 12 (1967), p. 209.
73. *SMH*, 19 April 1841, 28 April 1842.
74. *Teetotaller*, 27 September 1843.
75. *SMH*, 25 November, 9 December 1841.
76. Evidence of Reverend Alfred H. Stephen to the Select Committee on Intemperance, N.S.W., *V & PLC*, 1854, vol. 2, p. 575.
77. See for example *SMH*, 6, 8, 20 July 1841.
78. See *Teetotaller*, 6, 27 September 1843.
79. See Brian Harrison, "Pubs", in H. J. Dyos and Michael Wolff (eds.), *The Victorian City: Images and Realities* (London, 1973), vol. 1, pp. 161, 181;

Gusfield, *Symbolic Crusade,* especially pp. 4, 50–51; Brian Harrison and Barrie Trinder, "Drink and Sobriety in an Early Victorian Country Town: Banbury 1830–60", *English Historical Review,* Supplement 4 (London, 1969), p. 9.

80. *Australian Temperance Magazine,* 1 July 1837. Total abstainers or teetotallers, as distinct from temperance advocates, placed greater emphasis on reclaiming drunkards.

81. Evidence of Reverend William Binnington Boyce to the Select Committee on Intemperance, N.S.W., *V & PLC,* 1854, vol. 2, p. 584.

82. *SMH,* 12 April 1842.

83. [Colony of N.S.W.] 2 Vic., No. 18, sec. 68.

84. [Colony of N.S.W.] 13 Vic., No. 29, sec. 62.

85. [Colony of N.S.W.] 6 Wm. 4, No. 6, sec. 2.

86. *Temperance Advocate,* 7 October 1841. *Advocate's* emphasis.

87. Evidence of Alfred Stephen to the Select Committee on Intemperance, N.S.W., *V & PLC,* 1854, vol. 2, p. 606. Stephen apparently changed his ideas in later years, asserting that the proper place for treating drunkards was not prison, but a sanitarium or "hospital for inebriates". Alfred Stephen, *Address on Intemperance and the Licensing System, Delivered in the Masonic Hall, on the 11th December, 1869* (Sydney, 1870), pp. 12, 20.

88. *Teetotaller,* 18 June 1842.

89. *Sydney Gazette,* 18 May 1839.

90. Evidence of James Sheen Dowling to the Select Committee on Intemperance, N.S.W., *V & PLC,* 1854, vol. 2, p. 537.

91. *Bell's Life,* 27 January 1849.

92. Evidence of Robert H. Mariner Forster to the Select Committee on the Management of the Central Police Office, N.S.W., *V & PLA,* 1862, vol. 2, p. 509.

93. Evidence of James Sheen Dowling to the Select Committee on Intemperance, N.S.W., *V & PLC,* 1854, vol. 2, p. 539.

94. Evidence of George Hill to the Select Committee on the Management of the Central Police Office, N.S.W., *V & PLA,* 1862, vol. 2, pp. 496–97.

95. See for example Charles Windeyer's Address to Temperance Society, *Australian Temperance Magazine,* 1 July 1838; Mundy, *Our Antipodes,* p. 18.

96. See for example Meredith, *Notes,* p. 54; Byrne, *Wanderings,* vol. 1, p. 136; Fowler, *Southern Lights,* pp. 51–52.

97. Freeland, *Australian Pub,* p. 204; Lane, "Urbanization and Violence", p. 475.

98. The ratio for Sydney is based on *SMH,* 1 May 1841; Census of New South Wales, 1841. The figure for Glasgow is from Marjoribanks, *Travels,* p. 152. The ratio for Banbury is given by Harrison and Trinder, "Drink in Banbury", p. 2.

99. Report from the Select Committee on the Condition of the Working Classes of the Metropolis, N.S.W., *V & PLA,* 1859–60, vol. 4, p. 1273.

8

Police and Public Order

No Public Department in the Colonial Service has been so well-abused as the Police, whether of Sydney or the Country districts, and certainly no department so richly deserves it.[1]

The police are only one mechanism for maintaining order within a network of social control, which ranges from religious organizations to recreational facilities. As the most obvious law enforcement agency, however, as well as the most immediate link between the legal system and community, the police deserve special attention. In dealing with police-public relations in nineteenth-century Australia, historians typically emphasize the existence of popular disrespect for the constabulary, and point to anti-authoritarianism inherited from a large convict and Irish population.[2] A contempt for the police, however, was not unique to Australia. Even in Britain resistance to the police continued well into the nineteenth century. Pre-modern police forces were in general staffed by constables of poor quality in order to minimize expense.[3] Low recruitment standards and, more importantly, the interaction of New South Wales' constabulary with the community, provide ample explanation of its unpopularity without reference to inherent attitudes. Reform of the police, nevertheless, did not result so much from public animosity as from elite fears concerning a breakdown in public order. Again, this was a development which paralleled that in many other communities.

The fragmentary evidence available suggests that the Sydney force was composed largely of men drawn from those groups which are traditionally regarded as most antithetical to the police. — Irish and convicts. About seventy per cent of Sydney's police were originally from Ireland. Until at least 1840 police were also recruited largely from ex-convicts and ticket of leave holders, although the proportion appears to have quickly diminished after that date.[4] In country districts police with convict backgrounds may have made up a larger and more lasting proportion of the constabulary, particularly since ex-convicts constituted a larger proportion of the rural population. During the 1830s prisoners holding tickets of leave were frequently recruited as constables not only because of the difficulty in obtaining "proper persons", but because they were considered "more under control than free men".[5]

Whether the recruitment of a large percentage of the police from marginal groups in the community contributed toward anti-authoritarianism or not is debatable. Given sensitivity to the colony's origins, it is possible that the employment of ex-convict constables contributed to popular animosity. But it is perhaps more important to emphasize that constables were drawn largely from the least employable in the community. At least from the mid-1840s, it also appears that ex-soldiers formed a much larger proportion of the constabulary than did ex-convicts.[6]

Both the poor quality of constables and the unattractiveness of police work was reflected in the high rate of dismissal and resignation. Between 1844 and June 1847 eighty-two men were dismissed from the Sydney force, and within the same period another eighty-three men resigned.[7] During 1854 seventy men resigned from the Sydney police, two absconded, and another seventy-two were dismissed, when the entire force consisted of 179 men.[8] According to Henry Croasdaile Wilson, who superintended Sydney's force from 1833 to 1839, a constable's weaknesses were easily exploited. "As soon as they are sworn, every temptation is open to them for the gratification of their tastes free of expense — liquor, women, and bribes are employed to corrupt them, and many are corrupted".[9] Liquor in particular took a heavy toll. Of the seventy-two men dismissed from Sydney's constabulary during 1854, fifty-four were discharged for drunkenness and related offences.[10] In fact, this figure probably understates the extent of the problem, since many constables were dismissed only after repeated offences, or when drunkenness was compounded by another breach of discipline. Police were also charged with more serious offences. Cases in which policemen allegedly robbed prisoners in their custody were not uncommon, at least until the early 1840s.[11]

The public image of the police was rarely improved by their leaders. Henry Wilson, who noted the inducements to corruption to which policemen were liable, was dismissed himself following a rash of complaints and formal inquiries into his character. Among other charges, it was proved to the satisfaction of Governor Gipps and the Executive Council that Wilson employed constables in his private service, frequently in livery. He also appeared guilty of appropriating bread from the Police Office for feeding his dogs and poultry, although Wilson insisted the bread, an estimated fourteen pounds a day, was delivered to his home without his knowledge.[12] William Augustus Miles, who superintended Sydney's police from September 1841, was forced from office in 1848 following repeated charges of corruption and accusations of being drunk on duty.[13] His successor, Joseph Long

Innes, was dismissed the following year after disclosures by a select committee on Darlinghurst Gaol where he served as visiting magistrate. It was demonstrated that Innes employed prisoners and turnkeys from Darlinghurst in his private service, and his prevarication to the committee alone was sufficient grounds for his dismissal from all government posts.[14] The new superintendent, Edward Denny Day, was distinguished as a rural police magistrate for leading the capture of the Myall Creek murderers and the "Jewboy" bushranging gang. He was dismissed in less than a year for being intoxicated while on duty.[15]

It is more difficult to generalize concerning the quality of constables in rural areas. Police in Campbell Town were considered satisfactory, and were praised by the local magistracy for their "general good conduct" and long service. All of the force's seven members in 1847 had served at least four years.[16] The Campbell Town police, however, may well have been exceptional. Charles Lockhart, a Cooma magistrate, characterized rural constables generally as "quite unfit". He believed many, "Very many!", were confirmed drunkards, while many others were infirm, old and destitute men appointed out of pseudo charity.[17]

As in the case of the Sydney force, there was a high rate of dismissal. During 1837, 95 men were dismissed from the rural constabulary, out of a total strength of 263.[18] While in Sydney constables were summarily dismissed by the superintendent, the matter rested with the magistracy in country areas. As a result, there was a good deal of latitude between districts, which may help account for the longevity of Campbell Town's constables. Policemen found drunk on duty were often only fined like other drunkards. At Mudgee, for example, constable Terrence O'Donnell was dismissed from the force only after he was brought before the bench for drunkenness four times in the space of a year.[19] On the other hand, William Moore was expelled from Patrick's Plains force simply for using abusive language to a publican's wife.[20] The readiness or reluctance of JPs to dismiss police probably depended to some extent on how easily the police could be replaced.

The stereotyped rural policeman, embodied in Alexander Harris's fictional character Harry Grimsby, was too indolent and too fond of a debauched life to work at any other occupation.[21] Whether the police generally conformed to this stereotype, of course, is questionable. But this was frequently their image as projected in the press. Police at Bathurst, for example, were portrayed as spending their time "lounging about public-houses, and in doing worse". Their "immoral lives and habits" were denounced as "really disgraceful".[22] Goulburn's constabulary was similarly portrayed as consisting of "idlers" and "loiterers", who acted as "a source of annoyance to the respectable portion of the inhabitants".[23] Constables were often described with the same sarcasm generally reserved for drunkards and other supposed reprobates. *Bell's Life,* in reference to Newcastle's lock-up keeper, found it most disgusting to see a man holding so mean a situation as he now holds, although he but a short time back filled the important office of Boots in one of the Newcastle inns, and was pew opener and grave digger to the parish church, yet he now struts forth with princely grandeur, snuffing the breeze of the morning with a gold chain about his neck . . . again he is seen attired in the same glittering and ornamental manner mounted on his high-spirited steed, enjoying the luxury of an Havanah, sometimes setting at defiance all laws for the suppression of furious driving. Again he is seen with his young and enchanting wife, noted for her meekness, charity, and piety, taking an evening's drive in a neatly-finished jaunting-car, cutting and dashing in a more than ducal style; 'tis most refreshing to catch the beautiful scent emanating from the vehicle as it passes, which often acts as a restorative to many a way-worn traveller upon the road-side, who often takes the fellow to be the most important personage in the town, and therefore touches his hat with the most profound respect.[24]

Chief constables, who commanded ordinary constables under the supervision of the magistracy, were a special object of contempt. More often than not, they were characterized as petty tyrants, whose only claim to office was their superior ignorance.[25]

As continually noted by colonial officials and the press, low rates of pay acted as the main impediment to recruiting "respectable and efficient men" as police. Nevertheless, both for the sake of economy, and as a protest against the home government's transfer of the expense to the colonial revenue, the Legislative Council was determined to keep police costs to a minimum. The low wages offered to police were made even less attractive by the irregular intervals at which they were paid in some districts.[26] Nor did constables receive any additional compensation for frequently travelling great distances to serve subpoenas and escort prisoners.[27] The only "fringe benefit" was a small clothing allowance. Even the police uniform, however, was believed to deter recruits. Modelled on those worn by the London constabulary, the coats and hats provided were considered too heavy for New South Wales' climate.[28]

The low wages of the police were partly rationalized on the basis that they might supplement their incomes by earning rewards, but this system created problems in itself. It was complained that the police refused to act unless there was some prospect of remuneration. Even the *Sydney Morning Herald,* which confessed a reluctance to criticize the police, believed there was reason to suppose that the police did not exert themselves to capture bushrangers unless a reward was offered.[29] At the same time, the offer of rewards could inspire interference with or the arrest of innocent people.

This was especially the case under the Bushranging Act, first enacted in 1834 and renewed until it was allowed to expire in December 1853.[30] Under the Act any person suspected of being a runaway convict could be apprehended by the police, and either detained until he proved his freedom, or forwarded to Sydney to be identified. The apprehension of some of the colony's leading personages as suspected runaways, including Chief Justices Francis Forbes and James Dowling, is a common anecdote in contemporary accounts. The Act posed a more serious threat to travelling labourers, particularly as New South Wales' free population increased.[31] Arrests under the Act seemed all the more galling since they were frequently made by police who were themselves ticket of leave holders or ex-convicts. Although it was sometimes believed that apprehensions were made out of pure spite, constables were probably motivated by the offer of government rewards, either in the form of money or a remittance of sentence.

Even more obnoxious was the system in which informing constables received a portion of the fines for certain offences. It was suggested that the police devoted their time dealing with minor offences which involved fines, while neglecting more serious crimes.[32] More importantly perhaps, the system inspired the apprehension of normally law-abiding people for petty offences. Since it was in the direct economic interest of police to obtain convictions, their evidence was rendered suspect, while they were open to charges of entrapment. Police were accused of actively encouraging illicit stills in order to gain a reward for their seizure.[33] Many charges of assault made by constables were considered to be "of the most frivolous description".[34] Apprehensions for drunkenness, which accounted for the largest proportion of arrests by the police, were particularly objectionable. According to the *Heads of the People*, the police had so little legitimate business to look after that they turned their attention to other pursuits, and in particular, to offences through which they might secure a portion of the fines.[35]

It was consistently urged, both by police officials and by the public, that the pay of the police should be increased, while abolishing the system of rewards and fines altogether. Under Acts passed in 1849 and 1850 police no longer received a portion of the fines for drunkenness, while fines for other offences went to a "police reward fund" rather than to the informing constable.[36] Nevertheless, provisions which excluded police from receiving a portion of penalties were to some extent circumvented. The Gold Police, who were not under the jurisdiction of the Police Act, still received a share of fines for informations against sly-grog selling. Even ordinary police might have a friend file an information in order to collect rewards.[37]

Resentment against the constabulary was manifest in the numerous assaults on policemen which took place and their frequent harassment by crowds. Resistance to police interference, particularly with recreational activities, sometimes erupted into spontaneous riots. In October 1841, crowds led by men from the *HMS Favourite* attacked police watch-houses two nights in succession following the rumoured arrest of some sailors.[38] An attempt by a constable to interfere with disorderly sailors in 1845 resulted in another attack on a station house, in which seven constables were severely injured.[39] Prisoners were liberated from a watch-house in 1848 by a crowd following the arrest of some boys charged with setting off fireworks in the streets.[40] During 1851 two disturbances approaching riot proportions were precipitated by police action. The first occurred on the evening of Anniversary Day when constables attempted to clear a public house at Circular Quay. Later in the year a series of attacks were made on watch-houses following the arrest of some man-of-war sailors charged with drunkenness and attending church services dressed in women's clothing.[41]

Resentment against police interference was a feature of other communities during the period. But in New South Wales the comparatively large numbers of police, as well as their habit of closely regulating the personal conduct of convicts, probably increased the potential for conflict with citizens. In 1846, based on available returns, the average ratio of country police to inhabitants in England was 1:2700. At about the same time, 1848, the ratio of police to population was less than 1:1000 in sixty-five per cent of England's boroughs.[42] By comparison the ratio of police to population in New South Wales' settled districts in 1846, excluding Sydney and exclusive of the colony's specialized forces, was 1:344.[43]

In general, the character and performance of the colony's more specialized police forces were regarded little more favourably than the regular constabulary. There were frequent complaints against the Water Police, particularly in relation to their "overbearing conduct" towards ship's officers.[44] Ordinary seamen had even more reason to resent the force. Under the Water Police Act of 1840, seamen on shore after nine o'clock without a pass were liable to a fine, or in default of payment up to three days imprisonment. The same Act provided that seamen guilty of insubordination or refusing to work could be imprisoned at hard labour for up to three months.[45] The *Australian* expressed fears that the oppressive nature of the Act, as well as police interference with sailors on shore leave, might even result in ships refitting at other ports.[46] Although the harshest provisions of the Act were repealed in 1843,[47] it is doubtful whether relations between seamen and police significantly improved.

The composition of the Border Police was particularly open to objection, since the force was composed largely of convicts under sentence. As initially formed, the force was staffed mainly by soldiers transported for desertion.[48] By the mid-1840s, convicts and ticket of leave holders continued to make up about half the Border Police.[49] Such a force, critics asserted, was inappropriate in light of the colony's increasing free population.[50] What was probably more objectionable, however, was the mode of its support. Under the Border Police Act of 1839, the force was financed by an assessment on livestock beyond the boundaries of location. Instead of providing protection, squatters claimed that the police devoted their energies almost entirely to collecting taxes for their own maintenance.[51] Further resentment was fostered by the autocratic powers vested in commissioners of crown lands, which according to S. H. Roberts, made their unpopularity pre-destined. The variety of problems dealt with, the lack of legal precedents, and the difficulty of appealing against their decisions, tended to make the commissioners appear arbitrary and despotic.[52]

The Native Police proved more popular than the Border Police, probably because their activities were mainly limited to suppressing Aborigines. It was also the colony's least expensive force. Aboriginal troopers were initially unpaid, and in 1850 received only three pence a day plus rations.[53] Nevertheless, the force was not without its problems. Squatters resented the recruitment of Aboriginal labourers to act as police, while workers believed that they tended to lower wages.[54] Following a long period of complaints by residents, magistrates and finally officers of the corps, a board of inquiry was appointed in September 1854 to investigate the general management of the Native Police. Suspicions that its commandant, Frederick Walker, was of intemperate habits seemed confirmed when he appeared before the board "in a state of intoxication, bordering on stupidity".[55] The accounts of the force were found in a similar state of confusion, with large arrears due in back pay. As a result, Walker was relieved of command in January 1855.[56] After Walker's dismissal the force was reduced, and criticized for its relative inefficiency, improper distribution and general deterioration in discipline.[57]

The most important auxiliary police force, both in terms of its numbers and duties, was the Mounted Police. Troopers for the Mounted Police were selected from the regiments by their commanding officers, who were hardly inclined to send their best men. The commandant of the force, Major Jeffrey Nicholson, characterized his men generally as "only a tolerable average".[58] Turnovers in the Mounted Police were less frequent than in the regular constabulary,[59] but this probably reflects in part the fact that mounted policemen could not simply resign. One may also suspect that they were less readily dismissed. Edward Warrington, who joined the Mounted Police in October 1838, was punished for no less than twenty breaches of discipline before his record ended in October 1849.[60] As with Sydney's constabulary, the most common offence leading to disciplinary action was drunkenness.[61] Nevertheless, the colonial secretary was probably justified in claiming that mounted policemen were in general better behaved than the regular constabulary.[62] Warrington held the dubious distinction of being punished for more offences than any other member of the force, and as his record indicates, the incidence of misconduct was inflated by offences committed by the same men.

Criticism of the Mounted Police was directed mainly at the force's paramilitary organization, its alleged brutality in dealing with suspected criminals, and its contempt for civil authorities.[63] As with the regular constabulary, it was complained in some districts that Mounted Police refused to pursue bushrangers until they were "worth catching".[64] To some extent the protective function of the Mounted Police was also perverted by local magistrates. Contrary to official intentions, troopers were frequently employed in the duties of ordinary constables, serving subpoenas and escorting prisoners.[65] Until an order of 1848 prohibited the practice, troopers at some stations were sent on long journeys to apprehend absconding servants, leaving districts unprotected.[66]

The efficiency of the Mounted Police was further undermined by lack of co-operation from the regular constabulary. Commandant Jeffrey Nicholson complained that the force encountered great difficulty in obtaining early intelligence of robberies and other crimes. Rural constables often withheld information until their own efforts failed, in hopes of gaining any credit or reward for the capture of offenders. By the time the Mounted Police heard of a crime, it was often too late to apprehend any suspects.[67]

The lack of communication and co-operation between rural constables and the Mounted Police was symptomatic of relations between all of the colony's forces. Along with the poor quality of constables recruited, the fragmented organization of the police was long considered a major obstacle to efficiency. Sydney police magistrate Charles Windeyer asserted in 1839 that persons who committed offences in the city and then moved to the remote interior were as safe as if they had left the colony.[68] The police of neighbouring districts apparently not only failed to co-operate, but exhibited an "unseemly jealousy".[69]

As in many other communities, the impetus for police reform in New South Wales came largely from fears of public disorder.[70] A riot on New Year's Day 1850 was the principal catalyst which changed desultory criticism of the police into vigorous agitation for their reform. The disturbance apparently began with a brawl between some off-duty soldiers and merchant seamen. A crowd estimated at three to four hundred gradually assembled, consisting largely of boys, which smashed windows along Pitt, George and Elizabeth Streets, tore down fences at one street corner, and set fire to a watch-box at the racecourse. In Pitt Street one of the alleged ringleaders encouraged stone throwing by waving his hat over his head, cocking one leg, and shouting "Hurrah! Go it, boys!". There was no pillaging, although a publican on George Street testified that some of the rioters came to his door demanding a bottle of rum. He eventually gave them the liquor, and one of the crowd waved a stick over his head, crying "no stones here lads", before they moved on to the next door.[71]

One of the most alarming features of the riot was the youth of many participants, who included the sons of "respectable citizens". Of sixteen persons apprehended by the police, seven were reported to be under fifteen years of age. Still more galling was the absence of any apparent cause for the riot other than "the pure love of mischief".[72] The *Herald* asserted that:

> In Europe and America, when the masses break out into violence, the passions have been inflamed by some real or imaginary wrong. ... But the riot which on New Year's morning spread terror and dismay amongst so many of the peaceful families of Sydney, was altogether without provocation or pretext of any kind. . . . Sydney is threatened with riots of a perfectly novel genus. We have nothing to fear from mobs goaded to madness by starvation, nor from mobs fired with political disaffection. But the experience of the last few years shows that we have very much to fear from mobs of giddy boys, who love rioting for rioting's sake, and with whom midnight violence is an amusing pastime.[73]

Following the riot, public meetings were held which protested against the inefficiency of the police, and pressed for measures to ensure the security of citizens' lives and property.[74] A similar campaign was waged by the press. In a series of leading articles, the *Sydney Morning Herald* underlined the inadequacies of the constabulary, while alluding to the dangers posed by the "mob".[75] Protests in Sydney were reinforced by a flurry of agitation in country areas. To some extent residents in country districts probably took their cue from the metropolis in pressing for greater police protection. Concern was mainly motivated, however, by plans to abolish the Mounted Police. Between 1849 and 1850 the force was reduced from 131 men to only thirty-five, before it was disbanded completely at the end of the year.[76] The disbandment was regretted by many persons who considered the force was foolishly sacrificed for economy. Anne Deas Thomson wrote to her father that it seemed "perfect nonsense doing away with such a very efficient body of men", and that some would no doubt feel their loss "when the winter nights come on and bushranging begins again".[77]

There was nothing novel in the report of the select committee of the Legislative Council appointed to investigate the police in the wake of popular agitation. For the most part, it simply echoed the conclusions drawn by previous select committees on police in 1835, 1839 and

1847. Unlike previous committees, however, its recommendations were acted upon. The select committee, as well as a board of inquiry appointed to investigate the New Year's riot, recommended a generous augmentation of the Sydney constabulary. Following their reports twenty-four ordinary constables were added to the city force, the first increase since the "crime wave" of 1844. A Horse Patrol was also formed, consisting of sixteen men, primarily to facilitate crowd control. The most important innovation which followed the inquiries was the introduction of a centralized form of control over the colony's various police forces.[78] Under the Colonial Police Act of 1850 the governor was authorized to appoint an inspector-general of police for New South Wales, and up to six provincial inspectors.[79]

In general, these reforms failed to silence criticism of the police, and their impact was to prove transitory. The appointment of inspectors at high salaries, while ignoring the pay of ordinary constables, was denounced as flagrant jobbery.[80] The system of general superintendence over the police remained in effect for only two years, and even during that time was operative in only a few districts.[81]

Inadequate administrative machinery, the poor choice of provincial inspectors, and lack of co-operation from magistrates, were considered the major reasons for the system's failure.[82] Because of their extensive districts, it was thought that not enough officers were appointed to effectively supervise the police.[83] At the same time, some of the officers appointed were considered less than satisfactory. William Spain, who arrived in New South Wales only a short time before to practise as a lawyer, became the colony's first inspector-general of police in January 1851. His appointment was initially criticized on the grounds that better qualified colonists were passed over for "a comparative stranger".[84] Lack of public and government confidence led Spain to resign later the same year.[85] The provincial inspectors appointed included Edward Denny Day, despite his recent dismissal as supe-intendent of Sydney's force for drunkenness.[86] The inspector of Bathurst, Captain Wentworth, was described as a sexagenarian who knew absolutely nothing about the district.[87] The efficiency of the police was further hindered by the country magistracy, who were inclined to view the system as an infringement on their authority.

In 1852 a select committee amended the Police Regulation Bill limiting control of the inspector-general to the Sydney police and Road Patrols. Although the inspector-general's office remained a channel of communication for the colony's various forces, control of the constabulary in each district was returned to local JPs.[88] A centralized system of police in New South Wales was not permanently re-established until 1862.[89] While changes in 1850 were inspired largely by the New Year's Day riot, reorganization of the police a decade later was largely in response to riots against the Chinese, as well as a new outbreak of bush-ranging.

In addition to placing the police under centralized control, the Police Regulation Act of 1850 established more stringent guidelines for the appointment of constables. Police were to be able bodied, under forty years of age, literate, and with "a good character for honesty fidelity and activity".[90] But significant improvement in the quality of constables was probably precluded by the discovery of gold in 1851. As before 1850, the major obstacle to obtaining desirable men to act as police was insufficient pay. Charles Henry Green, gold commissioner for the western district, pointed out that as long as police pay was "not equal to what a labouring man can earn within two or three hundred yards of them, they will not be satisfied".[91] William Colburn Mayne, who was appointed inspector-general of police following Spain's resign-ation, considered that the high rate of resignations from the police was less the result of men being lured to the goldfields, than of the pressure of increasing rents and prices.[92]

One means repeatedly urged for improving the quality and efficiency of the police was to recruit constables in the United Kingdom. Under the pressure of large scale resignations, steps for recruiting men acting as constables in Britain, as well as "other eligible persons", to serve in the colonial force were finally taken with the Police Recruiting Act of 1853. Under the Act recruits were to be given free passage to the colony with their families. They were engaged to serve in the police for a minimum of three years, and persons deserting or guilty of mis-conduct were liable to imprisonment with hard labour for up to six months, as well as forfeiture of all wages due.[93]

Although it was hoped to engage one hundred and fifty men from the Dublin and London constabularies to serve in Sydney, difficulties were encountered in getting recruits. Commissioners of the Dublin Metropolitan Police objected to sending volunteers to New South Wales, where they would receive increased pay, on the grounds that it would undermine the morale of an already understaffed Irish constab-ulary.[94] At the same time, volunteers from the London force were far less numerous than expected.[95] During 1855 two detachments of men from England arrived to serve on Sydney's police force. A little over one-third of the men had served as police in England. The remainder were mostly labourers, although a wide range of former occupations were also represented.[96]

According to police magistrate James Dowling, police from England improved the tone of the force and "commanded respect for it".[97] Compared to other men appointed constables in Sydney during 1855, the imported recruits did appear to represent an improvement. Of ninety men appointed in the colony, thirty-one were dismissed within a year of their appointment, and another twenty-four resigned. A total of 118 men arrived from England to act as police during the same period. Only one was dismissed during his first year of service, although eleven more men were dismissed within two years of their appointment. They were prohibited from resigning before three years service, but seventeen men absconded during their first year on the force.[98]

The low dismissal rate of English recruits may reflect a reluctance to dismiss men who represented an investment. At the same time, the lower rate of resignations was perhaps indicative of the fact that a larger proportion were committed to police work as a career. But even if it is assumed they raised the tone of the constabulary, their acceptance by the community is questionable. Critics of the plan noted that colonial recruits were more amenable to local opinion, and more likely to possess public confidence than imported policemen. As a result, a better force, if decently paid, could be raised in the colony than Britain.[99] In the long term, a tightened labour market following the gold rushes, and more attractive service conditions, were the most important changes in improving the quality of constables.[100]

On the goldfields, the problem was not only providing enough police, but not too many. As one gold commissioner indicated, the police had to be sufficient to afford protection, "but not in such numbers as to offend the prejudices of any".[101] Particularly where the Gold Police exceeded their authority, they might become regarded as more a nuisance than a protection. Russel Ward suggests that a hatred for the police was perhaps "the most prominent feature of the diggers' ethos".[102]

On the other hand, oppression by the Gold Police is easily exaggerated. Some of the more obnoxious gold regulations were either easily circumvented or not enforced. One of the most objectionable regulations required that licences be issued only to persons producing a certificate of discharge from their last employment, or who could prove to the satisfaction of the commissioners that they were not improperly absent from hired service. But this regulation was considered a dead letter. Miners were rarely required to give an account of themselves, while forged discharges could be obtained at any public house for the price of a drink. Similarly, regulations requiring non-British subjects to pay a double licence fee were easily evaded. Americans were difficult to distinguish, and could claim to be Englishmen. Chinamen could insist they came from the British possession of Hong Kong. All "dark men" and Dutchmen reportedly claimed to come from the Cape of Good Hope, and Frenchmen could maintain they were from Canada.[103]

Contemporary descriptions of the Gold Police as corrupt, overbearing and inefficient, generally refer to Victoria. There is at least some evidence which suggests the police in New South Wales conducted themselves better. William Johnson, a commissioner for the western district, characterized the Gold Police as "a steady and efficient body", and considered that communication and co-operation between police on the various goldfields was an improvement over most other parts of the colony. According to Johnson, the orderly state of the diggings owed as much to police supervision "as to any abstract love of order" among the miners.[104] In general, the all-important gold commissioners were believed popular with the diggers.[105] When a mass disturbance seemed imminent on the Turon in February 1853, the tact of the gold commissioners was largely credited with averting an armed confrontation.[106] By regulating disputed claims, the commissioners also contained what was potentially a major source of violence.[107]

The importance of the police in maintaining order was most apparent in their absence. Despite denunciations of Californian "lynch law", diggers in New South Wales were not above resorting to vigilante action where police protection appeared inadequate. Before the arrival of police at the Ophir gold field, a man caught robbing his mate was run down by diggers and severely kicked.[108] Residents at Maitland Point on the Turon formed a vigilance association in 1851, which while acting in conjunction with the police, apparently lacked discrimination in serving out punishments.[109] Diggers at Stoney Creek, where in 1856 there was only one commissioner and two police for the regulation of two to three thousand inhabitants, also formed a vigilance committee, and on one occasion reportedly came close to hanging a thief.[110] It was later reported that two men were narrowly saved from lynching on the Kiandra gold fields in 1860.[111] That such incidents were not more frequent undoubtedly owed much to a police presence, which helps account for the stark contrast to America where there were no less than 119 documented vigilante killings between 1850 and 1859.[112]

Larger disturbances also usually took place when constituted authority was at its weakest. The first attack on Chinese in New South Wales, at the Rocky River gold field in September 1856, occurred only after fruitless requests for more men by the resident gold commissioner. At the time of the "collision", four policemen were responsible for the control of about 3,000 persons. Although the population was serviced by sixteen public houses, it was not until the following year that there was a lock-up for detaining offenders, or a court house to try them in.[113]

The more infamous anti-Chinese riots at Lambing Flat occurred as well when the machinery for social control appeared relatively ineffectual.[114] It was not until nine months after the discovery of gold at Lambing Flat in March 1860 that the area was proclaimed a goldfield and a commissioner appointed. The new commissioner, David Dickson, was formerly a sub-commissioner at Kiandra, where he was allegedly renowned for his arrogance in dealing with miners.[115] The police camp was initially located twelve miles from the diggings, and the construction of police quarters and a lock-up was only sanctioned in February 1861.[116] Although the arrival of a strong force of police and troops on the goldfield in March 1861 temporarily quelled disturbances, they were withdrawn in May amid racial tension and against the advice of resident officials. The small number of police left proved powerless to prevent a subsequent conflict between Chinese and Europeans at Native Dog Creek, a field which was neglected by the authorities even though violence was anticipated there.[117] The riots culminated with an attack on the police camp itself in July 1861, while order was quickly restored when a strong force was again deployed to the field.

Ultimately, levels of collective violence on the goldfields depended on colonists' frustrations (whether attributed to the economy, government or Chinese) on the one hand, and the ability of authorities either to contain or placate those frustrations on the other. At the same time, disorders at Lambing Flat shared some of the "issueless" characteristics of the 1850 New Year's Day riot. The fact that four anti-Chinese riots took place on a Sunday suggests some correlation with miners' leisure activity.[118] Chinese camps were not only destroyed but looted. Following an attack on Chinese at Back Creek and Blackguard Gully in June 1861, one gold commissioner reported that "the object of the Rioters seemed to be more for the sake of the plunder to be obtained than from repugnance to the Chinese".[119] The procession of banners and flags added a festive air to "roll ups", while at least four riots were accompanied by band music. In this respect, the Lambing Flat riots combined aspects of disorders which were largely spontaneous, communal or recreational, with the use of force to achieve articulated objectives.

There was some attempt to credit the disturbances at Lambing Flat to the influence of the "criminal class". The *Sydney Morning Herald* insisted that persons responsible for attacks on the Chinese were not to be confused with the digging population.

> They are the vendors of illicit drink — the receivers of stolen goods — the plotters of sticking-up and gold robberies — and generally the main strength and stay of all schemes for the demoralization of the people. A popular grievance therefore is to them a centre of operation, and assuming the character of reformers they disguise their latent purpose and give something like eclat to their career of crime.[120]

This view received some support from men on the spot. Assistant-Commissioner J. H. Griffin, noting the harvest of plunder reaped by "roll ups", asserted that there were more "scoundrels" at Lambing Flat than he had witnessed anywhere else in the colony since he joined the

Gold Police in 1852.[121] Historians as well have tacitly accepted a causal relationship between rioting and a concentration of criminals on the gold field.

Whether criminals played an instrumental part in the Lambing Flat riots seems doubtful. It is difficult to rationalize their alleged role with the fact that an attack on Chinese in December 1860 was immediately preceded by the burning of sly-grog shanties and other supposed criminal haunts on the gold field. Captain Henry Zouch, who commanded the Southern Road Patrol, contended that shanty keepers instigated the attack on the Chinese to discredit those who destoyed their property.[122] This seems a rather lame explanation at best, and typically imputes a degree of organization to law-breakers which probably did not exist. As D. L. Carrington points out, it also seems unlikely that riots involving several thousand people did not include a substantial proportion of genuine diggers.[123] Nor is there any reason to assume that looting which accompanied the riots was the work of "criminals" rather than of diggers taking an opportunity to obtain goods with little chance of being prosecuted. Attributing disorders to the "criminal class" was a standard response to riots. It was believed that thieves and pickpockets encouraged the New Year's Day riot of 1850 as a cover for their nefarious activities, while the *Herald* stated as a matter of fact that fifteen per cent of those in the Eureka Stockade were "known thieves".[124] The association of disturbances with criminals served both to satisfy the need for an explanation of collective violence, while denying the legitimacy of popular grievances.

Underlying the portrayal of Lambing Flat rioters as criminals was fear that the tactics used against the Chinese might be employed to achieve other objectives. The *Herald*'s apparent sympathy for the Chinese barely obscured its less humanitarian concerns. Following a clash between Europeans and Chinese at Native Dog Creek it reported that:

> these riots and disorders are a pretext, and that they are expressive of a state of things which may endanger the safety of the British as well as the Chinese population. These men will not confine their grievances to one department. . . . . they contemplated no end of political and social reforms. Entering upon this path they may soon find that many other classes of the population are in the way and they will probably extend the range of their depredations beyond the limits of the goldfields.[125]

One may question the contention of Ted Robert Gurr, Peter Grabosky and Richard Hula that by mid-century public order was no longer a dominant issue in New South Wales due to the end of transportation, an influx of free immigrants and rising prosperity.[126] During the 1840s fear of convict insurrection quickly gave way to that of the anonymous city "mob". When troops were diverted from New South Wales to New Zealand in 1847, William Wentworth warned that, "It was in the crowded cities that internal violence was most easily excited, and most to be expected".[127] The anti-transportation movement in particular created apprehensions of mob violence. Governor FitzRoy reacted to the *Hashemy* protest in 1849 by placing a double guard around Government House with fixed bayonets, quartering reinforcements in the kitchen and stable, and, it was rumoured, training the cannon at Fort Macquarie on Circular Quay.[128] Following an anti-transportation meeting in August 1850, Wentworth and others presented an address to the governor stating their belief that "an anti-British and democratic spirit" was springing up which was both "violent and dangerous".[129] Fear of a "democratic spirit" was not simply indicative of Wentworth's conservatism. Against the backdrop of revolutions in Europe during 1848 and Chartism, "democracy" was often equated with republicanism and rebellion.[130]

To some extent, fears of disorder were exacerbated by the very conditions which other researchers note as minimizing them. With the cessation of transportation, apprehensions of rebellious prisoners were displaced by fear of an urban mob inflamed by democratic ideas. The withdrawal of troops and reductions of police which accompanied the dismantling of the penal system made élites feel that much more vulnerable. A dramatic increase in free immigrants brought a population more conscious and assertive of their rights. They could be neither as blatantly repressed as convicts, nor ignored as moral inferiors. Rising prosperity, at least to the extent that it improved the bargaining position of labour, created further fears of social revolution. It was precisely because public order was a dominant issue that police reforms were implemented in 1850 and 1862.

Notes

1. *Heads of the People,* 24 April 1847.
2. See for example Ward, *Australian Legend,* especially pp. 6, 160, 245; Cyril Pearl, *Wild Men of Sydney* (London, 1958), p. 112; Michael Cannon, *Who's Master? Who's Man? Australia in the Victorian Age* (Melbourne, 1971; reprint ed., 1976), p. 76.
3. See Gurr, *Rogues, Rebels, and Reformers,* pp. 120–21; Robert D. Storch, "The Policeman as Domestic Missionary: Urban Discipline and Popular Culture in Northern England, 1850–80", *Journal of Social History* vol. 9 (June 1976), pp. 481, 502–8.
4. Papers referred to in Evidence of Henry Croasdaile Wilson to the Committee on Police and Gaols, N.S.W., *V & PLC,* 1839, vol. 2, p. 377; Return enclosed in W. A. Miles to Col. Sec., 7 January 1846, Col. Sec., Letters

Received, N.S.W. SA, 2/8028.2; Colonial Secretary's Address, LC, *SMH*, 7 June 1844; "One of the Inferior Grade" to Editor, *People's Advocate*, 14 September 1850. Since there was a high rate of turnover in the police, the returns represent only a sample for the years indicated.

5. Final Report of the Committee on Police and Gaols, N.S.W. *V & PLC*, 1835, p. 431; Evidence of John Street to the Committee on Police and Gaols, N.S.W., *V & PLC*, 1839, vol. 2, p. 286.
6. Return enclosed in W. A. Miles to Col. Sec., 7 January 1846, Col. Sec., Letters Received, N.S.W. SA, 2/8028.2; Returns of the Sydney Constabulary for 1854, Police, N.S.W. SA, 7/93.
7. Appendix referred to in Evidence of William Augustus Miles to the Select Committee on Police, N.S.W., *V & PLC*, 1847, vol. 2, p. 64.
8. Compiled from Returns of the Sydney Constabulary for 1854, Police, N.S.W. SA, 7/93.
9. Report from H. C. Wilson, 1 May 1835, Appendix to the Minutes of Evidence taken before the Committee on Police and Gaols, N.S.W., *V & PLC*, 1835, p. 362.
10. Compiled from Returns of the Sydney Constabulary for 1854, Police, N.S.W. SA, 7/93.
11. See for example *Sydney Gazette*, 7 July, 9 October 1838; *SMH*, 2 September 1841, 22 March 1842; Harris, *Settlers and Convicts*, pp. 56–57.
12. Col. Sec. to H. C. Wilson, 27 February 1839, Col. Sec., Letters Sent, N.S.W. SA, 4/3843; Gipps to Normanby, 5 December 1839, *HRA*, ser. 1, vol. 20, pp. 415–19.
13. See O'Brien, *Australian Police*, p. 22; Knight, *Illiberal Liberal*, p. 243.
14. Report from the Select Committee on the Darlinghurst Gaol, N.S.W., *V & PLC*, 1849, vol. 2, pp. 210–11.
15. See Ben W. Champion, "Captain Edward Denny Day, of the 46th and 62nd Regiments", *JRAHS* vol. 22, pt 5 (1936), pp. 345–57; *ADB*, vol. 1, p. 300; *SMH*, 4 September 1850.
16. *Australian*, 11 January 1840; Campbell Town Police Office to Col. Sec., 14 May 1847, Col. Sec., Letters Received, N.S.W. SA, 4/2777.
17. Lockhart, "Proposed System of Police", Police, N.S.W. SA, 2/674.15, pp. 5–6.
18. Return of Police Dismissals, Letters, Petitions and Statistical Returns Received by Judge Burton, 1834–43, Supreme Court, N.S.W. SA, 4765.
19. Mudgee Bench Book, 16 February, 23 March 1849, 4 January, 9 April 1850, N.S.W. SA, 4/5591.
20. Singleton (Patrick's Plains) Bench Book, 17 May 1841, N.S.W. SA, 4/5662.
21. Harris, *Emigrant Family*, vol. 1, p. 103.
22. *Australian*, 11 January 1840.
23. *SMH*, 8 May 1850.
24. *Bell's Life*, 3 January 1846.
25. See for example "A Reformer" to Editor, *Atlas*, 21 June 1845; Edward C. Laman to Editor, *Empire*, 13 August 1851.
26. See for example *SMH*, 9 March 1841; *Bathurst Free Press*, 26 July 1851; "An Interested Party" to Editor, *SMH*, 12 March 1861.
27. Report of the Committee on Police and Gaols, N.S.W., *V & PLC*, 1839, vol. 2, p. 185.
28. *SMH*, 9 October 1849; Lockhart, "Proposed System of Police", Police, N.S.W. SA, 2/674.15, p. 19.
29. *SMH*, 5, 19 February 1844.
30. [Colony of N.S.W.] 5 Wm. IV, No. 9; 6 Wm. IV, No. 17; 1 Vic., No. 2;

3 Vic., No. 29; 5 Vic., No. 23; 8 Vic., No. 5; 9 Vic., No. 31; 11 Vic., No. 45.

31. See for example Col. Sec. to Parramatta Police Magistrate, 12 September 1838, Col. Sec., Letters Sent, N.S.W. SA, 4/3842, p. 265; Gipps to Russell, 1 January 1841, *HRA*, ser. 1, vol. 21, p. 149; Petition of Sydney Operatives, enclosed in FitzRoy to Grey, 1 February 1847, vol. 25, p. 350.

32. See for example Evidence of Joseph Long Innes to the Select Committee on the Insecurity of Life and Property, N.S.W., *V & PLC*, 1844, vol. 2, p. 425; Evidence of James Macarthur to the Select Committee on Police, N.S.W., *V & PLC*, 1847, vol. 2, p. 129.

33. *Guardian*, 8 June 1844; *SMH*, 28 November 1844.

34. *SMH*, 5 January 1841.

35. *Heads of the People*, 24 April 1847.

36. [Colony of N.S.W.] 13 Vic., No. 29, sec. 86; 13 Vic., No. 32, sec. 2; 14 Vic., No. 38, sec. 26.

37. Evidence of Saul Samuel and Charles Henry Green to the Select Committee on the Police Regulation Bill, N.S.W., *V & PLC*, 1852, vol. 1, pp. 932, 939.

38. *Sydney Herald*, 7, 8, 11 October 1841; *Sydney Gazette*, 7, 9 October 1841.

39. *SMH*, 3 November 1845; W. A. Miles to Col. Sec., 24 November 1845, Col. Sec., Letters Received, N.S.W. SA, 2/8026.4; Col. Sec. to Commissioner of Police, 28 November 1845, Col. Sec., Letters Sent, N.S.W. SA, 4/3850.

40. *Bell's Life*, 27 May 1848.

41. Dowling, "Reminiscences", ML, MS. C194, pp. 244–48; *Empire*, 28 January, 28 February, 25, 26 August 1851; *SMH*, 28 February, 26, 27 August 1851.

42. Macnab, "Crime in England and Wales", pp. 23, 283. These figures actually overstate the ratio of police to population in England, since they refer only to counties with police forces organized under the County Police Act of 1839, and boroughs with police established under the Municipal Corporations Act of 1835.

43. Ratio is based on Returns of the Colony, "Blue Book", 1846, CO 206/88; Census of New South Wales, 1846.

44. *Sydney Gazette*, 2 April 1842.

45. [Colony of N.S.W.] 4 Vic., No. 17, sec. 19, 23.

46. *Australian*, 9 October 1841.

47. [Colony of N.S.W.] 7 Vic., No. 21, sec. 3, 10.

48. King, "Problems of Police Administration", p. 62.

49. Constitution of the Border Police for February 1845 and January 1846, Col. Sec., Letters Received, Special Bundle, N.S.W. SA, 4/1141.1.

50. Report from the Select Committee on Crown Land Grievances, N.S.W., *V & PLC*, 1844, vol. 2, p. 129; LC, *SMH*, 26 October 1843, 3 October 1844.

51. See *Sydney Gazette*, 6 June 1840; LC, *SMH*, 20 August 1842, 3 October 1844; John Henderson, *Excursions and Adventures in New South Wales* (London, 1851), pp. 278–83.

52. Roberts, *Squatting Age*, pp. 348–55.

53. Bridges, "Native Police", pp. 124–25; *SMH*, 10 January 1850.

54. Skinner, *Native Police*, pp. 84–85, 121.

55. Board of Inquiry to Col. Sec., 20 December 1854, N.S.W., *V & PLC*, 1855, vol. 1, p. 871.

56. Col. Sec. to Frederick Walker, 19 January 1855, ibid., pp. 874–75.

57. Skinner, *Native Police,* pp. 164, 226, 252.

58. Evidence of Major Jeffrey Nicholson to the Select Committee on Police, N.S.W., *V & PLC,* 1847, vol. 2, p. 81.

59. See Nominal Roll of Men belonging to the Mounted Police Corps, 31 March 1848, Police, N.S.W. SA, 2/671.

60. Record of offences by members of the Mounted Police, 1839–50, Police, N.S.W. SA, 2/671; Jeffrey Nicholson to Col. Sec., 9 November 1844, 8 May 1846, Mounted Police, Letters Sent, N.S.W. SA, 4/5720; Col. Sec. to Commandant of Mounted Police, 12 May 1846, Col. Sec., Letters Sent, N.S.W. SA, 4/3863; General Order No. 108, 19 June 1846, Orders to Mounted Police Troops, Police, N.S.W. SA, 4/5718.

61. Compiled from Record of Offences by Members of the Mounted Police, 1839–50, Police, N.S.W. SA, 2/671.

62. LC, *SMH,* 30 August 1849.

63. See for example Report from the Select Committee on Police, N.S.W., *V & PLC,* 1847, vol. 2, p. 27; Evidence of Charles Windeyer to the Committee, pp. 47–48; A. L. Haydon, *The Trooper Police of Australia. A Record of Mounted Police Work in the Commonwealth from the Earliest Days of Settlement to the Present Time* (London, 1911), p. 70.

64 Evidence of John Street to the Committee on Police and Gaols, N.S.W., *V & PLC,* 1839, vol. 2, p. 289.

65. See for example Report of the Committee on Police and Gaols, N.S.W., *V & PLC,* 1839, vol. 2, p. 169; Jeffrey Nicholson to W. O'Brien, 29 May 1846; Jeffrey Nicholson to Col. Sec., 9 June 1846, Mounted Police, Letters Sent, N.S.W. SA, 4/5720.

66. Troop Order No. 36, 2 December 1848, Orders to Mounted Police Troops, Police, N.S.W. SA, 4/5718.

67. Jeffrey Nicholson to Col. Sec., 3 March 1845, Mounted Police, Letters Sent, N.S.W. SA, 4/5720; Evidence of Major Jeffrey Nicholson to the Select Committee on Police, N.S.W., *V & PLC,* 1847, vol. 2, p. 85.

68. Evidence of Charles Windeyer to the Committee on Police and Gaols, N.S.W., *V & PLC,* 1839, vol. 2, p. 401.

69. Report from the Select Committee on Police, N.S.W., *V & PLC,* 1850, vol. 2, p. 402.

70. See Roger Lane, *Policing the City. Boston 1822–1885* (Cambridge, Mass., 1967), p. 26; Richard Maxwell Brown, "Historical Patterns of Violence in America", in Graham and Gurr (eds.), *Violence in America,* pp. 54, 60; Gurr, *Rogues, Rebels and Reformers,* pp. 122–23; Philips, *Crime in Victorian England,* pp. 57–58.

71. *SMH,* 4, 5, 7, 10 January; 4 March 1850; *Bell's Life,* 5 January, 9 March 1850.

72. *SMH,* 23 January 1850.

73. *SMH,* 12 January 1850.

74. *Bell's Life,* 5 January 1850; *SMH,* 5, 17 January 1850.

75. *SMH,* 23, 25, 31 January, 29 May, 19 June 1850.

76. LC, *SMH,* 30 August 1849; Returns of the Colony, "Blue Books" (xerox copy), 1849–50, ML, CY 4/282–283.

77. Anne Deas Thomson to Richard Bourke, 1 January 1850, Bourke Papers, ML, Uncatalogued MSS, Set 403, Item 7.

78. Report from the Board appointed to Inquire into the Conduct of the Sydney Police on the occasion of the recent Riots, and into the means of rendering the Force more Efficient, N.S.W., *V & PLC,* 1850, vol. 1, p. 385;

Report from the Select Committee on Police, N.S.W., *V & PLC,* 1850, vol. 2, pp. 402–6, 411–12.

79. [Colony of N.S.W.] 14 Vic., No. 38, sec. 1–2.

80. See for example *People's Advocate,* 31 August 1850; *Empire,* 21 March 1851; *Goulburn Herald,* 7 June 1851.

81. Evidence of William Colburne Mayne to the Select Committee on the Administration of Justice and Conduct of Official Business in Country Districts, N.S.W., *V & PLA,* 1856–57, vol. 1, p. 947.

82. Ibid.; Report of Board of Inquiry on Police, 26 July 1856, N.S.W., *V & PLA,* 1856–57, vol. 1, p. 1149.

83. LC, *Empire,* 8 December 1852; Lockhart, "Proposed System of Police", Police, N.S.W. SA, 2/674.15, p. 13.

84. *Bell's Life,* 15 March 1851.

85. LC, *SMH,* 15 December 1851; William Spain to FitzRoy, enclosed in FitzRoy to Grey, 3 January 1852, CO 201/450, ff. 20–21.

86. *Empire,* 24 January 1851.

87. *Bathurst Free Press,* 1 February 1851.

88. Final Report from the Select Committee on the Police Regulation Bill, N.S.W., *V & PLC,* 1852, vol. 1, p. 929; [Colony of N.S.W.] 16 Vic., No. 33, sec. 1–3.

89. [Colony of N.S.W.] 25 Vic., No. 16.

90. [Colony of N.S.W.] 14 Vic., No. 38, sec. 7.

91. Evidence of Charles Henry Green to the Select Committee on the Police Regulation Bill, N.S.W., *V & PLC,* 1852, vol. 1, p. 940.

92. W. C. Mayne to Col. Sec., 8 July 1852, Col. Sec., Letters Received, N.S.W. SA, 4/3118.

93. [Colony of N.S.W.] 17 Vic., No. 30, sec. 1, 5, 7.

94. J. Browne to Under Secretary, 17 July 1854, enclosed in Henry FitzRoy to Herman Merivale, 29 July 1854, CO 201/478, ff. 155–56.

95. Grey to Denison, 17 October 1854, CO 202/63, ff. 305–6.

96. Compiled from Register of appointments, promotions, dismissals, retirements, 1855–61, Police, N.S.W. SA, 7/6362.

97. Dowling, "Reminiscences", ML, MSS. C194, p. 276.

98. Compiled from Register of appointments, promotions, dismissals, and retirements, 1855–61, Police, N.S.W. SA, 7/6362.

99. *Bell's Life,* 8 June 1850; *People's Advocate,* 22 June 1850.

100. Chappell and Wilson, *Police and Public,* p. 29.

101. Charles Lockhart to Chief Commissioner of Crown Lands, 1 November 1855, N.S.W., *V & PLC,* 1855, vol. 2, p. 609.

102. Ward, *Australian Legend,* p. 127.

103. Evidence of John Richard Hardy and William Essington King to the Select Committee on the Management of the Gold Fields, N.S.W., *V & PLC,* 1852, vol. 2, pp. 691–92, 743, 777–78; Evidence of Charles Henry Green and Robert George Massie to the Select Committee on the Gold Fields Management Bill, N.S.W., *V & PLC,* 1853, vol. 2, pp. 443, 448, 518; J. R. Godley, "Extracts from the Journal of a Visit to New South Wales in 1853", *Fraser's Magazine* vol. 48 (November 1853), p. 517.

104. Report from William Johnson, 5 October 1855, N.S.W., *V & PLC,* 1855, vol. 2, p. 617; William Johnson to Col. Sec., 11 October 1856, N.S.W., *V & PLA,* 1856–57, vol. 2, p. 517.

105. See for example *Empire,* 21 November 1851; *SMH,* 2 February 1853; *People's Advocate,* 21 June 1856.

106. *SMH,* 11, 12 February (Supplement), 19 February 1853.

107. See Commissioner Hardy to Col. Sec., 5 June 1851, enclosed in FitzRoy

to Grey, 15 August 1851, *PP*, 1852, vol. 34, [1430], p. 54; *SMH*, 19 September 1853.

108. Evidence of Charles Henry Green to the Select Committee on the Gold Fields Management Bill, N.S.W., *V & PLC*, 1853, vol. 2, p. 452.

109. *Empire*, 16 December 1851.

110. *Bathurst Free Press*, 8, 11, 15 October 1856; William Johnson to Col. Sec., 11 October 1856, N.S.W., *V & PLA*, 1856–57, vol. 2, pp. 516–17.

111. Assistant-Commissioner Lynch to Commissioner Cloete, 23 March 1860, N.S.W., *V & PLA*, 1861, vol. 2, p. 381.

112. Richard Maxwell Brown, "The American Vigilante Tradition", in Graham and Gurr (eds.), *Violence in America*, p. 175.

113. J. Buchanan to E. C. Merewether, August 1856; J. Buchanan to Chief Commissioner of Crown Lands, 30 August, 1 October, 1 December 1856, 2 February, 1 March 1857, Copies of Letters Sent to Officers and Private Individuals from Assistant Gold Commissioner, New England, Gold Commissioners, N.S.W. SA, 4/5475.

114. Concerning the Lambing Flat riots see D. L. Carrington, "Riots at Lambing Flat, 1860–61", *JRAHS* vol. 46, pt 4 (October 1960), pp. 223–43; R. B. Walker, "Another Look at the Lambing Flat Riots, 1860–61", *JRAHS* vol. 56, pt 3 (September 1970), pp. 193–205; P. A. Selth, "The Burrangong (Lambing Flat) Riots, 1860–61: A Closer Look", *JRAHS* vol. 60, pt 1 (March 1974), pp. 48–69; Clark, *History of Australia*, vol. 4, pp. 128–33; Markus, *Fear and Hatred*, pp. 29–31.

115. "A Bendigo Digger" to Editor, *SMH*, 23 February 1861.

116. M. FitzPatrick to P. L. Cloete, 27 February 1861, Department of Lands and Public Works, Letters Received, N.S.W. SA, 5/3626.

117. H. McLean, Memo, 15 May 1861, enclosed in Col. Sec. to Under Secretary for Lands, 17 May 1861, Department of Lands and Public Works, Letters Received, N.S.W. SA, 5/3626; Assistant Gold Commissioner Keightly to Commissioner of the Western Goldfields, 10 May 1861, enclosed in Col. Sec. to Under Secretary for Lands, 17 May 1861; Commissioner McLean to Under Secretary for Lands, 26 May 1861, Department of Lands and Public Works, Letters Received, N.S.W. SA, 5/3626; *SMH*, 1 June 1861.

118. Walker, "Lambing Flat", p. 197.

119. J. Lynch to Secretary for Lands, 3 July 1861, Department of Lands and Public Works, Letters Received, N.S.W. SA, 5/3627.

120. *SMH*, 26 February 1861.

121. J. H. Griffin to Under Secretary for Lands, 16 July 1861, Department of Lands and Public Works, Letters Received, N.S.W. SA, 5/3627.

122. Report of Henry Zouch, 2 January 1861, quoted in *SMH*, 14 January 1861.

123. Carrington, "Lambing Flat", p. 239.

124. *SMH*, 12 January 1850, 8 March 1861.

125. *SMH*, 6 July 1861.

126. Gurr, Grabosky and Hula, *Politics of Crime*, p. 679.

127. LC, *Atlas*, 29 May 1847.

128. *People's Advocate*, 16 June 1849; *SMH*, 19 June 1849.

129. Address of 1603 Inhabitants of Sydney and the Colony of New South Wales, enclosed in FitzRoy to Grey, 30 September 1850, *PP*, vol. 45, [1361], pp. 182–83.

130. W. J. V. Windeyer, "Responsible Government – Highlights, Sidelights and Reflections", *JRAHS* vol. 42, pt. 6 (1957), pp. 279–80.

Conclusion

Colonial Australia, one recent writer suggests, was "a society whose cohesion rested mainly on vice". The colony's penal origins had the effect of "warping all those who went there", and "left deep and disfiguring scars".[1] This view of New South Wales society may well seem justified. Certainly many nineteenth century observers reinforce this impression. But one may suspect that the colony's origins have been widely denigrated partly to magnify its subsequent progress. Contemporaries were also prone to confuse convict vices with what were in fact working class mores.

The social consequences of transportation often seem overemphasized or misconstrued. The inevitable association of crime with convictism overlooks other aspects of the community which shaped the incidence and type of offences committed. In relation to Britain, New South Wales was a "peculiar" society not only because of its penal origins, but also in terms of its environment, economy and free population. Interpretations which point to the assimilation of convict values, such as hard drinking and a contempt for the police, underplay important, if more mundane, influences at work.

This is not to argue that the impact of transportation on the community was negligible. But often the most important side-effects of convictism were more subtle or indirect than has been appreciated. The apparatus for social control inherited from the penal system probably had as profound an influence on colonial crime as convicts. Despite the obstruction to law enforcement posed by distance and isolation, New South Wales was over-policed by contemporary standards. It may be assumed as well, that in comparison with other frontier communities the magistracy and superior courts exercised a more pervasive influence. A reliance on formal agencies of law enforcement fostered by the convict system, was reinforced by the conditions of recent settlement. There was a relative absence of less blatant social control mechanisms such as "God's police", churches and schools. A lack of traditional channels for imposing authority and mediating relations encouraged colonists to resort to the courts.

A high crime rate is to be expected in a community which placed such heavy reliance on the law and its agents. The same reliance affected other aspects of community relations. Citizens brought personal and minor disputes before the courts for adjudication. Large numbers of police created resentment when their activities evolved from the regulation of convicts to monitoring the morality of more "respectable" residents. A strong police and military presence minimized the likelihood of collective violence. The infrastructure established to control convicts in remote districts probably inhibited as well the growth of a vigilante tradition.

Dominant values, at least as defined by the upper and middle classes, were more profoundly shaped by a reaction against convictism than by the dissemination of a convict ethos. The community, which so often viewed itself as Britain's neglected offspring, demonstrated an obsessional concern with repudiating its origins and raising its status in the Empire. The gold rush in particular was embraced as a "moral passage" which assured the colony's new image. Stuart A. Donaldson, New South Wales' first prime minister, told a British select committee on transportation in 1861 that a stranger coming to the colony would notice nothing unusual about society, and that the amalgamation of the second generation was "nearly perfect".[2] Another observer, applauding the mechanisms of social Darwinism, claimed that the last convicts to die of drink did so shortly after gold was discovered.[3] Nevertheless, colonists remained sensitive to the stigma of convictism. When sentencing the bushranger Gardiner in 1864, the colony's chief justice noted the degradation which he had brought on New South Wales, which was already regarded in England and elsewhere as "nothing but a den of thieves".[4] Colonial sensitivities were no doubt heightened by the insistence of British visitors that there was still an "ingrained taint", although they were usually vague about what this consisted of.[5] The most lasting consequence of transportation was the convict stain itself, which fostered feelings of social inferiority throughout the nineteenth century.

The convict stain in fact played a functional role in the community's consciousness. Historians are prone to overemphasize the influence of the convict era as an attractive explanation of Australian culture. For contemporaries, convictism served as a rationale for thwarted expectations in building a better society. By the 1850s attention was shifting from problems associated with transportation to those of a rapidly expanding society. A select committee on the working classes in 1859—60 pointed to more fundamental dilemmas posed by urbanization, poor housing, sanitation, juvenile delinquency, land policies and unemployment.[6] It was still tempting, however, to fall back on the penal system in explaining social problems rather than seeking more basic causes. When addressing itself to the presence of destitute children in a new and enterprising country, the *Herald* asserted in 1861 that:

> Although moral traces of convictism are wonderfully obliterated, there has never been a rooting out of all its traditional haunts, and all its old associations. . . . Death has been the great social purifier. Property and plenty have done their share in the reformation; dispersion has distributed and concealed much of the evil. But there is a residuum, and this we have to dissolve and scatter by moral means.[7]

Convictism obscured the existence of poverty and inequality, and served to absolve the community of social responsibility.

Historians have concerned themselves much less with the after-effects of transportation than with the criminality of those transported. Whereas convicts were formerly romanticized as political prisoners and victims of oppression, more recent scholarship has cast them in the mould of more or less hardened and professional criminals. Both of these categories can be equally misleading. While quantitative studies of the convict records fail to discern the social implications of offences committed, they make it clear that those who can be documented as political prisoners represented only a small minority. But to assume that those transported were drawn principally from a distinct criminal subculture is probably just as erroneous. At least one must consider the motives and prejudices of those who defined "crime" and officially stigmatized certain people as "criminals".

In New South Wales there was a clear distinction between those who defined the community's moral standards, and those typically designated as breaching those standards. As occasionally became apparent, deviance was by no means the preserve of the lower classes, although those with some measure of power were much less likely to suffer the full consequences of the law. Criminality was largely a conferred status which depended only in part on the commission of a criminal offence. As such, the criminality of convicts must be considered in the light of their social and economic position in the colony, their closer supervision by the police and magistracy, the greater likelihood of their prosecution and conviction, as well as the motives and interests of those who labelled them criminals. Similar motives and interests must be taken into account in relation to the stigmatizing of other social groups, whether Irish, Chinese or rebellious gold diggers.

As a social product, perceptions of crime reflected in large part contemporary fears. The notions of a "criminal class" and "contamination" were wedded in the 1830s to fears of emancipist domination. By the 1840s, as the initiative in defining moral issues was transferred from large landholders to the urban middle classes, these notions were associated with the economic, social and political threat posed by a resumption of penal transportation. With the gold rushes, crime was increasingly identified with the menace of an independent working class and democratic reform. Following a visit to fellow refugee William Wentworth, Roger Therry wrote from England in 1863 that:

> He tells me that universal suffrage has quite ruined the Colony, and that society is so much altered and so little for the better, that I would scarcely recognize it as the same place I left five years ago. Bushranging is worse than in the worst days of convictism.[8]

While probably unconscious, the juxtaposition of democracy and crime was hardly coincidental.

Counterpoised against crime and vice was the concept of respectability. Whereas perceptions of crime were shaded by fear, respectability was closely identified with colonial aspirations. In its crudest form, respectability was a synonym for upper-middle class pretensions to moral superiority and power. At a more subtle level, respectability entailed a "competitive struggle" for status by persons anxious to confirm their place in a new and rapidly changing social environment. For New South Wales as a community, respectability meant overcoming the stigma of convictism.

Not only were the concepts of criminality and respectability set against each other, but they were to some extent mutually dependent. For some people to assume a role as "respectable" members of the community, it was necessary to identify other persons as disreputable. The attempt to impose "respectable" standards of behaviour, whether through the overt coercion of the penal system or by more subtle means such as the press, tended to dramatize crime and make it more visible. New South Wales' reputation as a "vicious" society depended at least in part on the very fervour with which vice was suppressed in the colony.

Notes

1. Patrick O'Farrell, *The Catholic Church in Australia. A Short History: 1788–1967* (Melbourne, 1968), pp. 10, 16; Patrick O'Farrell, *The Catholic Church and Community in Australia. A History* (Melbourne, 1977), pp. 10–11.
2. Evidence of Stuart Alexander Donaldson to the Select Committee on Transportation, *PP*, 1861, vol. 13 (286), p. 77.
3. Curr, *Recollections of Squatting*, p. 437.
4. Quoted in G. O. Preshaw, *Banking Under Difficulties or Life on the Gold Fields of Victoria, New South Wales and New Zealand* (Melbourne, 1888; reprint ed., Christchurch, 1971), p. 98.
5. See for example William Howitt, *Land, Labour, and Gold; or Two Years in Victoria: with Visits to Sydney and Van Diemen's Land* (London, 1855), vol. 2, p. 344.
6. Report from the Select Committee on the Condition of the Working Classes of the Metropolis, N.S.W., *V & PLA*, 1859–60, vol. 4, pp. 1272–75.
7. *SMH*, 30 April 1861.
8. R. Therry to James Macarthur, 19 October 1863, Macarthur Papers, ML, A2930, vol. 34, pp. 282–83.

Appendix I

Male and Female Population of New South Wales, 1831–61.

Year	Male No.	Male %	Female No.	Female %	Total
1831	38,088	74.3	13,147	25.7	51,155
1832	39,554	73.9	14,077	26.3	53,631
1833	44,644	73.4	16,150	26.6	60,794
1834	48,269	72.9	17,943	27.1	66,212
1835	51,976	72.6	19,759	27.6	71,735
1836	55,539	72.0	21,557	28.0	77,096
1837	60,284	70.7	25,068	29.4	85,352
1838	66,483	67.9	31,429	32.1	97,912
1839	75,871	66.3	38,515	33.7	114,386
1840	87,004	67.2	42,459	32.8	129,463
1841	96,112	64.2	53,557	35.8	149,669
1842	100,507	62.9	59,382	37.1	159,889
1843	103,329	62.4	62,212	37.6	165,541
1844	106,309	61.3	67,068	38.7	173,377
1845	112,618	62.0	68,938	38.0	181,556
1846	118,927	60.5	77,777	39.5	196,704
1847	123,890	60.4	81,119	39.6	205,009
1848	131,742	59.8	88,732	40.2	220,474
1849	144,829	58.8	101,470	41.2	246,299
1850	154,575	58.2	110,928	41.8	265,503
1851	113,032	57.3	84,136	42.7	197,168
1852	118,687	57.0	89,567	43.0	208,254
1853	131,368	56.8	99,920	43.2	231,288
1854	144,121	37.3	107,194	42.7	251,315
1855	158,523	57.1	119,056	42.9	277,579
1856	161,882	56.1	126,796	43.9	288,678
1857	171,673	56.2	133,814	43.8	305,487
1858	199,537	58.3	142,525	41.7	342,062
1859	196,126	58.3	140,446	41.7	336,572
1860	213,021	59.1	147,406	40.9	360,427
1861	202,099	56.4	156,179	43.6	358,278

Source: Returns of the Colony, "Blue Books", 1831–57 (xerox copy), **ML, CY** 4/270–4/290; N.S.W., Registrar General's Office, *Statistical Register of New South Wales,* 1858–61.

Note: Male and female population figures for 1830–32, 1834–35 and 1837 are interpolated.

Appendix II

Convict Population of New South Wales, 1831–61.

Year	Assigned Service	Govt. Service, Establishments, or Under Punishment	Ticket of Leave Holders	Total	% of Total Pop.
1831				21,825	42.7
1832				24,154	43.1
1833				24,543	40.4
1834	18,304	5,147	3,800	27,251	41.2
1835	19,247	6,285	3,650	29,182	40.7
1836	20,934	5,772	4,480	31,186	40.5
1837	21,153	9,277	5,679	36,190	42.3
1838	25,929	6,018	6,026	37,973	38.8
1839	25,577	2,503	6,955	35,035	30.6
1840	22,999	6,824	9,292	38,415	29.7
1841	13,181	7,637	6,159	26,977	20.6
1842	7,591	6,382	10,975	24,948	15.6
1843	3,688	5,333	12,405	21,426	12.9
1844	2,877	2,913	13,385	19,175	11.1
1845	476	2,601	13,766	16,843	9.3
1846	379	1,415	9,417	11,271	5.7
1847	58	657	5,949	6,664	3.2
1848		599	3,416	4,015	1.8
1849		699	2,818	3,517	1.4
1850		738	1,626	2,364	0.9
1851		657	1,708	2,359	1.2
1852		786	1,601	2,387	1.1
1853		748	1,495	2,243	1.0
1854		785	1,238	2,023	0.8
1855		714	780	1,494	0.5
1856		778	460	1,238	0.4
1857		676	450	1,126	0.4
1858		642	370	1,012	0.3
1859		544	340	884	0.3
1860		545	250	795	0.2
1861		514	190	704	0.2

Source: Returns of the Colony, "Blue Books", 1833–57 (microfilm), CO 206/73–99; N.S.W., Registrar General's Office, *Statistical Register of New South Wales*, 1858–61; C. M. H. Clark (ed.), *Select Documents in Australian History 1788–1850* (Sydney, 1950), p. 406; Crowley, "Working Class Conditions", pp. 663–64, 667, 671.

Note: Figures for some years differ between sources, presumably because they refer to different periods of the year. The figures above are generally from the "Blue Books" and refer to December of each year.

Appendix III

Total Convictions and Convictions per 100,000 Inhabitants for All Indictable Offences, Offences Against Property and Offences Against the Person, Before the Superior Courts in New South Wales from 1831 to 1861.

Year	All Offences		Against Property		Against the Person	
	Total	Per 100,000	Total	Per 100,000	Total	Per 100,000
1831	361	705.7	287	561.0	68	132.9
1832	425	794.0	311	581.0	84	156.9
1833	565	929.4	415	682.0	123	202.3
1834	685	1034.6	559	844.3	85	128.4
1835	771	1076.9	622	868.8	116	162.0
1836						
1837						
1838						
1839	912	797.3	696	608.5	165	144.2
1840	832	642.7	594	460.0	157	121.6
1841	725	484.4	522	348.8	150	100.2
1842	693	433.4				
1843	654	395.1	538	325.0	86	52.0
1844	616	355.3	474	273.4	93	53.6
1845	594	327.2	482	265.5	92	50.7
1846	651	331.0	511	259.8	116	59.0
1847	551	268.8	433	211.2	90	43.9
1848	571	259.0	436	197.8	91	41.3
1849	668	271.2	504	204.6	139	56.4
1850	666	250.8	525	197.7	108	40.7
1851	574	291.1	444	225.2	108	54.8
1852	527	253.1	398	191.1	113	54.3
1853	604	261.1	456	197.2	131	56.6
1854	637	253.5	444	176.6	136	54.1
1855	526	189.5	394	141.9	108	38.9
1856	461	159.7	340	117.8	78	27.0
1857	395	129.3	275	90.0	89	29.1
1858	415	121.3	288	84.2	93	27.2
1859	406	120.6	316	93.9	62	18.4
1860	405	112.4	295	81.3	83	23.0
1861	437	122.0	313	87.4	85	23.7

Source: Returns of the Colony, "Blue Books", 1831–57 (xerox copy), ML CY 4/262–290; N.S.W., Registrar General's Office, *Statistical Register of New South Wales* 1858–61.

Note: Figures 1, 2, 3, 5, 6, 7 and appendix 4 are based on the same sources.

Appendix IV

Total Conviction, and Conviction per 100,000 Inhabitants for Offences Against Property Without Violence, Offences Against Property with Violence, Forgery and Offences Against the Currency, and Malicious Offences Against Property, Before the Superior Courts in New South Wales from 1831 to 1861.

Year	Against Property Without Violence		Against Property With Violence		Forgery and Currency		Malicious Offences	
	Total	Per 100,000	Total	Per 100,000	Total	Per 100,000	Total	Per 100,000
1831	193	377.3	88	172.0	4	7.8	2	3.9
1832	222	414.8	77	143.9	8	14.9	4	7.5
1833	310	509.9	100	164.5	4	6.6	1	1.6
1834	411	620.7	128	193.3	17	25.7	3	4.5
1835	469	655.1	125	174.6	17	23.7	11	15.4
1836								
1837								
1838								
1839	531	464.2	136	118.9	26	22.7	3	2.6
1840	464	359.3	99	76.7	25	19.4	6	4.6
1841	389	260.0	101	67.5	27	18.0	5	3.3
1842								
1843	440	265.8	65	39.3	33	19.9	0	0.0
1844	357	205.9	83	47.9	33	19.0	1	0.6
1845	382	210.4	74	40.8	26	14.3	0	0.0
1846	418	212.5	53	26.9	36	18.3	4	2.0
1847	345	168.3	54	26.3	30	14.6	4	2.0
1848	347	157.4	54	24.5	34	15.4	1	0.5
1849	399	162.0	68	27.6	35	14.2	2	0.8
1850	418	157.4	62	23.4	44	16.6	1	0.4
1851	386	195.8	37	18.8	19	9.6	2	1.0
1852	334	160.4	52	25.0	12	5.8	0	0.0
1853	383	165.6	62	26.8	9	3.9	2	0.9
1854	386	153.4	40	15.9	18	7.2	0	0.0
1855	341	122.8	28	10.1	22	7.9	3	1.1
1856	297	102.9	30	10.4	10	3.5	3	1.0
1857	233	76.3	17	5.6	23	7.5	2	0.7
1858	240	70.2	25	7.3	20	5.8	3	0.9
1859	260	77.2	39	11.6	15	4.5	2	0.6
1860	224	62.1	46	12.8	17	4.7	8	2.2
1861	263	73.4	30	8.4	20	5.6	0	0.0

Appendix V

Total Convictions, and Convictions per 100,000 Inhabitants Before the Supreme Court and Courts of Quarter Sessions of England and Wales, Supreme Court and Courts of Quarter Sessions of Tasmania, Supreme Court of Victoria, and Supreme Court of South Australia, 1831–61.

Year	England and Wales No.	Per 100,000	Tasmania No.	Per 100,000	Victoria No.	Per 100,000	South Australia No.	Per 100,000
1831	13,830	98.8	223	941.8				
1832	14,947	105.5	302	1131.3				
1833	14,446	100.8	363	1144.5				
1834	15,995	110.2	606	1604.1				
1835	14,729	100.0	381	945.8				
1836	14,771	98.9	145	330.3				
1837	17,090	113.1	252	586.8				
1838	16,785	109.8	168	367.1				
1839	17,832	114.9						
1840	19,927	126.7					47	321.7
1841	20,280	127.3					37	231.3
1842	22,733	140.9	224	446.1			36	218.2
1843	21,092	129.1	212	369.2				
1844	18,919	114.4	493	813.5				
1845	17,402	104.0	377	591.0				
1846	18,144	107.1	255	380.7			40	154.5
1847	21,542	125.6	217	309.3			31	99.5
1848	22,900	131.9					45	116.4
1849	21,001	119.6					116	219.3
1850	20,537	115.6					93	146.0
1851	21,579	120.0					103	154.8
1852	21,304	117.1			471	279.8	37	53.9
1853	20,756	112.8			562	252.7	73	92.5
1854	23,047	123.8	267	352.2			69	74.6
1855	19,971	106.1	345	444.0	309	84.8	77	79.4
1856	14,734	77.4	195	245.0	272	68.4	85	81.2
1857	15,307	79.5	162	198.8	425	91.8	73	66.4
1858	13,246	68.0	178	212.0	535	106.0	75	63.4
1859	12,470	63.3	184	212.8	582	109.8	93	75.8
1860	12,068	60.6	168	190.8	416	77.3	73	58.8
1861			107	118.9	462	85.3	62	47.5

Source: Macnab, "Crime in England and Wales", appendix pp. 6–7, 10; *Statistics of the State of Tasmania* [Van Diemen's Land], 1831–61; *Statistics of the Colony of Victoria,* 1851–53, 1855–61; Returns of the Colony of South Australia, "Blue Books", 1841–43, CO 17/13–15; *Statistics of South Australia,* 1850, 1854, 1856, 1859–61.

Note: Statistics for Victoria and South Australia refer only to convictions before the Supreme Court.

Appendix VI

Per Capita Consumption of Spirits in New South Wales and the United Kingdom, 1838–55.

Year	Gallons		Per Capita Consumption		Per Capita Consumption of Males	
	NSW	UK	NSW	UK	NSW	UK
1838	278,802	30,855,000	2.85	1.19	4.19	2.43
1839	315,792	29,216,000	2.76	1.11	4.16	2.28
1840	341,651	25,503,000	2.64	.97	3.93	1.96
1841	284,114	24,106,000	1.90	.90	2.96	1.84
1842	277,333	22,043,000	1.73	.82	2.76	1.67
1843	192,263	22,026,000	1.16	.81	1.86	1.65
1844	169,317	23,852,000	.98	.87	1.59	1.77
1845	194,764	26,673,000	1.07	.96	1.73	1.96
1846	314,281	28,352,000	1.60	1.01	2.64	2.07
1847	338,679	24,543,000	1.65	.92	2.73	1.79
1848	334,822	26,830,000	1.52	.97	2.54	1.97
1849	356,073	28,228,000	1.45	1.02	2.46	2.08
1850	402,534	28,666,000	1.52	1.04	2.60	2.13
1851	496,087	28,755,000	2.52	1.05	4.39	2.15
1852	713,999	30,063,000	3.43	1.10	6.02	2.24
1853	964,160	30,164,000	4.17	1.10	7.34	2.24
1854	1,092,147	31,023,000	4.35	1.13	7.58	2.29
1855	856,857	26,746,000	3.09	.96	5.41	1.97

Source: Return of Spirits, N.S.W., *V & PLA*, 1856–57, vol. 2, p. 3; George B. Wilson, *Alcohol and the Nation (A Contribution to the Study of the Liquor Problem in the United Kingdom from 1800 to 1935)* (London, 1940), p. 332. Population figures used in calculating per capita consumption of males in the United Kingdom are from B. R. Mitchell and Phyllis Deane, *Abstract of British Historical Statistics* (London, 1962), pp. 8–9.

Bibliography

OFFICIAL PAPERS – MANUSCRIPT
    Correspondence
    Police Records
    Magistrates' Bench Records
    Superior Court Records
OFFICIAL PAPERS – PRINTED
PRIVATE PAPERS
NEWSPAPERS
CONTEMPORARY BOOKS AND ARTICLES
COLLECTED DOCUMENTS
SECONDARY SOURCES

OFFICIAL PAPERS – MANUSCRIPT

Correspondence

Attorney-General. Copies of Letters Sent to the Colonial Secretary, 1847–50. N.S.W. SA, 7/2678.
————. Copies of Letters Sent to Magistrates, 1839–42, 1846–49. N.S.W. SA, 4/6658–6659.
Colonial Office. Despatches from Governor of New South Wales, 1849–56. CO 201/414, 433, 440, 450, 454, 467, 478, 493. Australian Joint Copying Project – microfilm copies in the National Library.
————. Despatches from Secretary of State, 1849–56. CO 202/66, 83.
————. Miscellaneous and Individual Correspondence, 1836–37, 1854. CO 201/257, 267, 478.
————. Returns of the Colony, "Blue Books", 1831–57. CO 206/71–99. (Xerox copies also held in the Mitchell Library, CY 4/262–290.)
Colonial Secretary. Letters Received relative to the Police, 1835, 1838–49. N.S.W. SA, 4/2275, 4/2292.1, 4/2415.2, 4/2421.2, 4/2469.3, 4/2508.5, 4/2545.1, 4/2587.2, 4/2625.1, 2/8022.2, 2/8026.4, 2/8028.2, 4/2775–2779, 4/2817–2820, 4/2870.

Letters received from 1850 are in various bundles referenced in the indexes and registers of correspondence.

Colonial Secretary. Letters Received relative to Convicts, 1844. N.S.W. SA, 4/2641, 4/2674.3.

———. Letters Received from Sheriff and Gaolers, 1844. N.S.W. SA, 4/2670.

———. Letters Sent to Benches of Magistrates and Police, 1834–56. N.S.W. SA, 4/3837–3859.

———. Letters Sent to Magistrates Beyond the Settled Districts, 1847–55. N.S.W. SA, 4/3860–3862.

———. Letters Sent to Gold Commissioners, 1851–56. N.S.W. SA, 4/3732–3733.

———. Letters Sent to Mounted Police, 1846–50. N.S.W. SA, 4/3863.

Department of Lands and Public Works. Copies of Letters Sent to Gold Commissioners, 1857–63. N.S.W. SA, 4/6854, 2/1805.

———. Letters Received, 1861. N.S.W. SA, 5/3626–3627.

Despatches from Governor of New South Wales. 1831–32, 1836, 1838, 1842, 1844. ML, A1209, A1210, A1216, A1218, A1228, A1233.

———. Enclosures, etc., 1832–35, 1841–43. ML, A1267–B, A1267–20.

Gold Commissioners. Copies of Letters to Officials and Private Individuals from Assistant Gold Commissioner, Nundle, 1852–61. N.S.W. SA, 9/2696, 4/5480.

———. Copies of Letters to Officials and Private Individuals from Assistant Gold Commissioner, Sofala, 1852–74. N.S.W. SA, 4/6264, 4/5664.

———. Copies of Letters to Officials and Private Individuals from Assistant Gold Commissioner, New England, 1856–60. N.S.W. SA, 4/5475.

———. Copies of Letters Sent to Gold Commissioners, 1851–52. N.S.W. SA, 4/421.

———. Letters Received from Gold Commissioners, 1851–52. N.S.W. SA, 5/3770.

Petitions to the King, 1835–37. ML, A284.

Supreme Court. Chief Justice's Letterbooks, 1836–66. N.S.W. SA, 4/6652–6654.

———. Copies of Semi-Official Letters and Opinions by Chief Justice Dowling, 1833–40. N.S.W. SA, 4765.

———. Letters, Petitions and Statistical Returns Received by Judge Burton, 1834–43. N.S.W. SA, 4765.

Police Records

Abstracts and Returns of the Windsor Police Establishment, 1843—53. N.S.W. SA, 4/5692.

Minute by J. Long Innes, Superintendent of Police, to the Governor on the State of the Sydney Police, 1 February 1849. N.S.W. SA, 2/674.13.

Mounted Police. Orders to Mounted Police Troops, 1850. N.S.W. SA, 4/5718.

————. Copies of Letters Sent, Adjutant's Office, Sydney, 1842—46. N.S.W. SA, 4/5720.

————. Troop Order Books, 1828—41. NLA, 3221.

Nominal Roll of Men Belonging to the Mounted Police Corps 31 March 1848. N.S.W. SA, 2/671.

Record of Offences by Members of the Mounted Police, 1839—50. N.S.W. SA, 2/671.

Register of Sydney Police Establishment, 1838—51. N.S.W. SA, 7/92.

Register of Sydney Police Establishment, 1853—56. N.S.W. SA, 7/94.

Report on Conduct and Employment of the Border Police, 1842. N.S.W. SA, 4/1132.

Reports of Commissioners of Crown Lands on Border Police in the various Districts, 1843—47. N.S.W. SA, 4/1141.1.

Returns of Police, Sydney and Country Districts, 1838—55. N.S.W. SA, 4/7390—7407.

Returns of Sydney Constabulary, 1854. N.S.W. SA, 7/93.

Sketch of a Proposed System of Police for the Colony of New South Wales by Charles George Norman Lockhart, c. 1851. N.S.W. SA, 2/674.15.

Sydney Police. Register of Appointments, Promotions, Dismissals and Retirements, 1855—61. N.S.W. SA, 7/6362.

Magistrates' Bench Records

Armidale Bench Books, 1844—59. N.S.W. SA, 4/5488—5490.

Balranald Bench Book, 1850—66. N.S.W. SA, 4/5505.

Bathurst Register of Convictions, 1848—77. N.S.W. SA, 7/91.

Bendencer Bench Book, 1859—76. N.S.W. SA, 7955.

Braidwood Bench Books, 1838—56. N.S.W. SA, 4/5516—5517.

Camden Bench Books, 1847—54. N.S.W. SA, 4/5527—5528.

Dungog Bench Books, 1843—53. N.S.W. SA, 4/5536—5537.

Gundagai Bench Book, 1856—58. N.S.W. SA, 4/5568.

Kiama Bench Book, 1860—63. N.S.W. SA, 4/5577.

Maitland Bench Book, 1853—54. N.S.W. SA, 4/5541.

Merriwa Bench Book, 1850—66. N.S.W. SA, 4/5583.

Mudgee Bench Book, 1846–56. N.S.W. SA, 4/5591.
Muswellbrook (Merton) Bench Books, 1838–43. N.S.W. SA, 4/5601–5602.
Newcastle Bench Book, 1836–38. N.S.W. SA, 4/5607.
Parramatta Bench Books, 1849–55. N.S.W. SA, 4/5613–5615.
Picton (Stonequarry) Bench Books, 1833, 1837, 1843. N.S.W. SA, 4/7572–7573; 4/5627.
Port Macquarie Bench Book, 1830–32. N.S.W. SA, 4/5637.
Port Macquarie Deposition Book, 1839–55. N.S.W. SA, 4/5647.
Queanbeyan Bench Books, 1841–62. N.S.W. SA, 4/5652–5653.
Queanbeyan Deposition Book, 1838–44. N.S.W. SA, 4/5650.
Singleton (Patrick's Plains) Bench Books, 1835–44. N.S.W. SA, 4/5562; 5/7685–7686.
Singleton (Patrick's Plains) Register of Convicts Tried Before the Bench, 1833–39. N.S.W. SA, 7/3714.
Tenterfield Bench Book, 1856-63. N.S.W. SA, 7/74.
Wagga Wagga Bench Book, 1848–51, 1858. N.S.W. SA, 4/5676.
Warialda Bench Book, 1848–57. N.S.W. SA, 4/5679.
Windsor Bench Book, 1836–40. N.S.W. SA, 4/5697.
Windsor Judgment Book of Cases Involving Free Persons, 1837–44. N.S.W. SA, 4/5695.
Yass Bench Books, 1840–67. N.S.W. SA, 4/5703–5704.

Superior Court Records

Bathurst Circuit Court Judgment Book, 1841. N.S.W. SA, 4/5741.
Bathurst Quarter Sessions Judgment Book, 1846–53. ML, A1455.
Brisbane Circuit Court Judgment Book, 1851. N.S.W. SA, 4/5747.
Calendars of persons tried on Criminal Charges in Sydney Courts, 1838–43, 1847–56. N.S.W. SA, X852; 4/6649.
Notes of Criminal Cases Tried before Mr Justice Burton in New South Wales, 1844. N.S.W. SA, 2/2451.
Prisoners Tried at the Circuit Courts held at Maitland, Berrima and Bathurst, 1841. N.S.W. SA, X901.
Register of Criminal Cases Tried at Berrima Quarter Sessions, 1839–43. N.S.W. SA, 3015.
Register of Criminal Cases Tried at Campbell Town Quarter Sessions, 1839–43. N.S.W. SA, 3012.
Registers of Criminal Cases Tried at Parramatta Quarter Sessions, 1839–43, 1848–52. N.S.W. SA, 2997; 5/2999.
Register of Criminal Cases Tried at Sydney Quarter Sessions, 1841. N.S.W. SA, 2916.
Register of Criminal Cases Tried at Windsor Quarter Sessions, 1839–43. N.S.W. SA, 3008.

Returns of Prisoners Tried and Convicted at the Berrima Circuit Court, 1841–47. N.S.W. SA, X884.

Returns of Prisoners Tried and Convicted at the Brisbane Circuit Court, 1851–55. N.S.W. SA, X885.

Returns of Prisoners Tried and Convicted at the Maitland Circuit Court, 1841–66. N.S.W. SA, X894A.

Returns of Prisoners Tried and Convicted in Courts of Quarter Sessions, 1844–45. N.S.W. SA, X50.

Returns of Prisoners Tried and Convicted in the Supreme Court, Sydney, 1838–48. N.S.W. SA, X43; X44.

Session Returns of Prisoners Tried and Convicted in the Supreme Court, Port Phillip, 1841–45. N.S.W. SA, X46A.

Official Papers – Printed

Great Britain. *Parliamentary Papers*. Report of the Commission of Inquiry on the Judicial Establishments of New South Wales, and Van Diemen's Land, 1823, vol. 10 (33), pp. 515–606.

————. Report from the Select Committee on Secondary Punishments; together with the Minutes of Evidence, Appendix and Index, 1831–32, vol. 7 (547), pp. 559–720.

————. Report from the Select Committee on Transportation; together with the Minutes of Evidence, Appendix and Index, 1837, vol. 19 (518), pp. 1–755; 1837–38, vol. 22 (669), pp. 1–424.

————. Report from the Select Committee of the House of Lords appointed to Inquire into the Execution of the Criminal Law, especially respecting Juvenile Offenders and Transportation, 1847, vol. 7 (447), pp. 1–3; 1847, vol. 7 (534), pp. 5–12.

————. Correspondence on the Subject of Convict Discipline and Transportation, 1849, vol. 43 [1121], pp. 359–81; 1850, vol. 45 [1153], pp. 11–75; 1850, vol. 45 [1285], pp. 325–62; 1850, vol. 45 (40), pp. 397–418; 1851, vol. 45 [1361], pp. 153–226; 1851, vol. 45 [1418], pp. 325–50; 1852, vol. 41 [1517], pp. 279–333; 1852–53, vol. 82 [1601], pp. 117–31; 1852–53, vol. 82, [1677], pp. 393–412.

————. Papers Relative to the Discovery of Gold in Australia, 1852, vol. 34 [1430], pp. 5-80; 1852, vol. 34 [1508], pp. 89-131; 1852–53, vol. 64 [1684], pp. 475–522; 1854, vol. 44 [1719], pp. 187–252; 1854–55, vol. 38 [1859], pp. 115–91.

————. Report from the Select Committee on Transportation; together with the Proceedings of the Committee, Minutes of Evidence, Appendix and Index, 1861, vol. 13 (286), pp. 505–714.

Great Britain. *Statutes at Large*, 1823, 1828, 1839.
Historical Records of Australia, 1832–48. Series 1, vols. 16–26.
New South Wales. *Votes and Proceedings of the Legislative Council*, 1832–55.
New South Wales. *Votes and Proceedings of the Legislative Assembly*, 1856–62.
New South Wales Government Gazette, 1835–36, 1838–41, 1844, 1851, 1853, 1858.
Public General Statutes of New South Wales, 1824–62.
Statistical Register of New South Wales, 1858–61.
Statistical Register of South Australia, 1850, 1854, 1856, 1859–61.
Statistics of the Colony of Victoria, 1851–53, 1855–61.
Statistics of Van Diemen's Land and the State of Tasmania, 1831–61.

Private Papers

Bingle, John. Papers, 1829–37. ML, A1825.
Bourke, Richard. Papers. ML, CY A1737; Uncatalogued MSS., Set 403/ Items 7–8.
Burton, William Westbrooke. Correspondence, 1832–38. ML, MSS. 834.
Dowling, James. Commissions, Correspondence, Addresses, 1810–44. ML, D266.
———. Correspondence. ML, A486, A489.
———. "James Sheen Dowling's Recollections of 'Old Sydney', 'Parramatta' and 'The Hawkesbury' Including Windsor and Richmond", 1889. (Typescript). ML, Ad 69.
———. "Reminiscences of Judge Dowling". ML, C194.
Eyre, Edward John. Autobiography, 1832–39. (Microfilm). ML, CY Reel 118.
Fox, Henry Thomas. Diary, 1850–53. (Typescript). ML, MSS. 1045/3.
Gipps-LaTrobe Correspondence, 1840–46. (Microfilm). NLA, G10, 422–424.
Hyde Park Committee. Alfred Stephen to Superintendent of Police, 2 May 1849, re Orders to the Constabulary to patrol the Park and assist the Park Ranger to keep law and order. (Xerox Copy). ML, Document 2427.
Knatchbull, John. "The Life of John Knatchbull, written by himself 23 January 1844, in Woolloomooloo Gaol". ML, MSS. 798.
Lowe, Robert. Papers. (Microfilm). NLA, G2040.
Macarthur Papers. ML, A2923, A2924, A2930, A2931, A2955.
Mowle, S.M. "Journal in Retrospect", 1822–51. (Typescript). NLA, MS. 1042.

Selwyn, Reverend Arthur E. Correspondence, 1850–81. NLA, MS. 3542.

Stephen, Alfred. Diaries and Notebooks, 1837–93. ML, MSS. 777/2.

──────. Letterbook, 1837–47. ML, A673.

Thomson, Edward Deas. Papers. ML, A1531–2, A1531–3.

Townsend, Joseph Phipps. Papers. ML, MSS. 1461/1, 1461/3.

Newspapers

Atlas
Australian
Australian Temperance Magazine
Bathurst Free Press
Bell's Life in Sydney, and Sporting Reviewer
Colonist
Empire
Freeman's Journal
Goulburn Herald and County of Argyle Advertiser
Guardian
Heads of the People
Illustrated Sydney News
Maitland Mercury and Hunter River General Advertiser
Omnibus and Sydney Spectator
People's Advocate and New South Wales Vindicator
Port Phillip Patriot and Melbourne Advertiser
Press
Satirist and Sporting Chronicle
Star, and Working Man's Guardian
Sydney Gazette and New South Wales Advertiser
Sydney Herald
Sydney Monitor and Commercial Advertiser
Sydney Morning Herald
Teetotaller, and General Newspaper
Temperance Advocate and Australasian Commercial and Agricultural Intelligencer
Weekly Register of Politics, Facts and General Literature

Contemporary Books and Articles

Alison, Archibald. "Crime and Transportation". In *Essays: Political, Historical, and Miscellaneous*, vol. 1, pp. 543–617. Edinburgh: William Blackwood and Sons, 1850.

Anon. *A Memoir of Knatchbull, The Murderer of Mrs Jamieson, Com-*

prising an Account of His English and Colonial History. Sydney: 1844.

Anon. "Anti-Transportation Movement in Sydney". *Colonial Magazine and East India Review* vol. 18 (July-December 1849), pp. 179–84.

————. "Transportation and Convict Colonies". *Colonial Magazine and East India Review* vol. 18 (July-December 1849), pp. 27–37.

Backhouse, James. *A Narrative of a Visit to the Australian Colonies*. London: Hamilton and Adams, 1843.

Bland, William. *New South Wales. Examination of Mr James Macarthur's Work, "New South Wales, Its Present State"*. Sydney: 1838.

Braim, Thomas Henry. *A History of New South Wales, From Its Settlement to the Close of the Year 1844*. 2 vols. London: Richard Bentley, 1846.

Burrows, William (pseud.). *Adventures of a Mounted Trooper in the Australian Constabulary: Being Recollections of Seven Years' Experience of Life in Victoria and New South Wales*. London: Routledge, Warne and Routledge, 1859.

Burton, William Westbrooke. *The State of Religion and Education in New South Wales*. London: J. Cross, Simkin and Marshall, 1840.

————. "State of Society and of Crime in New South Wales, During Six Years' Residence in that Colony". *Colonial Magazine and Commercial-Maritime Journal* vol. 1 (January-April 1840), pp. 421–40; vol. 2 (May-August 1840), pp. 34–54.

Byrne, J. C. *Twelve Years' Wanderings in the British Colonies. From 1835 to 1847*. 2 vols. London: Richard Bentley, 1848.

————. *Emigrants' Guide to New South Wales Proper, Australia Felix and South Australia*. 7th ed. London: Effingham Wilson, 1848.

Chisholm, Caroline. *Emigration and Transportation Relatively Considered; In a Letter, Dedicated, By Permission, to Earl Grey*. London: 1847.

Corbyn, Charles Adam. *Sydney Revels of Bacchus, Cupid and Momus; Being Choice and Humorous Selections from Scenes at the Sydney Police Office, and Other Public Places, During the Last Three Years*. Sydney: 1854.

Cozens, Charles. *Adventures of a Guardsman*. London: Richard Bentley, 1848.

Curr, Edward M. *Recollections of Squatting in Victoria Then Called the Port Phillip District (From 1841 to 1851)*. Melbourne: George Robertson, 1883; facsimile ed., Adelaide: Libraries Board of South Australia, 1968.

Darwin, Charles. *Charles Darwin's Diary of the Voyage of H.M.S. "Beagle"*. Edited by Nora Barlow. Cambridge: Cambridge University Press, 1933.

Denison, Sir William. *Varieties of Vice-Regal Life.* 2 vols. London: Longmans, Green and Company, 1870.

Fowler, Frank. *Southern Lights and Shadows: Being Brief Notes of Three Years' Experience of Social, Literary and Political Life in Australia.* London: Sampson Low, 1859; facsimile ed., Sydney: Sydney University Press, 1975.

Godley, J. R. "Extracts from the Journal of a Visit to New South Wales in 1853". *Fraser's Magazine* vol. 48 (November and December 1853), pp. 506–18, 634–47.

Harris, Alexander. *The Emigrant Family: or, The Story of an Australian Settler.* Edited by W. S. Ramson. London: Smith, Elder and Company, 1849; reprint ed., Canberra: Australian National University Press, 1967.

————. [An Emigrant Mechanic]. *Settlers and Convicts, or Recollections of Sixteen Years' Labour in the Australian Backwoods.* London: 1847; reprint ed., Melbourne: Melbourne University Press, 1954.

Haygarth, Henry William. *Recollections of Bush Life in Australia, During a Residence of Eight Years in the Interior.* London: John Murray, 1848.

Hayter, Henry Heylyn. *Crime in New South Wales. A Paper Written For, But Rejected by the Royal Society of that Colony.* Melbourne: 1884.

Henderson, John. *Excursions and Adventures in New South Wales; with Pictures of Squatting and Life in the Bush; An Account of the Climate, Productions and Natural History of the Colony, and of the Manners and Customs of the Natives, with Advice to Emigrants, etc.* 2 vols. London: W. Shoberl, 1851.

Howitt, William. *Land, Labour, and Gold; or, Two Years in Victoria: with Visits to Sydney and Van Diemen's Land.* London: Longmans, Brown, Green and Longmans, 1855.

Lancelott, F. *Australia As It Is: Its Settlements, Farms and Gold Fields.* 2 vols. London: Hurst and Blackett, 1853.

Lang, John Dunmore. *An Historical and Statistical Account of New South Wales, Both as a Penal Settlement and as a British Colony.* 2 vols. 2nd ed. London: A. J. Valpy, 1837.

————. *Transportation and Colonization; or, The Causes of the Comparative Failure of the Transportation System in the Australian Colonies: With Suggestions for Ensuring Its Future Efficiency In Subserviency to Extensive Colonization.* London: A. J. Valpy, 1837.

Legge, J. Gordon. *A Selection of Supreme Court Cases in New South Wales, from 1825 to 1862.* 2 vols. Sydney: Government Printer, 1896.

MacAlister, Charles. *Old Pioneering Days in the Sunny South.* Goulburn: 1907; facsimile ed., Sydney: Library of Australian History, 1977.

Macarthur, James. *New South Wales; Its Present State and Future Prospects: Being A Statement with Documentary Evidence, Submitted in Support of Petitions to Her Majesty and Parliament.* London: D. Walther, 1837.

McCombie, Thomas. "Distinguished Convicts". *Simmond's Colonial Magazine and Foreign Miscellany* vol. 8 (May-August 1846), pp. 365–73.

Maconochie, Alexander. "Criminal Statistics and Movement of the Bond Population of Norfolk Island, to December, 1843". *Journal of the Statistical Society of London* vol. 8 (1845), pp. 1–49.

Macqueen, T. Potter. *Australia As She Is and As She Might Be.* London: J. Cross, 1840.

Marjoribanks, Alexander. *Travels in New South Wales.* London: Smith, Elder and Company, 1847.

Mayhew, Henry. *London Labour and the London Poor.* Extra vol.: *Those That Will Not Work.* London: Griffin, Bohn and Company, 1862.

Melville, Henry. *The Present State of Australia, including New South Wales, Western Australia, South Australia, Victoria and New Zealand, with Practical Hints on Emigration; to which are added the Land Regulations, and Description of the Aborigines and Their Habits.* London: G. Willis, 1851.

Meredith, Louisa Anne. *Notes and Sketches of New South Wales During A Residence in that Colony from 1839 to 1844.* London: John Murray, 1844; facsimile ed., Harmondsworth: Penguin Books, 1973.

Mortlock, J. F. *Experiences of a Convict Transported for Twenty-one Years.* Edited by G. A. Wilkes and A. G. Mitchell. London: 1864–65; reprint ed., Sydney: Sydney University Press, 1965.

Mounted Police. *Standing Orders of the Mounted Police, New South Wales.* Sydney: Government Printing Office, 1847.

Mudie, James. *The Felonry of New South Wales: Being a Faithful Picture of the Real Romance of Life in Botany Bay with Anecdotes of Botany Bay Society and a Plan of Sydney.* Edited by Walter Stone. London: 1837; reprint ed., Melbourne: Lansdowne Press, 1964.

Mundy, Godfrey Charles. *Our Antipodes: or, Residence and Rambles in the Australasian Colonies with A Glimpse of the Gold Fields.* London: Richard Bentley, 1855.

Parkes, Henry. *An Emigrant's Home Letters.* Sydney: Angus and Robertson, 1896.

Plunkett, John Hubert. *The Australian Magistrate; or, A Guide to the Duties of a Justice of the Peace for the Colony of New South Wales.* Sydney: 1835.

Preshaw, G. O. *Banking Under Difficulties or Life on the Gold Fields of Victoria, New South Wales and New Zealand.* Melbourne: Edwards, Dunlop and Company, 1888; reprint ed., Christchurch: Caper Press, 1971.

Read, C. Rudston. *What I Heard, Saw and Did at the Australian Gold Fields.* London: T. and W. Boone, 1853.

Sadlier, John. *Recollections of a Victorian Police Officer.* Melbourne: George Robertson and Company, 1913.

Sidney, Samuel. *The Three Colonies of Australia: New South Wales, Victoria, South Australia; Their Pastures, Copper Mines and Gold Fields.* London: Ingram, Cooke, and Company, 1852.

Stephen, Alfred. *Address on Intemperance and the Licensing System, Delivered in the Masonic Hall, on the 11th December, 1869.* Sydney: John C. Sherriff, 1870.

Suttor, Edwin C. *Plunkett's Australian Magistrate: A Guide to the Duties of a Justice of the Peace, with Numerous Forms.* New ed. Sydney: 1847.

Therry, Roger. *Reminiscences of Thirty Years' Residence in New South Wales and Victoria.* London: Sampson Low, Son and Company, 1863; facsimile ed., Sydney: Sydney University Press, 1974.

Ullathorne, William. *The Catholic Mission in Australasia.* Liverpool: 1837; facsimile ed., Adelaide: Libraries Board of South Australia, 1963.

West, John. *The History of Tasmania.* 2 vols. Launceston: Henry Dowling, 1852; facsimile ed., Adelaide: Libraries Board of South Australia, 1966.

Westgarth, William. *Australia Felix; or, A Historical and Descriptive Account of the Settlement of Port Phillip, New South Wales: Including Full Particulars on the Manners and Condition of the Aboriginal Natives, with Observations on Emigration, on the System of Transportation, and on Colonial Policy.* Edinburgh: 1848.

Whatley, Richard. *Thoughts on Secondary Punishment, in a Letter to Earl Grey. To which are Appended, Two Articles on Transportation to New South Wales, and on Secondary Punishment; and Some Observations on Colonization.* London: B. Fellowes, 1832.

Collected Documents

Clark, C. M. H. (ed.) *Sources of Australian History*. London: Oxford University Press, 1957.

————. *Select Documents in Australian History 1851–1900*. Sydney: Angus and Robertson, 1955.

————. *Select Documents in Australian History 1788–1850*. Sydney: Angus and Robertson, 1950.

Evans, Lloyd, and Nicholls, Paul (eds.) *Convicts and Colonial Society 1788–1853*. Sydney: Caswell Stanmore: Caswell Australia, 1976.

Keesing, Nancy (ed.) *Gold Fever. The Australian Goldfields 1851 to the 1890s*. Sydney: Angus and Robertson, 1967.

Secondary Sources

Allars, Kenneth G. "Sir William Westbrooke Burton". *JRAHS* vol. 37, pt 5 (1951), pp. 257–94.

Atkinson, Alan. "The Political Life of James Macarthur". Ph.D. thesis, Australian National University, 1976.

————. "Four Patterns of Convict Protest". *Labour History* no. 37 (November 1979), pp. 28–51.

Banfield, Edward C. *The Unheavenly City. The Nature and Future of Our Urban Crisis*. Boston: Little, Brown and Company, 1968.

Barker, Sydney Kendall. "The Governorship of Sir George Gipps". *JRAHS* vol. 16, pts. 3–4 (1930), pp. 169–260.

Barry, John Vincent. *Alexander Maconochie of Norfolk Island. A Study of a Pioneer in Penal Reform*. London: Oxford University Press, 1958.

Bartholomew, Allen A. "Alcoholism and Crime". *Australian and New Zealand Journal of Criminology* vol. 1 (1968), pp. 70–99.

Becker, Howard S. *Outsiders. Studies in the Sociology of Deviance*. London: Collier-Macmillan, 1963.

Bennett, J. M. *A History of the Supreme Court of New South Wales*. Sydney: Law Book Company, 1974.

————. "Early Days of the Law in Country Districts". *Australian Law Journal* vol. 46 (November 1972), pp. 578–88.

————. "The Establishment of Jury Trial in New South Wales". *Sydney Law Review* vol. 3 (March 1961), pp. 463–85.

Berger, Peter L. *Invitation to Sociology. A Humanistic Perspective*. New York: Overlook Press, 1973.

Birch, Alan, and Macmillan, David S. *The Sydney Scene 1788–1960*. Melbourne: Melbourne University Press, 1962.

Blainey, Geoffrey. *The Tyranny of Distance. How Distance Shaped Australia's History*. Melbourne: Sun Books, 1966; reprint ed., 1970.

————. *The Rush That Never Ended. A History of Australian Mining.* Melbourne: Melbourne University Press, 1963.

Blair, Sandra J. "The Revolt at Castle Forbes: A Catalyst to Emancipist Emigrant Confrontation". *JRAHS* vol. 64, pt 22 (September 1978), pp. 89–107.

Bolger, Peter. *Hobart Town.* Canberra: Australian National University Press, 1973.

Box, Steven. *Deviance, Reality and Society.* London: Holt, Rinehart and Winston, 1971.

Bridges, Barry. "The Native Police Corps, Port Phillip and Victoria, 1837–53". *JRAHS* vol. 57, pt. 2 (June 1971), pp. 113–42.

Buckley, K. "Gipps and the Graziers of New South Wales, 1841–46". *Historical Studies* vol. 7, no. 26 (May 1956), pp. 178–93.

Butlin, S. J. *Foundations of the Australian Monetary System 1788–1851.* Melbourne: Melbourne University Press, 1953.

Campbell, Walter S. "The Use and Abuse of Stimulants in the Early Days of Settlement in New South Wales". *JRAHS* vol. 18, pt 2 (1932), pp. 74–99.

Cannon, Michael. "Violence: The Australian Heritage". *National Times Magazine,* 5 March 1973, pp. 16–21; 12 March 1973, pp. 28–30.

————. *Who's Master? Who's Man? Australia in the Victorian Age.* Melbourne: Thomas Nelson, 1971; reprint ed., 1976.

Carrington, D. L. "Riots at Lambing Flat, 1860–61". *JRAHS* vol. 46, pt 4 (October 1960), pp. 223–43.

Castles, Alex C. *An Introduction to Australian Legal History.* Sydney: Law Book Company, 1971.

Champion, B. W. "Captain Edward Denny Day, of the 46th and 62nd Regiments". *JRAHS* vol. 22, pt 5 (1936), pp. 345–57.

Chappell, D. and Wilson, P. R. *The Police and the Public in Australia and New Zealand.* St Lucia: University of Queensland Press, 1969.

Clark, C. M. H. *A History of Australia.* Vol. 4: *The Earth Abideth For Ever 1851–1888.* Melbourne: Melbourne University Press, 1978.

————. *A History of Australia.* Vol. 3: *The Beginning of an Australian Civilization 1824–1851.* Melbourne: Melbourne University Press, 1973.

————. "The Origins of the Convicts Transported to Eastern Australia, 1787–1852". *Historical Studies* vol. 7, nos. 26–27 (May and November 1956), pp. 121–35; 314–27.

Clarke, F. G. *The Land of Contrarieties. British Attitudes to the Australian Colonies 1828–1855.* Melbourne: Melbourne University Press, 1977.

Coghlan, T. A. *Labour and Industry in Australia from the First Settlement 1788 to the Establishment of the Commonwealth in 1901.*

3 vols. London: Oxford University Press, 1918; reprint ed., Melbourne: Macmillan, 1969.

————. *General Report on the Eleventh Census of New South Wales.* Sydney: Government Printer, 1894.

Cohen, Stanley and Young, Jock (eds.) *The Manufacture of News. Social Problems, Deviance and the Mass Media.* London: Constable and Company, 1973; reprint ed., 1974.

Conlon, Anne. " 'Mine is a Sad Yet True Story': Convict Narratives 1818–50". *JRAHS* vol. 55, pt 1 (March 1969), pp. 43–82.

Connell, R. W. and Irving, T. H. *Class Structure in Australian History. Documents, Narrative and Argument.* Melbourne: Longman Cheshire, 1980.

Cressey, Donald R. and Ward, David A. (eds.) *Delinquency, Crime, and Social Process.* New York: Harper and Row, 1969.

Critchley, T. A. *A History of the Police in England and Wales 900–1966.* London: Constable and Company, 1967.

Crowley, F. K. "Working Class Conditions in Australia 1788–1851". Ph.D. thesis, University of Melbourne, 1949.

Currey, C. H. *Sir Francis Forbes. The First Chief Justice of the Supreme Court of New South Wales.* Sydney: Angus and Robertson, 1968.

————. "Chapters on the Legal History of New South Wales, 1788–1863". L.L.D. thesis, University of Sydney, 1929.

Dingle, A. E. "Drink and Drinking in Nineteenth-Century Australia: A Statistical Commentary". *Monash Papers in Economic History* no. 6 (1978).

————. " 'The Truly Magnificent Thirst': An Historical Survey of Australian Drinking Habits". *Historical Studies* vol. 19, no. 75 (October 1980), pp. 227–49.

Dixson, Miriam. *The Real Matilda. Woman and Identity in Australia, 1788–1975.* Ringwood: Penguin, 1976.

Donajgrodzki, A. P. (ed.) *Social Control in Nineteenth-Century Britain.* London: Croom Helm, 1977.

Douglas, Jack D. (ed.) *Deviance and Respectability. The Social Construction of Moral Meanings.* New York: Basic Books, 1970.

Dowd, B. T. and Fink, Averil. "Harlequin of the Hunter: 'Major' James Mudie of Castle Forbes". *JRAHS* vol. 54, pt 4 (December 1968), pp. 368–86; vol. 55, pt 1 (March 1969), pp. 83–110.

Downes, David and Rock, Paul (eds.) *Deviant Interpretations.* Oxford: Martin Robertson, 1979.

Dunlop, Eric W. " 'The Golden Fifties': Being the Story of the Influence of the Gold Discoveries in Australia in the 1850s". *JRAHS* vol. 37, pts 1–3 (1951), pp. 10–57, 96–142.

Dyster, Barrie. "The Fate of Colonial Conservatism on the Eve of the

Gold-Rush". *JRAHS* vol. 54, pt 4 (December 1968), pp. 329–55.

————. "Support for the Squatters, 1844". *JRAHS* vol. 51, pt 1 (March 1965), pp. 41–59.

Erikson, Kai T. *Wayward Puritans. A Study in the Sociology of Deviance.* New York: John Wiley and Sons, 1966.

Fall, Judith. "Crime and Criminal Records in Western Australia". *Studies in Western Australian History* no. 3 (November 1978), pp. 18–29.

Ferdinand, Theodore N. "The Criminal Patterns of Boston Since 1849". *American Journal of Sociology* vol. 73, no. 1 (July 1967), pp. 84–99.

Fletcher, Brian. "Sir John Jamison in New South Wales 1814–44". *JRAHS* vol. 65, pt 1 (June 1979), pp. 1–29.

Foster, S. G. *Colonial Improver. Edward Deas Thomson 1800–1879.* Melbourne: Melbourne University Press, 1978.

Freeland, J. M. *The Australian Pub.* Melbourne: Melbourne University Press, 1966.

Gatrell, V. A. C. and Haddon, T. B. "Criminal Statistics and Their Interpretation". In *Nineteenth-Century Society. Essays in the Use of Quantitative Methods for the Study of Social Data,* pp. 336–96. Edited by E. A. Wrigley. Cambridge: Cambridge University Press, 1972.

Glynn, Sean. *Urbanization in Australian History, 1788–1900.* Melbourne: Thomas Nelson, 1970.

Gollan, Robin. *Radical and Working Class Politics. A Study of Eastern Australia 1850–1910.* Melbourne: Melbourne University Press, 1960; paperback ed., 1967.

Gouldner, Alvin W. "The Sociologist as Partisan: Sociology and the Welfare State". *American Sociologist* vol. 3, no. 2 (May 1968), pp. 103–16.

Gove, Walter R. (ed.) *The Labelling of Deviance. Evaluating a Perspective.* New York: Sage Publications, 1975.

Grabosky, Peter N. *Sydney in Ferment. Crime, Dissent and Official Reaction 1788 to 1973.* Canberra: Australian National University Press, 1977.

————. "Patterns of Criminality in New South Wales, 1788–1973". *Australian and New Zealand Journal of Criminology* vol. 7, no. 4 (December 1974), pp. 215–29.

Graham, Hugh Davis and Gurr, Ted Robert (eds.) *The History of Violence in America: Historical and Comparative Perspectives.* New York: Frederick A. Praeger, 1969.

Greenwood, Gordon (ed.) *Australia. A Social and Political History.* Sydney: Angus and Robertson, 1955; reprint ed., 1965.

Grocott, Allan M. *Convicts, Clergymen and Churches. Attitudes of Con-*

victs and Ex-convicts Towards the Churches and Clergy in New South Wales 1788–1851. Sydney: Sydney University Press, 1980.

Gurr, Ted Robert. Rogues, Rebels and Reformers. A Political History of Urban Crime and Conflict. London: Sage Publications, 1976.

Gurr, Ted Robert, Grabosky, Peter N. and Hula, Richard C. The Politics of Crime and Conflict. A Comparative History of Four Cities. London: Sage Publications, 1977.

Gusfield, Joseph R. Symbolic Crusade. Status Politics and the American Temperance Movement. Urbana: University of Illinois Press, 1963.

Harrison, Brian. "Pubs". In The Victorian City: Images and Realities, pp. 161–90. Edited by H. J. Dyos and Michael Wolfe. London: Routledge and Kegan Paul, 1973.

—————. Drink and the Victorians. The Temperance Question in England 1815–1872. London: Faber and Faber, 1971.

—————. "Drink and Sobriety in England 1815–72: A Critical Bibliography". International Review of Social History vol. 12 (1967), pp. 204–76.

Harrison, Brian and Trinder, Barrie. Drink and Sobriety in an Early Victorian Country Town: Banbury 1830–60. English Historical Review, Supplement 4. London: Longmans, Green and Company, 1969.

Harrison, J. F. C. The Early Victorians 1832–1851. London: Weidenfeld and Nicolson, 1971.

Hay, Douglas. "Property, Authority and the Criminal Law". In Albion's Fatal Tree. Crime and Society in Eighteenth-Century England, pp. 17–63. Edited by Douglas Hay, Peter Linebaugh and E. P. Thompson. London: Allen Lane, 1975.

Haydon, A. L. The Trooper Police of Australia. A Record of Mounted Police Work in the Commonwealth from the Earliest Days of Settlement to the Present Time. London: Andrew Melrose, 1911.

Hobsbawn, E. J. Primitive Rebels. Studies in Archaic Forms of Social Movement in the 19th and 20th Centuries. Manchester: Manchester University Press, 1959.

Hobsbawn, E. J., Samuel, Raphael, May, Margaret. Thompson, E. P., Linebaugh, Peter, Hay, D., Hirst, Paul and Rock, P. E. "Conference Report". Society for the Study of Labour History Bulletin no. 25 (Autumn 1972), pp. 5–21.

Holt, H. T. E. A Court Rises. The Lives and Times of the Judges of the District Court of New South Wales (1859–1959). Sydney: The Law Foundation of New South Wales, 1976.

Hume, L. J. "Working Class Movements in Sydney and Melbourne before the Gold Rushes". *Historical Studies* vol. 9, no. 35 (November 1960), pp. 263–78.

Inglis, K. S. *The Australian Colonists. An Exploration of Social History 1788–1870.* Melbourne: Melbourne University Press, 1974.

Irving, T. H. "The Development of Liberal Politics in New South Wales, 1843–1855". Ph.D. thesis, University of Sydney, 1967.

Jackson, R. V. *Australian Economic Development in the Nineteenth Century.* Canberra: Australian National University Press, 1977.

Jeans, D. N. *An Historical Geography of New South Wales to 1901.* Sydney: Reed Education, 1972.

Jeffries, Charles. *The Colonial Police.* London: Max Parrish, 1952.

Jones, Howard. *Crime in a Changing Society.* Hammondsworth: Penguin Books, 1965.

————. *Alcoholic Addiction. A Psycho-Social Approach to Abnormal Drinking.* London: Tavistock Publications, 1963.

King, Hazel. "Problems of Police Administration in New South Wales, 1825–51". *JRAHS* vol. 33, pt 2 (1958), pp. 49–70.

————. "Some Aspects of Police Administration in New South Wales, 1825–51". *JRAHS* vol. 42, pt 5 (1956), pp. 205–30.

————. "Police Organization and Administration in the Middle District of New South Wales, 1825–1851". MA thesis, University of Sydney, 1956.

Knight, Ruth. *Illiberal Liberal. Robert Lowe in New South Wales, 1842–1850.* Melbourne: Melbourne University Press, 1966.

Lane, Roger. "Crime and Criminal Statistics in Nineteenth-Century Massachusetts". *Journal of Social History* vol. 2 (Winter 1968), pp. 156–63.

————. *Policing the City. Boston 1822–1885.* Cambridge: Harvard University Press, 1967.

Larcombe, F. A. *A History of Local Government in New South Wales.* Vol. 1: *The Origin of Local Government in New South Wales 1831–58.* Sydney: Sydney University Press, 1973.

Leroy, Paul Edwin. "The Emancipists from Prison to Freedom: The Story of the Australian Convicts and Their Descendants". Ph.D. thesis, Ohio State University, 1960.

Lippman, Mathew. "Crime Coverage in Melbourne". *Media Information Australia* no. 8 (May 1978), pp. 9–15.

MacDougall, D. J. "Law". In *The Pattern of Australian Culture,* pp. 252–75. Edited by A. C. McLeod. New York: Cornell University Press, 1963.

Mackinolty, Judy and Radi, Heather (eds.) *In Pursuit of Justice. Australian Women and the Law 1788–1979.* Sydney: Hale and Iremonger, 1979.

McLachlan, N. D. "Larrikinism: An Interpretation". M.A. thesis, University of Melbourne, 1950.

McLaughlin, John Kennedy. "The Magistracy and the Supreme Court of New South Wales, 1824–50: A Sesqui-Centenary Study". *JRAHS* vol. 62, pt 2 (September 1976), pp. 91–113.

————."The Magistracy in New South Wales, 1788–1850". LL.M. thesis, University of Sydney, 1973.

Macnab, K. K. "Aspects of the History of Crime in England and Wales Between 1805 and 1860". Ph.D. thesis, University of Sussex, 1965.

Macnab, Ken and Ward, Russel. "The Nature and Nurture of the First Generation of Native-Born Australians". *Historical Studies* vol. 10, no. 39 (November 1962), pp. 289–308.

McQueen, Humphrey. *A New Britannia. An Argument Concerning the Social Origins of Australian Radicalism and Nationalism.* Ringwood: Penguin Books, 1970; revised ed., 1975.

————. "Convicts and Rebels". *Labour History* no. 15 (November 1968), pp. 3–30.

McQuilton, John. *The Kelly Outbreak 1788–1880. The Geographic Dimension of Social Banditry.* Melbourne: Melbourne University Press, 1979.

Madgwick, R. B. *Immigration into Eastern Australia 1788–1851.* London: Longmans, Green and Company, 1937.

Magarey, Susan. "The Invention of Juvenile Delinquency in Early Nineteenth-Century England". *Labour History* no. 34 (May 1978), pp. 11–27.

————. "The Reclaimers: A Study of the Reformatory Movement in England and Wales, 1846–1893". Ph.D. thesis, Australian National University, 1975.

Marcus, Steven. *The Other Victorians. A Study of Sexuality and Pornography in Mid-Nineteenth Century England.* 2nd ed. New York: Basic Books, 1974.

Markus, Andrew. *Fear and Hatred. Purifying Australia and California 1850–1901.* Sydney: Hale and Iremonger, 1979.

————. "The Burden of Hate: The Australian Inter-Racial Experience, 1850–1901. A Comparative Study of the Australian Mainland Colonies and California, With Special Emphasis on the Working Classes". Ph.D. thesis, La Trobe University, 1974.

Martin, A. W. *Henry Parkes. A Biography.* Melbourne: Melbourne University Press, 1980.

————. "Drink and Deviance in Sydney: Investigating Intemperance, 1854–55". *Historical Studies* vol. 17, no. 68 (April 1977), pp. 342–60.

Marx, Gary T. "Issueless Riots". *Annals of the American Academy of Political and Social Science* no. 391 (September 1970), pp. 21–33.

Mayne, Alan. "A Land of Promise Across the Seas: The Making of a Civilization in Sydney during the Years of Renewed Convict Transportation, 1844–1851". B.A. Honours thesis, Australian National University, 1976.

Melbourne, V. A. C. *Early Constitutional Development in Australia.* 2nd ed. Edited by R. B. Joyce. St Lucia: University of Queensland Press, 1963.

Menham, James George. "The Molesworth Committee: British Ideas and Colonial Reality". B.A. Honours thesis, Australian National University, 1973.

Merritt, Adrian. "The Development and Application of Masters and Servants Legislation in New South Wales – 1845 to 1930". Ph.D. thesis, Australian National University, 1981.

————. "Methodological and Theoretical Implications of the Study of the Law and Crime". *Labour History* no. 37 (November 1979), pp. 108-19.

Miller, Wilbur R. "Police Authority in London and New York City 1830–70". *Journal of Social History* vol. 8 (Winter 1975), pp. 81–101.

Milte, Kerry L. *Police in Australia. Development, Functions and Procedures.* Sydney: Butterworths, 1977.

Mitchell, B. R. and Deane, Phyllis. *Abstract of British Historical Statistics.* London: Cambridge University Press, 1962.

Molony, John N. *An Architect of Freedom. John Hubert Plunkett in New South Wales 1832–1869.* Canberra: Australian National University Press, 1973.

Moore, James F. H. *The Convicts of Van Diemen's Land 1840–1853.* Hobart: Cat and Fiddle Press, 1976.

Nadel, George. *Australia's Colonial Culture. Ideas, Men and Institutions in Mid-Nineteenth-Century Eastern Australia.* Melbourne: F. W. Cheshire, 1957.

O'Brien, G. M. *The Australian Police Forces.* London: Oxford University Press, 1960.

O'Farrell, Patrick. *The Catholic Church and Community in Australia. A History.* Melbourne: Thomas Nelson, 1977.

————. *The Catholic Church in Australia. A Short History: 1788–1967.* Melbourne: Thomas Nelson, 1968.

O'Malley, Pat. "Class Conflict, Land and Social Banditry: Bushranging in Nineteenth-Century Australia". *Social Problems* vol. 26, no. 3 (February 1979), pp. 271–83.

O'Sullivan, John. *Mounted Police in N.S.W.* Adelaide: Rigby, 1979.

Parsons, T. G. "The Limits of Technology or Why Didn't Australians Drink Colonial Beer in 1838?" *Push From the Bush* no. 4 (September 1979), pp. 22–29.

Pearl, Cyril. *Wild Man of Sydney*. London: W. H. Allen, 1958.

Perry, T. M. *Australia's First Frontier. The Spread of Settlement in New South Wales 1788–1829*. Melbourne: Melbourne University Press, 1963; reprint ed., 1965.

Philips, David. *Crime and Authority in Victorian England. The Black Country 1835–1860*. London: Croom Helm, 1977.

————. "Crime and Authority in the Black Country 1835–60: A Study of Prosecuted Offences and Law-Enforcement in an Industrializing Area". Ph.D. thesis, Oxford University, 1973.

Pike, Douglas and Nairn, Bede (gen. eds) *Australian Dictionary of Biography*. Vols. 1–6. Melbourne: Melbourne University Press, 1966–76.

Pittman, David J. and Snyder, Charles R. (eds.) *Society, Culture and Drinking Patterns*. New York: John Wiley and Sons, 1962.

Powell, Alan. *Patrician Democrat. The Political Life of Charles Cowper 1843–1870*. Melbourne: Melbourne University Press, 1977.

Priestly, Alison M. "The Molesworth Committee and New South Wales". M.A. thesis, Australian National University, 1967.

Quinault, R. and Stevenson, J. (eds.) *Popular Protest and Public Order. Six Studies in British History 1790–1920*. London: George Allen and Unwin, 1974.

Quinney, Richard. *Class, State and Crime. On the Theory and Practice of Criminal Justice*. New York: David McKay Company, 1977.

Radzinowicz, Leon. *Ideology and Crime: A Study of Crime in its Social and Historical Context*. London: Heinemann Educational Books, 1966.

Radzinowicz, Leon and Wolfgang, Marvin E. (eds.) *Crime and Justice*. Vol. 1: *The Criminal in Society*. New York: Basic Books, 1971.

Reece, R. H. W. *Aborigines and Colonists. Aborigines and Colonial Society in New South Wales in the 1830s and 1840s*. Sydney: Sydney University Press, 1974.

Reynolds, Henry. "Violence, the Aboriginals, and the Australian Historian". *Meanjin Quarterly* vol. 31, no. 4 (December 1972), pp. 471–77.

————. " 'That Hated Stain': The Aftermath of Transportation in Tasmania". *Historical Studies* vol. 14, no. 53 (October 1969), pp. 19–31.

Ritchie, John. "Towards Ending an Unclean Thing: The Molesworth Committee and the Abolition of Transportation to N.S.W., 1837–40". *Historical Studies* vol. 17, no. 67 (October 1976), pp. 144–164.

————. *Punishment and Profit. The Reports of Commissioner John Bigge on the Colonies of New South Wales and Van Diemen's Land, 1822–1823; Their Origins, Nature and Significance.* Melbourne: William Heinemann, 1970.

Ritter, Ann Lenora. "Concepts and Treatment of Juvenile Delinquency in Nineteenth-Century England, New South Wales and South Australia", M.A. thesis, University of New England, 1974.

Roberts, Stephen Henry. *The Squatting Age in Australia 1835–1847.* Melbourne: Melbourne University Press, 1935.

Robson, L. L. *The Convict Settlers of Australia. An Enquiry into the Origin and Character of the Convicts Transported to New South Wales and Van Diemen's Land 1787–1852.* Melbourne: Melbourne University Press, 1965.

Rock, Paul. *Deviant Behaviour.* London: Hutchinson and Company, 1973.

Rock, Paul and McIntosh, Mary (eds.) *Deviance and Social Control.* London: Tavistock Publications, 1974.

Roderick, Colin. *John Knatchbull from Quarterdeck to Gallows (Including the Narrative Written by Himself in Darlinghurst Gaol 23rd January-13th February 1844).* Sydney: Angus and Robertson, 1963.

Roe, Michael. *Quest for Authority in Eastern Australia 1835–1851.* Melbourne: Melbourne University Press, 1965.

————. "Colonial Society in Embryo". *Historical Studies* vol. 7, no. 26 (May 1956), pp. 149–59.

Rosenberg, Sidney. "Black Sheep and Golden Fleece: A Study of Nineteenth-Century English Attitudes Towards Australian Colonies". Ph.D. thesis, Columbia University, 1954.

Rowley, C. D. *Aboriginal Policy and Practice.* Vol. 1: *The Destruction of Aboriginal Society.* Canberra: Australian National University, 1970.

Rubington, Earl and Weinberg, Martin S. (eds.) *Deviance: The Interactionist Perspective. Text and Readings in the Sociology of Deviance.* New York: Macmillan, 1968.

Rudé, George. *Protest and Punishment. The Story of the Social and Political Protesters Transported to Australia 1788–1868.* London: Oxford University Press, 1978.

————. *The Crowd in History. A Study of Popular Disturbances in France and England 1730–1848.* New York: John Wiley and Sons, 1964.

Sagarin, Edward. *The Anatomy of Dirty Words.* New York: Lyle Stuart, 1962.

Schedvin, M. B. and Schedvin, C. B. "The Nomadic Tribes of Urban

Britain: A Prelude to Botany Bay". *Historical Studies* vol. 18, no. 71 (October 1978), pp. 254–76.

Scott, Ernest. "The Resistance to Convict Transportation in Victoria," 1844–53". *Victorian Historical Magazine* vol. 1, no. 4 (December 1911), pp. 101–42.

Sellin, Thorsten and Wolfgang, Marvin E. *The Measurement of Delinquency*. New York: John Wiley and Sons, 1964.

Selth, P. A. "The Burrangong (Lambing Flat) Riots, 1860–61: A Closer Look". *JRAHS* vol. 60, pt 1 (March 1974), pp. 48–69.

Serle, Geoffrey. *The Golden Age. A History of the Colony of Victoria 1851–1861*. Melbourne: Melbourne University Press, 1963; reprint ed., 1968.

Shaw, A. G. L. "Reformatory Aspects of the Transportation of Criminals to Australia". In *Law and Crime. Essays in Honor of Sir John Barry*, pp. 135–54. Edited by Norval Morris and Mark Perlman. New York: Gordon and Breach, 1972.

————. *Convicts and the Colonies. A Study of Penal Transportation from Great Britain and Ireland to Australia and Other Parts of the British Empire*. London: Faber and Faber, 1966.

————. *Heroes and Villains in History. Governors Darling and Bourke in New South Wales*. Sydney: Sydney University Press, 1966.

————. "Violent Protest in Australian History". *Historical Studies* vol. 15, no. 60 (April 1973), pp. 545–61.

————. "The British Criminal and Transportation". *Tasmanian Historical Research Association, Papers and Proceedings* vol. 2, no. 2 (March 1953), pp. 29–33.

Silver, Alan. "The Demand for Order in Civil Society: A Review of Some Themes in the History of Urban Crime, Police and Riot". In *The Police: Six Sociological Essays*, pp. 1–24. Edited by David J. Bordua. New York: John Wiley and Sons, 1967.

Skinner, L. E. *Police and the Pastoral Frontier. Native Police 1849–59*. St Lucia: University of Queensland Press, 1975.

Storch, Robert D. "The Policeman as Domestic Missionary: Urban Discipline and Popular Culture in Northern England, 1850–80". *Journal of Social History* vol. 9 (June 1976), pp. 481–509.

Sturma, Michael. "Police and Drunkards in Sydney, 1841–51". *Australian Journal of Politics and History* vol. 27, no. 1 (1981), pp. 48–56.

————. "Eye of the Beholder: The Stereotype of Women Convicts, 1788–1852". *Labour History* no. 34 (May 1978), pp. 3–10.

————. "Vice in a Vicious Society: Crime and the Community in Mid-Nineteenth-Century New South Wales". Ph.D. thesis, Australian National University, 1980.

Sundin, Jan. "Theft and Penury in Sweden 1830–1920: A Comparative

Study at the Country Level". *Scandinavian Journal of History* vol. 1 (1976), pp. 265–92.

Taylor, Ian, Walton, Paul, and Young, Jock (eds.) *Critical Criminology*. London: Routledge and Kegan Paul, 1975.

Thomas, J. E. and Stewart, Alex. *Imprisonment in Western Australia. Evolution, Theory and Practice*. Nedlands: University of Western Australia Press, 1978.

Thompson, E. P. *Whigs and Hunters. The Origin of the Black Act*. London: Allen Lane, 1975.

Tilly, Charles, Tilly, Louise, and Tilly, Richard. *The Rebellious Century 1830–1930*. London: J. M. Dent and Sons, 1975.

Tobias, J. J. *Crime and Police in England 1700–1900*. Dublin: Gill and Macmillan, 1979.

————. *Crime and Industrial Society in the 19th Century*. London: B. T. Batsford, 1967.

Townsend, Norma. "The Molesworth Enquiry: Does the Report Fit the Evidence". *Journal of Australian Studies* no. 1 (June 1977), pp. 33–51.

Vaile, P. J. "Free Society and the Range of Crime in the Bathurst Disttrict before the Gold Rush". *JRAHS* vol. 64, pt 3 (December 1978), pp. 192–203.

————. "Aspects of Law and Order in the Bathurst District 1813-c. 1850". M.A, thesis, University of Sydney, 1974.

Waldersee, James. *Catholic Society in New South Wales 1788–1860*. Sydney: Sydney University Press, 1974.

Walker, Nigel. *Crime and Insanity in England*. Vol. 1: *The Historical Perspective*. Edinburgh: Edinburgh University Press, 1968.

Walker, Robin B. *The Newspaper Press in New South Wales, 1803–1920*. Sydney: Sydney University Press, 1976.

————. "Another Look at the Lambing Flat Riots, 1860–61". *JRAHS* vol. 56, pt 3 (September 1970), pp. 193–205.

————. "Bushranging in Fact and Legend". *Historical Studies* vol. 11, no. 42 (April 1964), pp. 206–221.

Ward, John M. *Earl Grey and the Australian Colonies 1846–1857. A Study of Self-Government and Self-Interest*. Melbourne: Melbourne University Press, 1958.

Ward, Paul and Woods, Greg. *Law and Order in Australia*. Sydney: Angus and Robertson, 1972.

Ward, Russel. "The Australian Legend Re-Visited". *Historical Studies* vol. 18, no. 71 (October 1978), pp. 171–90.

————. *The Australian Legend*. London: Oxford University Press, 1958; reprint ed., 1970.

Wilson, George B. *Alcohol and the Nation (A Contribution to the*

Study of the Liquor Problem in the United Kingdom from 1800 to 1935). London: Nicholson and Watson, 1940.

Wilson, Paul R. and Braithwaite, John (eds.) *Two Faces of Deviance. Crimes of the Powerless and the Powerful.* St Lucia: University of Queensland Press, 1978.

Wilson, P. R. and Brown, J. W. *Crime and the Community.* St Lucia: University of Queensland Press, 1973.

Windeyer, Victor. *Sir Charles Nicholson. A Place in History.* St Lucia: University of Queensland Press, 1978.

Windeyer, W. J. V. "Responsible Government – Highlights, Sidelights and Reflections". *JRAHS* vol. 42, pt 6 (1957), pp. 257–312.

Wright, Martin (ed.) *Use of Criminology Literature.* London: Butterworths, 1974.

Zehr, Howard. *Crime and the Development of Modern Society. Patterns of Criminality in Nineteenth Century Germany and France.* London: Croom Helm, 1976.

————. "The Modernization of Crime in Germany and France, 1830–1913". *Journal of Social History* vol. 8 (Summer 1975), pp. 117–41.

Index

a'Beckett, William, 124, 150–51
Aboriginals, 6, 42, 58, 60, 72, 76, 91–92, 95–97, 113, 169
Albury, 70
alcohol, 89, 144–51, 153, 158, 193
Americans, 60, 174. *See also* California; United States
anti-authoritarianism, 90, 136, 163, 164
anti-transportation, 8, 47, 51–59, 178
Anti-Transportation Association, 52
Armidale, 70, 98, 122
arson, 60, 65
assault, 19, 56, 88–90, 95–98, 132, 133, 137, 151–52, 167; statistics, 65, 80, 94, 124, 152
assignment: abolition of, 27, 41, 87, 101, 127; regulations of, 25–26
Atlas, 119
Australian, 13, 24, 25, 38, 40, 43, 126, 132, 168
Australian Patriotic Association, 20, 26
Australian Temperance Magazine, 149

Bathurst, 52, 54, 70, 97, 105, 107, 123, 144, 155; police, 165, 172
beer, 146–47, 150, 153
Bell's Life in Sydney, 4, 124, 127, 154, 157, 165
Berrima, 70, 103
bestiality, 3, 98
Bigge, John Thomas, 27
Black Country, 2, 89
Border Police, 72–74, 168–69
Border Police Act, 169
Bourke, Richard, 12–16, 18–21, 23–26, 29, 54, 69, 71
Braidwood, 131, 132
Brisbane, Thomas, 72, 123
Britain, 4, 28, 56, 57, 113, 135, 185;

crime in, 2, 89, 94, 97, 107, 108, 110, 113, 127, 151–52, 192; drink in, 144–46, 155, 157–58, 193; magistrates in, 119, 122; police in, 80, 163, 168, 173–74
Broughton, William Grant, 153
Burdett, Thomas, 37–41
burglary, 35, 53–54, 65, 111, 150
Burton, William Westbrooke, 12–14, 21, 28, 35, 37, 38, 75, 127, 150
bushrangers, 99–102, 170, 185
bushranging, 6, 54, 98–102, 112, 171, 173, 187
Bushranging Act, 102, 166–67
bush workers, 29, 101, 105, 148, 158
Byrne, J. C., 3

California, 60, 61, 175
Camden, 130
Campbell Town, 70, 165
Cannon, Michael, 96
capital punishment, 23, 55, 97, 98, 102, 103. *See also* executions
Castle Forbes, 15–16, 19
cattle stealing. *See* stock theft
Chinese, 124, 174, 186; riots against, 61, 173, 175–77
circuit courts, 64, 69–70, 86
Clarke, C. M. H., 2
Cockatoo Island, 41
Colonial Magazine, 64
Colonial Office, 21, 51, 53
commissioners of crown lands, 72, 73, 119, 121, 169. *See also* gold commissioners
common scolds, 91
Constitution Act (1842), 42
Constitutional Association, 53, 57
contamination, 1–3, 6, 28, 30, 53–56, 61, 78, 148, 186
convictism, influence of, 6, 8, 28, 53, 59, 82, 101, 110, 134, 135, 156, 163, 184–87